# Rev. Leonard Whitney

## His Search for Answers

Lois K. Lefler

Editor and Publisher Charleen Stroup, Michigan USA

Published in the USA

Paperback ISBN: 979-8-9906911-0-0

Hardback ISBN: 13-979-8-9906911-1-7

Library of Commerce Control Number. 2024912260

*There are those who may ask why all the fuss? Those folks are dead and gone. Let them rest in peace. We think they deserve more than that. Some of these people, their contemporaries and forebearers, apparently did not do the things nor catch the dreams that mattered on paper. We think it is tragic that such people, agrarian people with little or no worldly goods, some at least, illiterate, who lived and breathed, suffered, rejoiced, sinned or did Godly deeds, propagated, maybe religious, maybe not, should vanish from the memory of man, leaving virtually no path by which their origins can be traced and little, if any, proof that they ever existed.*

*Robert Athol Huston*

*November 1981*

# TABLE of CONTENTS

# EDITOR'S NOTE

Lois Koppenhafer Lefler preserved these literary artifacts for you, the reader. Lois dedicated several decades of her life to researching genealogy and other documents to augment the family stories about her ancestors. She only stopped when her eyesight faded and her commitment to caring for her family consumed her waking hours. Lois still thinks about these people as their lives became intimately entwined in succeeding generations through these documents. You will notice her enthusiasm and compassion parallels Rev. Leonard Whitney's as an honor for the ideals they both cherished. I type this in 2024 as a tribute to my cousin.

Abraham Lincoln died April 15, 1865, and could be counted in the number of those who died in the four years, one month and two weeks of the Civil War. This being the 80th score (160 years) after Abraham Lincoln's death and the end of the Civil War, it is a most fitting time to publish this treasure tome. The originals are preserved with her daughter, Lori Lefler Lewis, in Hamilton, Illinois, across the Mississippi bridge from Keokuk, Iowa. Just an hour drive south of this bridge is Hannibal, Missouri where Samuel Clemens, aka Mark Twain, was raised, who said:

*I didn't want to have anything to do with the war...so I went into hiding ... After a while I joined some of my schoolboy friends. We made up part of the Marion County militia...We didn't know what we were doing...We killed a Union soldier and thought that was wonderful until we went up and saw the man dying, mumbling about his wife and child. And it deemed an epitome of the war: that all war must be just that – killing the strangers against whom you feel no personal animosity. (Coffee With Mark Twain, p. 106. Duncan Baird Pub. 2008)*

Charleen Stroup, April 2024

# PREFACE

Lois K. Lefler

I write this of two men who touched my families' lives, and of whom, as I go through the old documents and papers left by my family, have touched my life also. I have become completely engrossed in the life and times of Rev. Leonard Whitney and his son, Harwood Otis Whitney.

In reading the letters and sorting the documents, I have put their lives together as much as I can. My heart goes out to Rev. Leonard who spent his life doing all the good he could while struggling to remain true to his ideals after the disillusionment and horrors of war; and the struggles of his family being left behind to continue. There is none of their family left only us and a pile of papers which I hope someone will read and not let be forgotten.

I have used mainly documented information and will interject only some of my own feelings and information where appropriate.

Although this is all that is left of two men, it is also a marvelous window into the life and times of the 1840's in Keokuk, Iowa, the Civil War, and the life struggles after the war. The letters by notable people of that time are also included in the story as they occurred.

What is written is quoted from various sources and all referenced. We have copies of all the original material. Some of the original letters were difficult to read, so the typed copies may contain "...?..." which indicates those deciphering challenges.

I never actually knew Aunt Lily. She was Grandfather Ehinger's sister and lived with grandfather and grandmother in the house on Grand Avenue in Keokuk during the 1920s and 30s. Most of the contents of that house belonged to Aunt Lily. She was married to

Harwood Whitney and lived there alone after Harwood died until grandfather and grandmother came to Keokuk to live with her.

Mother said the wooden house was built in Peoria by Rev. Leonard before the Civil War and taken apart, shipped by boat to Keokuk and reassembled at 728 Franklin Street in Keokuk. Rev. Leonard was living there when he mustered into the Civil War. After Ann Jenette died, Harwood inherited it and lived there with Aunt Lily. Aunt Lily lived there after Harwood died and added the porches and remodeled the interior by adding closets and bathrooms.

Mother came to live with Aunt Lily in 1917. Mother had fallen out of a hayloft and had some hemorrhaging and came to stay with Aunt Lily to convalesce. Aunt Lily was going with Harwood at the time. They were "courting", and she left a journal which we still have. She referred to him as "Sweetheart" in the journal, saying "I went for a walk with Sweetheart this evening" or "I had a lovely visit with Sweetheart this afternoon."

In 1920 Aunt Lily bought the brick house on Grand Avenue that I grew up in. It was built around 1856 by the Marshall family and Aunt Lily was its second owner. Mother inherited it, and then it was passed on to me.

Aunt Lily had invested in a farmland company which loaned money to farmers. There were about six farms involved, so she did not actually own the farms, but had a little income from the investment firm. After she died, Grandfather and Grandmother got those investments which did not pay much but it was a little income.

The Civil War letters were in a packet in one of the drawers of the desk in the living room. There were a lot of other treasures in the house, and I used to notice them but wasn't much interested in the history or genealogy at that time. After the kids were grown, I read the letters and started getting interested in genealogy and the other stuff that was left in the house.

My grandfather was Dr. Clyde Ehinger and grandmother was Ella (Long) Ehinger. They adopted mother when she was about 3 years old. Mother's biological mother died in childbirth. Mother's biological father was Dr. Sever Chauncy Ross, whose family came over on the second voyage of the Mayflower around 1630, and they fought in the American Revolution. Grandmother's family, Bower, comes from the Southwick's, and the poet John Greenleaf Whittier wrote the poem, "The Ballad of Cassandra Southwick" about Cassandra and her brother who were banned by the Pilgrims because they were Quakers.

Grandfather and Grandmother Ehinger were retired professors from what was then Westchester State Teachers College in Westchester, PA. He was Director of Physical Training for Men, and she was Director of Physical Training for Women. The gymnasium built in the 1920s was named in their honor. The name of the college has changed by now and a new gym has been built, and I don't know if it is still named for them.

Grandfather and Grandmother retired sometime in the 1920s and moved to a place in Washington state called Hidden Valley, near the current town of Bellevue. It was a wilderness then and they built a cabin and lived there until they moved to Keokuk to live with Aunt Lily in her final years.

Lois (Koppenhafer) Lefler

March, 1989

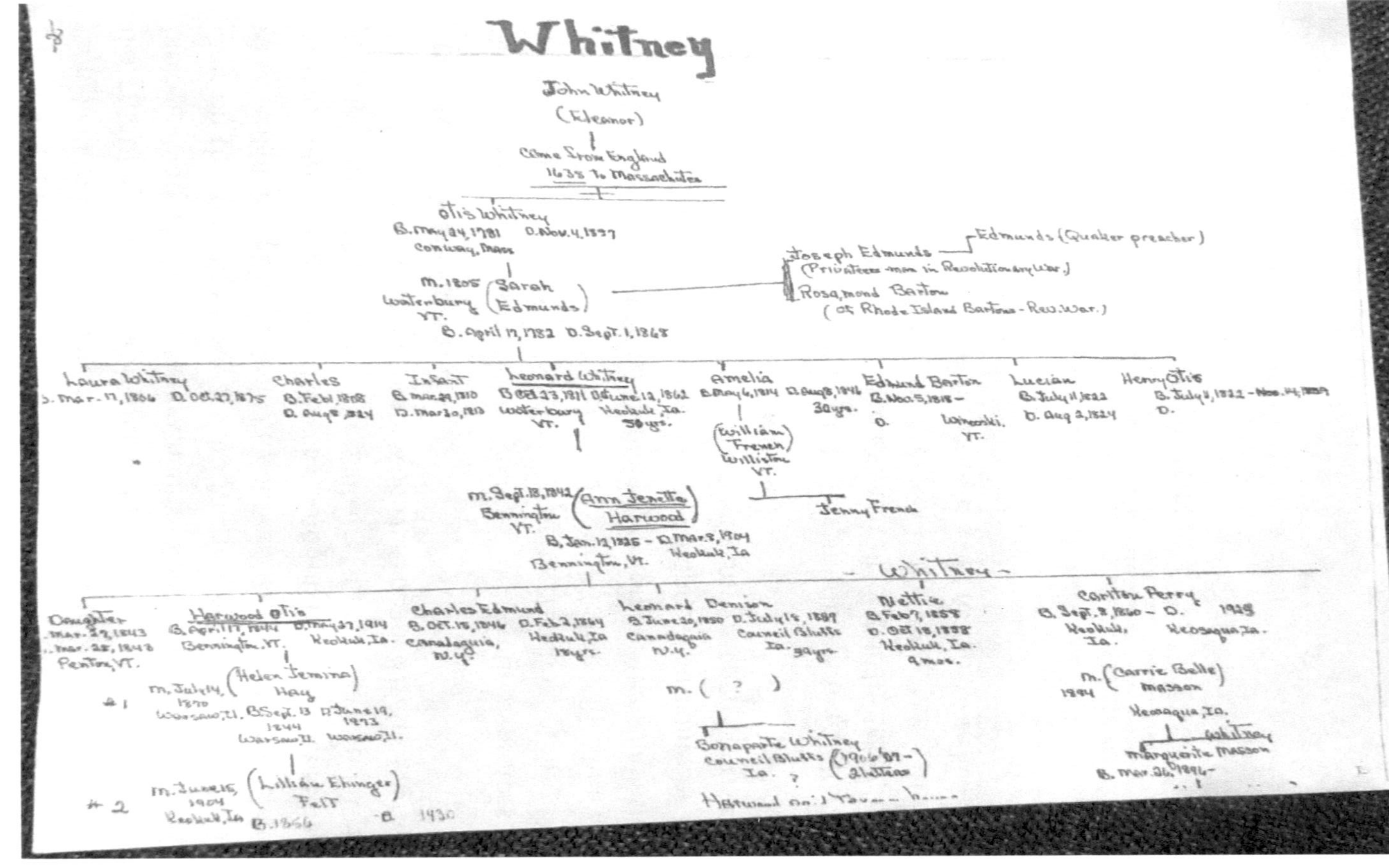
Whitney
John Whitney
(Eleanor)
Came from England
1635 To Massachusetts
Otis Whitney
B. May 24, 1781 D. Nov. 4, 1877
Conway, Mass
m. 1805
Waterbury VT.
(Sarah Edmunds)
B. April 17, 1782 D. Sept. 1, 1868
Joseph Edmunds
Edmunds (Quaker preacher)
(Privateer man in Revolutionary War.)
Rosamond Barton
(of Rhode Island Bartons - Rev. War.)
Laura Whitney
Charles
Infant
Leonard Whitney
Amelia
Edmund Barton
Lucian
Henry Otis
William French
Williston VT.
Jenny French
m. Sept. 18, 1842
Bennington VT.
(Ann Jenette Harwood)
Bennington, VT. Keokuk, Ia
Whitney
Daughter
Harwood Otis
Charles Edmund
Leonard Denison
Nettie
Carlton Perry
(Helen Jemima Hay)
m. ( ? )
Bonaparte Whitney
Council Bluffs Ia.
(Carrie Belle Masson)
Keosauqua, Ia.
Marguerite Masson Whitney
(Lillian Ehinger Felt)

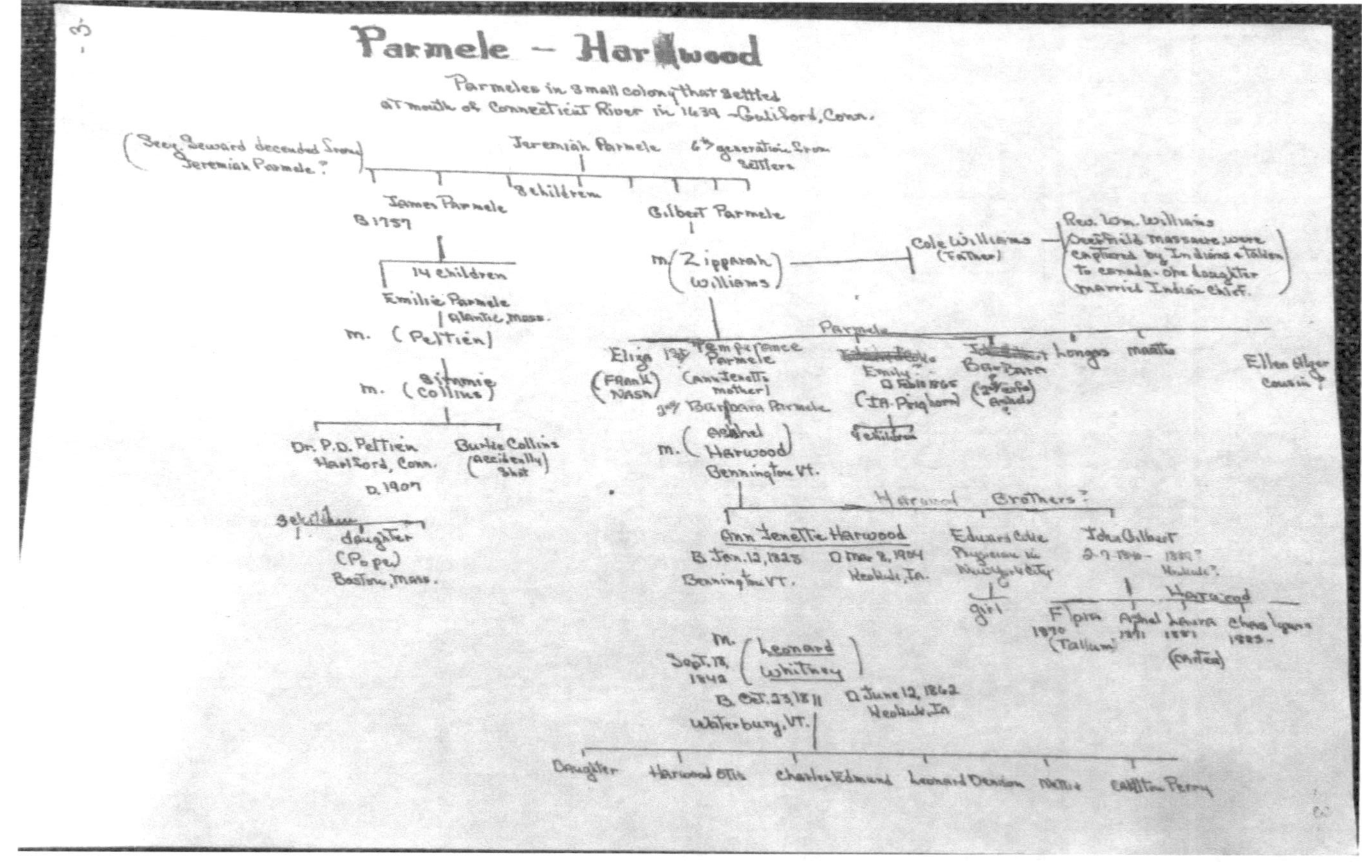
-3-
Parmele - Harwood
Parmeles in small colony that settled at mouth of Connecticut River in 1639 - Guilford, Conn.
(Sec. Seward decended from Jeremiah Parmele?)
Jeremiah Parmele
6th generation from settlers
8 children
James Parmele
B 1757
Gilbert Parmele
14 children
Emilie Parmele
Atlantic, Mass.
m. (Peltien)
m. (Collins)
Dr. P.D. Peltien
Hartford, Conn.
D. 1907
Burke Collins
(accidentally shot)
daughter
(Pope)
Boston, Mass.
m. (Zipparah Williams)
Cole Williams
(Father)
Rev. Wm. Williams
Deerfield massacre, were captured by Indians & taken to Canada - one daughter married Indian chief.
Parmele
Eliza
(Frank Nash)
Temperance Parmele
(Ann Jenette's mother)
3rd Barbara Parmele
Emily
(I.A. Pingham)
Barbara
Longs
Mattie
Ellen Alger
Cousin?
m. (Ashel Harwood)
Bennington Vt.
Harwood Brothers?
Ann Jenette Harwood
B. Jan. 12, 1825
Bennington VT.
D Mar 8, 1904
Keokuk, Ia.
Edward Cole
Physician in ...
girl
Ida Gilbert
Harwood
Aphel
1871
Laura
1881
(United)
m.
Sept. 18, 1842
(Leonard Whitney)
B. Oct. 23, 1811
Waterbury, VT.
D June 12, 1862
Keokuk, Ia
Daughter
Harwood Otis
Charles Edmund
Leonard Denison
Mattie
Carlton Perry

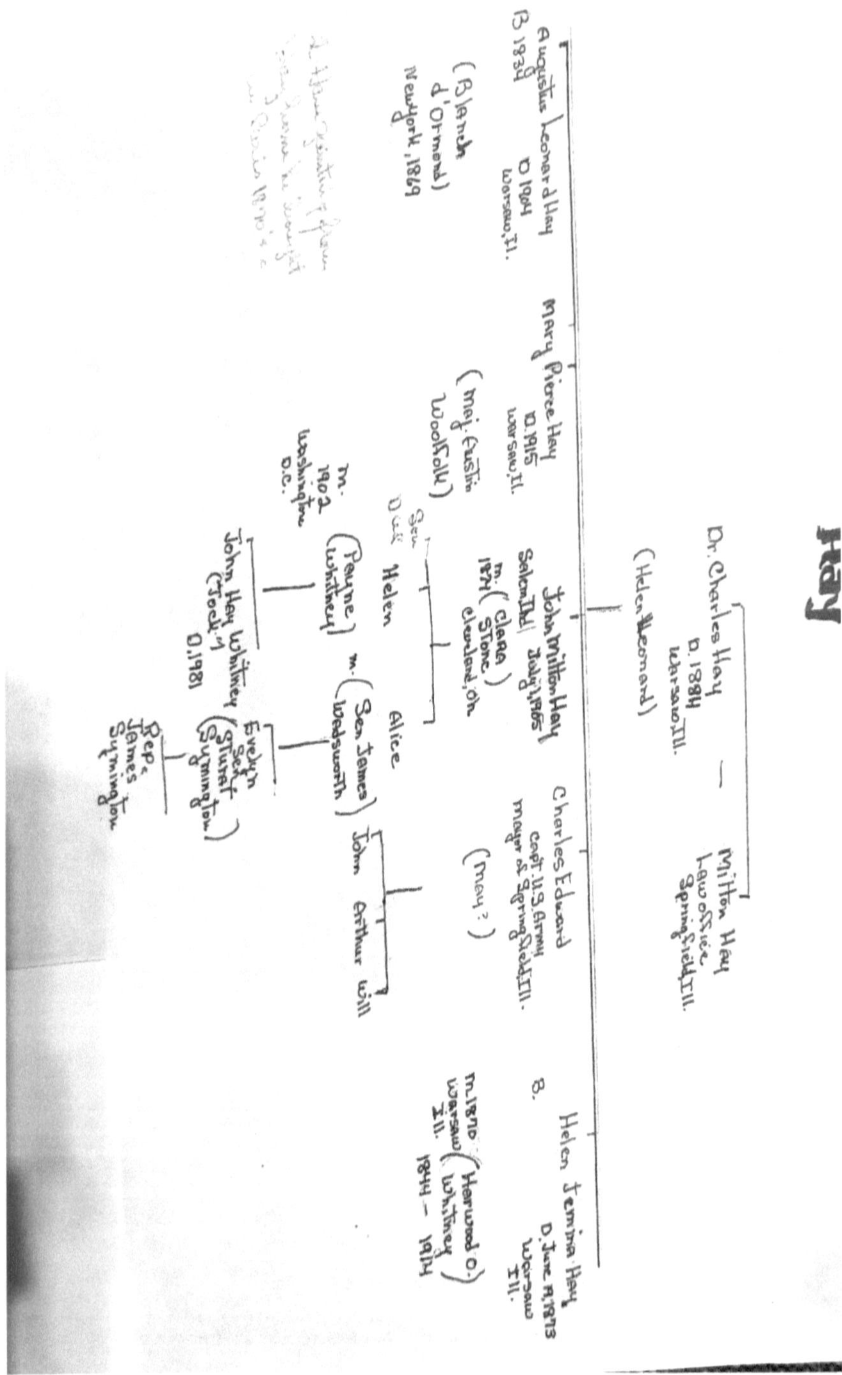
Hay
Dr. Charles Hay
D. 1884
Warsaw, Ill.
(Helen Leonard)
Milton Hay
Law office
Springfield, Ill.
Augustus Leonard Hay
B 1834
D 1904
Warsaw, Il.
(Blanch d'Ormond)
New York, 1869
Mary Pierce Hay
D. 1915
Warsaw, Il.
(Maj. Austin Woolfolk)
John Milton Hay
Salem, Ind.
July 1, 1865
m. 1874
(Clara Stone)
Cleveland, Oh
Charles Edward
Capt. U.S. Army
Mayor of Springfield, Ill.
(May?)
Helen Jemima Hay
B.
D. June 19, 1873
Warsaw
Ill.
m. 1870
Warsaw
Ill.
(Harwood O. Whitney)
1844 – 1914
Helen
Alice
m.
1902
Washington
D.C.
(Payne Whitney)
m. (Sen. James Wadsworth)
John
Arthur
Will
John Hay Whitney
("Jock")
D. 1981
Evelyn
(Sen. Stuart Symington)
Rep. James Symington

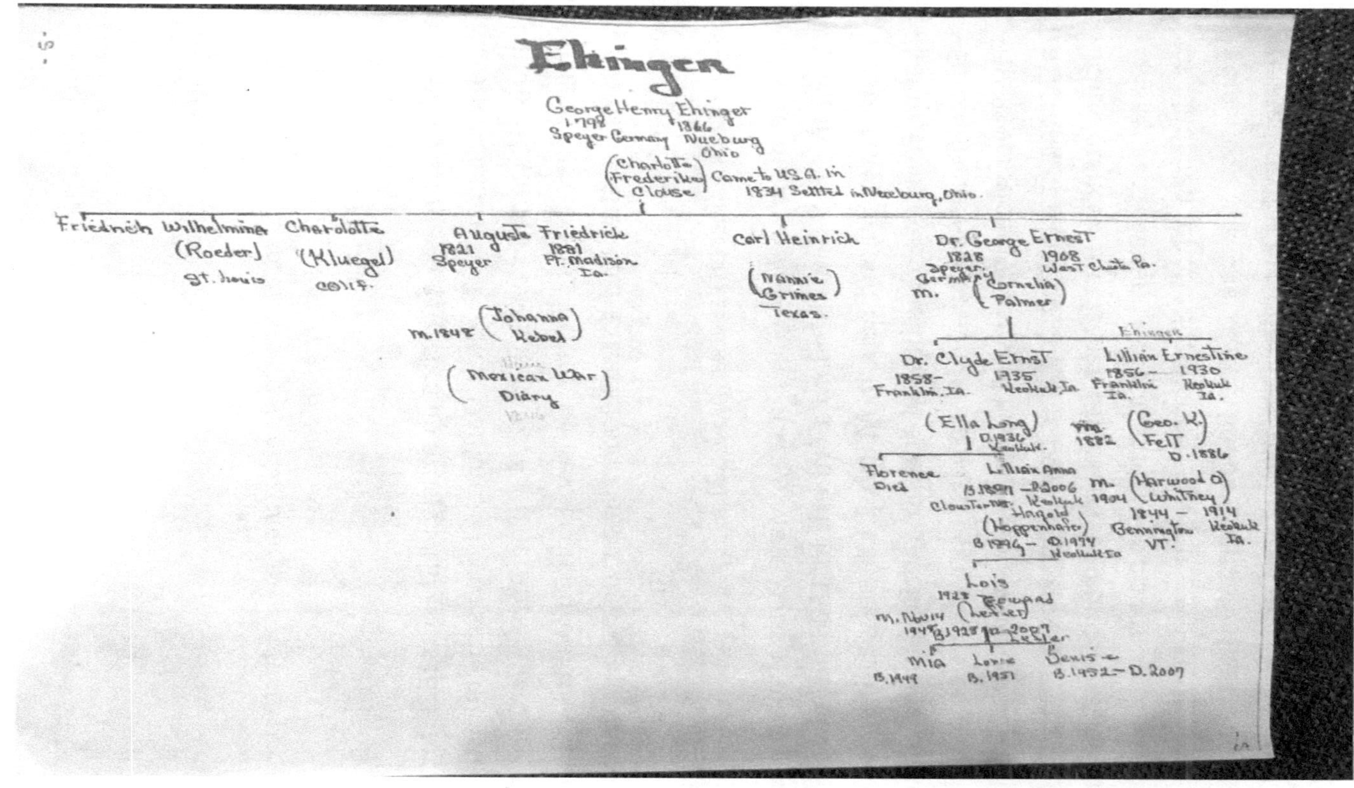
Ehingen
George Henry Ehinger
1798 1866
Speyer Germany Nuebury Ohio
(Charlotte Frederike Clouse)
Came to U.S.A. in 1834 Settled in Nuebury, Ohio.
Friedrich
Wilhelmine (Roeder) St. Louis
Charlotte (Kluegel)
Auguste Friedrick 1821 1881 Speyer Ft. Madison Ia.
m. 1848 (Johanna Hebel)
(Mexican War Diary)
Carl Heinrich
(Nannie Grimes) Texas.
Dr. George Ernest
1828 1908
Speyer, Germany
West Chester Pa.
m. (Cornelia Palmer)
Ehinger
Dr. Clyde Ernst
1858– 1935
Franklin, Ia. Keokuk, Ia.
Lillian Ernestine
1856– 1930
Franklin Ia. Keokuk Ia.
(Ella Long)
m. 1882
(Geo. K. Felt)
D. 1886
Florence
Died
Lillian Anna
m. 1904
(Harwood O. Whitney)
1844 – 1914
Bennington VT. Keokuk Ia.
Lois
Mia
B. 1949
Lorie
B. 1951
Denise
B. 1952 – D. 2007

# PART 1

*They lived. They died. They deserve more than to be forgotten.*
*Robert Athol Huston*

A portion of my story is taken from an article written in 1888 for the Iowa Historical Record by The Rev. O. Clute, who was the minister of The Unitarian Church in Keokuk in 1874. (See Appendix C for the entire article). The letters written by Rev. Leonard Whitney during the Civil War and the letters from Robert Ingersol are interlaced in chronological order.

The Iowa Historical Record states (p.50-52):

> In one of these homes in Conway, Mass., Otis Whitney was born in 1781 [Rev. Leonard's father]. In 1803 he moved to Waterbury, Vt. and here in March 1805 he was married to Sarah Edmunds, daughter of Joseph and Rosamond Barton Edmunds. Joseph Edmunds had been a privateers-man during the Revolutionary War, and his many stories of adventure had a strong fascination for the boys and young men of his acquaintance. The father of Joseph Edmunds had been a Quaker preacher and had transmitted to his son a noble strain of independence. Rosamond Barton, wife of Joseph Edmunds, was one of the Rhode Island Bartons and was related to the Bartons of Revolutionary fame, hence in the veins of Sarah Edmunds, wife of Otis Whitney, there pulsated a pure and strong love of justice and liberty for every human being and of that religion of the spirit that rises above the

narrow technicalities of creeds, and personally, she was a woman of strong mental and moral qualities.

Otis was a man of clear head and practical turn. His efficiency provided his family with the comforts usually found in a well-to-do New England home. He was a farmer, and his children grew up amid the freedom, the independence, the intelligence and industry that then characterized the rural population of New England. Both he and his wife were members of the Baptist church.

Among the children born to Otis and his wife came Leonard on Oct. 23, 1811. With such parentage he received vigor of body and mind. He grew to an active boy and became a leader of all the sports and mischief in the neighborhood. He was strong, quick, impulsive, wayward, and generous. He was by no means distressingly 'good' in the Sunday School library-book style. His parents and teachers found him difficult to manage. But he was the friend of the weak. He responded readily to what was generous, just and kind. The district school and academy gave him his early education which his father urged the restless boy to continue by going to college. But he had dreams of adventures amid strange scenes, fostered perhaps by the sea tales of his grandfather Joseph, the old privateers-man. When sixteen years old he went to Boston and shipped for a voyage. But before the vessel sailed, he had seen enough of the charms of sea life to change his mind. He succeeded in getting free from the engagement and never after had a return of the longing for the sea.

The experiences of his Boston trip, acting on a mind singularly receptive, turned his attention to the sober purposes of life.

He worked with interest on his father's farm. He attended school at Hinesburg, Vt., and made good progress in his studies. He chose the profession of law as his work for life and for several years gave himself to its study. In August 1835, he was admitted to practice at the Chittenden County Court, Bennington, Vt., 'by the unanimous consent of the bar.' He spent several years in the practice of law at Ann Arbor, Mich. and at Auburn, N.Y. There is no record accessible to me as to his success at the bar. Probably it was not promising. I suspect he was not by nature fitted in mind and morals to succeed in any but the higher field of law practice, and circumstances never allowed him to enter those fields. Work, study, anxiety brought him poor health, and he went to Saratoga Springs, N.Y. to rest. While there he visited, not infrequently, at the home of an old family friend, who was settled nearby, as pastor of the Baptist Church in Union Village - the Rev. William Arthur, father of the late President Arthur. His old friend had a strong influence over the young lawyer. During the summer he united with Mr. Arthur's church, decided to give up law, and to become a Baptist minister. That fall he began his ministerial work as pastor to the Baptist Church at Bennington, Vt. in his native state. Here he met the lady to whom the next year he was married, Ann Jennette Harwood, only daughter of Ashel Harwood of Bennington. He preached with ability and sincerity, and his work was acceptable among his people. Leaving Bennington, he preached at Penton, VT., at Reading, Pa., at Navy Yard Baptist Church in Washington, D.C. and then with the church at Canandaigua, N.Y.

Ann Jenette Harwood

Married at Bennington, Vt. Sept. 18, 1842, Leonard was 30 years of age, and Ann Jenette was 17 years of age. To them were born: Infant daughter, born at Penton, Vt., May 27, 1843, died May 28, 1843. Harwood Otis Whitney, born at Bennington, Vt. April 17, 1844. Charles Edmund Whitney, born at Canandaigua, N.Y. Oct. 15, 1846, Leonard Denison Whitney, born at Canandaigua, N.Y. June 20, 1850.

All the while his religion was growing too large for his creed. His humanity was too deep and loving to allow him to excuse crimes because they were popular and national. His religious opinions had been gradually changing for some years. Probably the anti-slavery agitation had much to do with helping this change. He soon found himself out of sympathy with the beliefs of a part of his Canandaigua flock, and with a dIfference of opinion there came among some ot his people bitterness of feeling. His conscience urged him on. He could not put a padlock on his lips. His hearers who disagreed with him, were doubtless, just as earnest and faithful. They believed the Baptist system, and it was their right to expect their minister to teach that system. A conflict came, church meeting was called, and Mr. Whitney was excluded from the church for heresy.

Following is a letter written by Rev. Leonard to his brother-in-law, William French, in Williston, Vt. I do not know if these were the final meetings of the church or if this occurred earlier. I feel this was a little earlier as it tells of his ordeal before the committees.

Canandaigua, March 16th, 1846

Dear Brother, - As I live, the reason I have not answered your letter is not that I did not receive in due time or was not glad to receive it, or the fact is I have been hurried and worried to death, and could not steal a scrap of time, only for the pressing duties of the present. I have just passed through the most important Trial of Faith, and it seems to me it was nothing less than the laying on of the hands of the Presbytery in solemn ordination. Tho I must confess I breathe freer and deeper, I don't know that I am a better man, a better Christian, or abler minister of the New Testament by the ceremony. My own opinion is, that a call by votes of any church to exercise the functions of a bishop, confers all the authority to do so, that man can confer. Nevertheless, to please the Jews, Timothy has been circumcised, and now to a certain intent in every particular is empowered to preach and practice what he believes the Bible to teach. We have called two ministers and 4 able councils to consummate the object. The first refused to ordain because I took exceptions to the term Total Depravity as defined by theologians alleging as a reason that if a man possessed a natural sense of right and wrong, he could not be totally depraved. If the conscience was totally depraved it would cease to be a conscience. 2. Asserted, if a heathen faithfully followed the light he had, he would be saved, even tho he in this life knew nothing of the Savior. 3. That men under the Gospel are saved because they believe, and do not believe because they are not elected to be saved. 4. That according to the scriptures, it is possible for men who really believe to fall. The second council met with us last Wednesday, and after laboring faithfully, by ingenious questions, and explanations to get orthodoxy enough down me to make me pass in a crowd concluded to commend me to diligent reflection and study on the mounted points and go on with the ordination. They did so but the way I was crammed with sound doctrine, in the ordination sermon by Br. Church, from Rochester, can never be beat. He settled the extent of man's depravity in his opening prayer, by confessing that by nature we are all devils and this appeal to the sympathies of the audience masterly as it was, was more than equaled on all the points at issue in the discourses that followed. It was a clincher. But I sat meek and submissive as a lamb in appearance but with such upheaving of internal emotion as we have all felt when pounced upon by larger boys in our schoolboy days, viz.: "if you don't catch it when I get big enough, then no matter." Well, I kept cool til this gentleman and others lifted me up on to their platform, where I too, could speak with authority. Yesterday in the forenoon I preached from Br. Church's text and if you want to know what ordination can do for a man, read and wonder at the following from that discourse, knowing in the meantime that Br. Ch. is pro slavery to the core. There will be time enough to sneer at a virtuous action flowing from the benevolence of the Natural Heart that lifts up the wounded man by the wayside--takes him to the Inn, and generously pays for his healing--as at best but a miserable residuum of total depravity--when theological regeneration ceases to be extended to the robber whose regenerative compassion beats him and robs him and leaves him by the wayside to die--when its holy discrimination ceases to embrace in the fold of God's chosen ones; as the special favorites of Heaven, men in those hearts is not a residuum only, but whose practices prove them to be Body, Soul & Spirit, a reeking, festering mess of moral putrefaction whose end is to be buried! If the discourse is published, I shall certainly send you a copy.

Private affairs, Baby has had the hooping cough for some weeks past but is getting better. Jannette is well as usual but has the dumps this evening. We have changed board, are not at Dea. Tisdale's, a fellow more like "Bill Tish" than any I have found here. We get board for $4 per week which is cheaper than we can keep house here and besides we never can get enough beforehand to commence housekeeping. I feel sometimes as if I must have me a home but don't know as even that would make me happy. If I am in the path of duty as I trust I am, I ought having food and raiment to be therewith content. That I have thus far, tho it isn't all paid for yet. The Ch. are behind about paying me. O how we should like to drop in and see you all in this sugar makin season and take a cup o' kindness yet, "for auld land syne." I hope Amelia is quite well by this time and all the rest. Some of the folks must write soon and tell us how you all get along and what the Ch. is doing, etc. Thank Amelia and Jenny for their part in the letter and will try to favor them with one if I don't get so I can't write a legible hand.

Yours affectionately, L. Whitney

Note: Amelia died Aug 8, 1846 - five months later. She was Leonard's sister.

The Iowa Historical Record continues: (pg.52-53):

> Many of his congregation were with him. These and others who became interested organized the 'Free Church of Canandaigua,' rented a hall and invited Mr. Whitney to be their word of Spirit as his eager ear caught its enchanting message. He preached justice for all, even if their skins were black. His moral perception was so strong and so sensitive that he was roused mightily by the Fugitive Slave Law and poured his impassioned feeling into his sermons. These sermons were not without wide influence. A friend who had heard of one of them wrote to him as follows:
>
> *Washington, Jan. 1851*
>
> *Friend Whitney: - I want you to send me a copy, prepared for publication, of the sermon preached by you in which you say: 'they had fugitive law in old times. The authorities commanded that if any knew where Jesus was, they should deliver him up. Undoubtedly many knew where he was; and doubtless, too, the chief priests preached as the Doctors of Divinity do now, that it was their duty to obey the civil authorities and deliver him up, but in all Judea there was found but one 'Silver Grey.'*
>
> *One of the merchant princes of New York, and a man high in influence as well as information, says he will print it in fine form, for gratuitous distribution, if I will procure the copy. Grave Senators scream and yell almost with joy, when the argument is thus told to them; they say that the minute it gets out it will go through all the papers, that it is just one of those things that must carry; that as soon as it is named, the wonder is that somebody had not thought of it before. Such was the*

> *effect when I told it at a dinner party of Senators, members of congress, etc. So, make it elevated, concise, sufficiently moderate, but unyieldingly conclusive and severe, and send it along. It will come into good hands. Very truly yours, M.O. Wilder.*

The printed copy appeared in the Ontario Messenger, EXTRA in 1851 (See Appendix A for the entire sermon). I share the first page here for a flavor of Rev. Leonard Whitney's commitment to antislavery.

> A Parallel between the traitor Judas Iscariot and the Authors & Supporters of the Fugitive Slave Bill. **A Sermon,** by L. Whitney, *Pastor of the Free Church of Canandaigua, N.Y.*
>
> Verily I say unto you inasmuch as ye have done it unto one of the least of them, my brethren ye have done it unto me. – Matt 25, 40.
>
> Most men in a Christian land are more ready to admit the doctrine of a judgment than to consider for what they are to be judged—more ready to confess themselves sinners in general terms than to consider what sin is. Their attention has been so much occupied with the doctrines of total depravity and the imputed sin of their father Adam, that they seem to have forgotten their own. If it is not so, why is it that as well in the church as out of the church, those very sins abound that, as sure as the words of Christ are true, shall be as a millstone about the neck, in that day when all men shall be judged according to their works? Our text seems well intended to bring men to their senses on this subject.
>
> And what are those great sins put on our Savior as the representatives of all others on this solemn occasion? And

what are those great duties of the gospel, of the Christian life, of such transcendent importance as to stand alone at the judgment seat of Christ? Are they what men in general—what the church even, puts foremost and uppermost as the test of Christian character? – of acceptance with God? If our Lord has truly described this scene, are men's great sins reckoned there, their supposed errors in doctrine? – their honest doubts of a Trinity, total depravity by Adam's fall, (a fact which Christ in all his teaching forgot to mention), a 'vicarious atonement' and such like? Are they neglect of the forms of religion? – of baptism, the supper, the meetings of the church, stated preachings, and the regular means of grace? No such thing. However important these things may be to some minds as means, they are neither the substance nor the end of true religion. I know not that Christ ever condemned a single sinner for such sins. Certain it is he has not dignified them with a place at his judgment seat.

And what are the great duties he has exalted there? The duty of possessing an evangelical faith – of experiencing a change of nature — of confessing him at the anxious seat of uniting with the church and of a good and regular standing there? Not one word of it. However well all this may be, it is not religion, or so much a sign of religion, as to be brought into account at that day when every man shall be rewarded according to his works.

But there are sins and there are duties which shall be remembered at the bar of God, at the judgment seat of Christ. They are of the substance of human character. They try the heart and reins of the children of men. They are indicted by

> that infallible standard of our Savior, 'ye shall know them by their fruits - by their works shall ye know them.' And what are these great sins and these great duties that determine the moral character of men? The passage of scripture standing in connection with our text, can leave us in no doubt what they are. They are sins against our fellow men, and duties to our fellow men. They are expressed in language so common and simple that a child can understand them, and with an obligation so apparent that every human heart must respond to them. They commend themselves to every man's conscience. Hear them. Learn of Christ what makes a righteous man, and what makes a sinner. 'Then shall the king say unto them on his right hand, come ye blessed of thy Father, inherit the kingdom prepared for you from the foundation of the world — For I was an hungered and ye gave me meat; I was thirsty and ye gave me drink: I was a stranger and ye took me in: naked and ye clothed me: I was sick and ye visited me: I was in prison and ye came unto me. Then shall the righteous answer him saying, Lord, when saw we thee were hungered and fed thee or thirsty and gave thee drink? When saw we thee a stranger and took thee in or naked and clothed thee? Or when saw we thee sick or in prison and came unto thee? And the King shall answer and say unto them, verily I say unto you, inasmuch as ye have done it unto one of the least of these my brethren, ye have done it unto me.'

Again, from the Iowa Historical Record (p.53):

All the time his thought was enlarging. He became acquainted with Dr. Hosmer, minister of the Unitarian Church in Buffalo, and with the noble Samual J. May of Syracuse, with both of whom he exchanged pulpits, and found himself in essential sympathy with both. He went west as a religious pioneer. He was called to a church in Peoria and to the new movement in Keokuk, Ia. His ambition was never great. Keokuk was the smaller place, with the smaller salary. He accepted its call and became its minister in Oct. 1853. He had been only a short time in Keokuk when he had an invitation to the pastorate of the Unitarian Church in Rochester N.Y., which he declined. His society in Keokuk erected a building which was dedicated in 1856 and Mr. Whitney entered upon his years of valuable service. The first church was a rented hall, then a frame building built at 4th and High St. in 1856, later to have the beautiful church built in 1874, which was the Unitarian Church until 1944-45 when it was disbanded.

Courtesy photo/The Organ Historical Society

This 1874 Boston-manufactured pipe organ glows like a jewel in the closed and decaying former Unitarian Church at Fourth and High streets. The instrument's case was constructed of black walnut; it has 58 notes, 17 ranks and more than 800 pipes. Renovated by Organ Historical Society member Phil Hoenig of Fort Madison, it will be heard for the first time in several decades during the society's 1986 National Convention tour. Two 30-minute demonstrations are scheduled for Thursday.

Prelude by former resident

Church built on old site in 1874 –

Organ performances scheduled here

Harwood O. Whitney wrote an article for the "Old and New, A Journal of Liberal Religion," p. 38, about the early years of the church and the family:

EARLY RECOLLECTIONS OF THE FIRST UNITARIAN SOCIETY OF KEOKUK, IOWA. By Harwood O. Whitney

The First Unitarian Society of Keokuk, Iowa, was incorporated November 22, 1853. The articles of incorporation were drawn up by the late Hon. Samuel F. Miller, associate justice of the United States Supreme Court, then a member of the bar at Keokuk, also of this Society.

The Rev. Leonard Whitney was the first minister called on October 10, 1853, and served until January 7, 1861, when he resigned and was later appointed by Colonel Robert G. Ingersoll, commanding the Eleventh Regiment of Illinois Cavalry, chaplain of that regiment.

The establishment of the first Unitarian Society required courageous effort on the part of its first minister. Prejudice was strong. Stories are told of orthodox revivalists who pointed out at their meetings the overwhelming disaster that would overtake their members should they venture to cross the threshold of the Unitarian Church, and the majority did not venture.

Financial matters were also embarrassing. Speculation in city property was rampant, real estate advanced daily. Fortunate purchasers counted themselves rich overnight. Soon came the downfall of the boom and those that had acquired the most real estate at the high prices were poor and in debt.

Stringency in money matters usually affects church subscriptions first. Grocery bills must be paid in order to obtain credit for more. The First Unitarian Society was young and did not seem to assume the responsibility as to the minister's support that it now does. The American Unitarian Association paid him $400 per annum. The Keokuk Society subscribed an equal or greater amount and paid the minister as it was collected. If collections were not good, the minister and his family seemed to suffer the loss. At this time collections were not good.

The minister had been brought up when a boy on a Vermont farm. He owned two cows and milked them himself. The children delivered the milk to customers and the minister delivered his sermons regularly. The family enjoyed a prolonged bread and milk diet; thus, hard times were tided over.

Chaplain Leonard Whitney died from exposure in caring for the sick and wounded soldiers at the battle of Pittsburg Landing. The Rev. Oscar Clute wrote a biographical sketch of his life which was published in the Iowa Historical Record April 1888. Among several letters published I find the following from Colonel Ingersoll, of the eleventh Illinois Cavalry:

*New York, Jan 6, 1888 - Rev O. Clute –*

*My Dear Sir: It gives me great pleasure to write a few words in reference to the Rev. Leonard Whitney. He was one of the best, one of the purest one of the noblest men I ever knew. He was in the highest sense a deeply religious man - that is to say he lived in accordance with his ideal. There was about him neither can't nor hypocrisy. He did not pretend to be better than others; he wished only to make others better. While I knew him his entire time was occupied in doing good to others. He was a perpetual consolation to the sick and wounded, an example for all. He won the respect of every man who knew him, and his influence was only good. He was a thorough believer in the religion of good works, and he lived in exact accordance with his belief. He as truly gave his life for his country as though he had died on the field of battle. Yours truly, R.G. Ingersoll, Keokuk*

The following letters were written by Rev. Leonard to his brother, or possibly his brother-in-law, in Williston, Vt. They are very interesting and show the rampant real estate market at that time. He also predicted the crash.

Keokuk, Feb 9, 1857

Dear Brother: Your letter and butter both arrived some time since. Both were about equally rare and welcome and both good articles. You did not say whether the butter was of your own make, and it is utterly incredible to some of our good neighbors that it can be winter butter. The express charges were only $4.25 which would not have made it cost more than ours if I had paid your price for it, which I understand from Mothers letter was 25 cents per lb. I think I can afford to pay you for my writer's stock next fall and will send so early that we need not forward by express.

I hope you will not infer that because our markets are high here that as a people we do not live well. On the contrary we have got so used to it that we buy just as much as if everything were dog cheap. For example, you might think apples are a luxury at $2 per bu., potatoes $1.80 and cranberries $5, but most of our citizens have them nevertheless. And yet the common rates interest are 25-30% at the banks, 40-50 of the shavers and brokers and it is always a tight time.

You inquire about investment in our lots and lands. I can only say I have always considered them much too high, have always been afraid to invest even if I had been able and yet they have more than doubled in price every year since I have been here, and the end is not yet. Our city lots are 50 ft. front by 140 deep and the highest sales on Main St are about $500 per front foot. On a street next to Main St. 3 lots (for a hotel larger than the Burnett House, Cincinnati) sold the other day for $30,000. Yet our city, except its large blocks of stores, is not larger or half as well built as your Burlington. They claim a population of 12 or 15,000.

Tho I think this an important convenient point and destined in a few years to become a large place, I have all along expected a crash and still do. When it comes, I will not venture to prophesy since my predictions have so often proved false. But this I can say without prophecy, from a pretty full knowledge of the East and West and the "comparative advantages." For almost anything but speculation, the Eastern emigrant who leaves a good house or a good farm to better his condition in the West will wake up to find it the most stupendous humbug ever imposed upon a romantic imagination. He may find a richer soil, but by the time he gets such fences and buildings as he left, it will cost him twice as much as the land he sold, and if he gets a better climate, better roads, society, schools or better anything else he must find a "West" I have not seen.

And yet I do not write as one disappointed or homesick, for I am doing well here and expect to stay. But I do pity the lot who leave good homes in the N.E. for these cold, bleak, naked prairies to live for years in miserable cabins built of lumber at $50 per m. hauled 100 miles and stuck down in the black mud, treeless, fenceless, neighborless, cheerless, all for the sake of a little more dirt. It is a sore evil under the sun and if the emigrant could see the reality and not the romance of the "Go West", Iowa would not count an annual immigration of over 100,000 and the old states would not be depopulated.

Our new church is filling up rapidly. We have let slips to the value of about $1800 and we have only 12 left. Our incidental expenses will be some 600 and they will pay me a salary of 10 or 1200. I delivered a Lect. before our Lyceum the other night on "Religion & Politics" which has been attacked by an editor of the Boyne Democracy, so I have plenty of work on hand.

Jeannette is up and about but not strong. Charley is down with a slow fever but not dangerous and hope will be well soon. Harwood saws most of our wood for 3 fires, and Leonard wonders if that butter did come all the way from Grandmas?

Yours as ever, Leonard Whitney

Keokuk, March 11, 1857

Dear Bro: Still the butter holds out and still we hold you all in daily grateful remembrance. But it is getting rather low. I write you in season that there may be no interruption of this precious extract of the "milk of human kindness." I will not beg any more but as the prospect is still as dubious as ever here, if you can get me 100 lbs. put up so as to keep for about $25 I think I can stand that and the freight and still feel very much your debtor. Is it possible that it was winter butter you sent us? If there is a chance to get it thru by a R.R. Freight Express in tolerable season the charges would be much less. Direct it via Quincy as we have daily boats from their R.R. Should you or should you not be able to get it, let me know by letter soon.

More about lots and lands here. Mother's cousin, Green Erskine, sold a quarter section (160 acres) about 2 miles from our city, to one of our land speculators the other day for, how much do you guess? $160,000!!! Well, $1000 per acre would be pretty high for farming purposes, but it has been mostly cut into city lots and resold for $2000 per acre. A dwelling house just on the opposite square from mine including 6 lots, 50-140 ft, was purchased at $2500. The house is new and gaudily finished but not large and the outbuildings and fences remain to be put on by the fortunate purchaser. He says they will cost at least $5000. Well, reckoning money at 20% the lowest rate here, his annual rent for dwelling will be only $6000.

If you doubt whether these prices are safe and will last, then come out and let your money at 20 to 30 per cent on good paper. Edward Boynton, a son of Uncle Jed of Hinesburg, is now here doing that very thing and they say there is no limit to the demand. Of course, this will not be while men can make 100 per cent in land speculation.

Col. Perry the other day gave me a clean deed to the lot I built on and says it is worth $2000 without the improvements. I am in favor of selling when I am offered $5000 for the place, but

Jannette objects and others say I could not better myself for a home.

We had quite a large gathering of our friends at our house last evening, treated them to hot coffee, biscuits and some of the Vt. butter and they seemed to enjoy it all, but especially the butter. Some of the natives, however, who never tasted any sweet butter before, think it lacks strength and seasoning. We have had an awfully muddy, disagreeable winter. The river has been open since the great flood East, but there is much running ice, some snow on the ground and the nights are still very cold.

Yours truly, L. Whitney

Keokuk, March 23, 1858

Dear Bro: I got your letter yesterday and in reply say send on your $1000. I have talked with my Friend Rudick, a money dealer, today and he says he thinks he can get 20 to 25 per cent for it with ample security besides selling the draft for about 3% if it comes on soon. He says I had better have you get it in about 4 drafts of $250 each. I will execute your mortgage as soon as I can get time and have it recorded according to our laws and send it to you. I think our security must be ample as naked lots are now selling near me for $1300 in cash down. I have not got the things Mother sent nor heard of them before your letter. Baby and wife not very well. You will remember to cut the $1000 into 4 drafts.

Yours in haste, Leonard Whitney

The Whitney home was at 8th and Franklin: 525 No. 8th, later changed to 728 Franklin. A family story was that he owned a house (can't figure out where it was located) had it torn down and shipped by boat to Keokuk and rebuilt on this lot in 1856 or 1857. I'm not sure about the story being true.

Ann Jenette (Rev. Leonard's widow) and Harwood both lived there until they died. Ann Jenette died in 1904 and Harwood died in 1914. Aunt Lilly, Harwood's widow, lived there until 1925. A kitchen was added in the back in 1885 at the cost of $131.25 by Geo Elrick. A porch was added about 1910 by Aunt Lilly.

Baby girl, Nettie, was born Feb. 7, 1858, and died Oct 18, 1858, at eight months old.

Later, in 1861, Rev. Leonard keeps mentioning a note owed him by Rudick that he keeps trying to collect on. I don't know if he invested some of his own money or if this was his brother's. This is a copy:

Ruddick note? 11-B

For the Consideration of Eleven Hundred & Twenty three $\frac{83}{100}$ Dollars I Wm Ruddick of City of Keokuk Iowa hereby convey to L. Whitney

the following tract of Land, to wit: Lot No. Ten in Block No. Thirty Eight And all my undivided one half interest in Lots No. Seven and eight in Block Sixty three – In the City of Keokuk

In the County of Lee and State of Iowa. And Warrant the Title against all persons whomsoever.

To be void upon the following conditions, to wit: That I pay or cause to be paid a certain promissary note bearing date April 12th – 1859 Payable Twelve Months after date to the order of L. Whitney – for the sum of Eleven hundred and Twenty three $\frac{83}{100}$ dollars. Signed by Wm & R. L. Ruddick.

In Witness Whereof, I have hereunto signed my name this Eighteenth day of June eighteen hundred and fifty Nine

Wm Ruddick (SEAL)

(SEAL)

STATE OF IOWA, Lee County } ss.

Be it remembered that on this Eighteenth day of June A. D., 1859. before me, R. L. Ruddick a Notary Public in and for said County, personally appeared Wm Ruddick who is personally known to me to be the identical person whose name is affixed to the above Deed as grantor and acknowledged the same to be his voluntary act and deed, for the uses and purposes therein expressed.

In Testimony Whereof, I have hereunto set my hand and affixed my Notarial Seal this day and date above written.

R. L. Ruddick

Keokuk Post Book and Job Office, print.

Rev. Leonard Whitney's story continues in the Iowa Historical Record, p.53:

> His geniality as a man, his generosity as a friend, his eloquence as a preacher, his power as a thinker, and the

> genuine religiousness of his nature called into his church a company of men and women of remarkable ability, some of whom have since reached a wider than national fame and influence. Hon. Samuel F. Miller, now senior Justice on the U.S. Supreme Court, was then a young lawyer in Keokuk. He became one of Mr. Whitney's most faithful friends. Hon. Geo W. McCrary, a rising young man from Van Buren Co. Iowa, went to Keokuk to study law. He and his amiable wife also found in the Unitarian church a congenial religious home. Mr. Briggs, editor of the Gate City, then as now one of the most influential papers in Iowa, became an attendant on Mr. Whitney's preaching, and one of his warmest admirers. Dr. Freeman Knowles, who had brought from his birthplace in Maine a keen New England mind and his wife, whose religious nature and mental power fitted her for the noblest society, and their daughter Emma were drawn to his preaching. Able businessmen were there not a few. George Williams, C.H. Perry, E. H. Harrison, Wm Leighton and their wives, were all fed mentally and spiritually by the power of their preacher. J.M. Hiatt, S.W. Tucker, R.B. Ogden and their wives found in him a leader whom they could gladly follow. Most of these early friends have crossed the river or have moved to other fields of business. But all of whom I have met are heartily loyal to this spiritual leader of their early or mature manhood and all are enthusiastic in their appreciation of his genius.

Evidently in 1859 or 1860 Harwood was sent to Vermont to live with Rev. Leonard's brother, Edmund, and to attend school at Williston Academy in Williston, Vt. I do not know how long he was there. In August 1861 he enlisted in the Iowa Volunteers at the age of 17, so he was 16 when Leonard wrote the following letter to him at

Williston, a father giving his son a lesson of when to stand up and fight and when not to.

Keokuk, April 8, 1860

Dear Harwood,

We got a line from you a day or two since and are always glad to hear from you, especially that you are growing and learning so fast. I wrote today to your Uncle Ed about your clothes & if he does not get them, I will send the money as soon as I can collect enough. I wish you were home last night to lick a boy that abused Charley. It was Henry Rickey with whom you once had a fight; & if with your present weight you could not lick him, I would lick you. He dragged Charley by the hair & pulled out some. I have just been up to see him about it & tell him the peril of repeating it with so much smaller than he. But how much better it would have been if you had been present to match him. I do hope you will never suffer yourself to be afraid when you are attacked, nor let anything of you siege conquer you & live. It is all in coolness & courage in conquering anything. Don't pick quarrels, be good natured & kind & forbearing - "If it be possible, as much as in you lies, live peaceably with all." But when it is not possible without a fight, let your wrath be dreadful - pitch in first & come out first - hit in the best place & give no breathing time til the job is done. This, in such cases is "overcoming evil with good". You do not write anything about what you want to do - whether remain in school or get into some business. I do not know of much chance here or whether you could find a place there. If not, you must put into your studies so as to get qualified for a teacher. How would it suit you or what

> business do you think you would like? Dr. Bartlett is with us & has gone to work in an Iron Foundry for his health. How would you like that? I suppose you must have had a good time with the maple sugar this spring. Have you been to any of the sugar camps? (--- can't read the last paragraph---) All send much love to you.
>
> Your father, L. Whitney

Carlton Perry Whitney was born in Keokuk on September 8, 1860, named for dear friend Col. C. Perry.

The Iowa Historical Record continues, p. 54:

> Still the strong man and the able leader found his labors hindered because some of those who loved him as a man, and who were in empathy with his religious philosophy could not agree with him in all respects in the practical application of that philosophy. Slavery was the all-absorbing topic in society and in politics. Mr. Whitney's soul was on fire with the love of liberty. His direct mind and sensitive moral nature went, sure as the needle to the pole, straight to the immediate freedom of the slave. Not all of his people were able to think with him. He could not rest except in sermon and in prayer, his love of justice and freedom found frequent and burning expressions. Not all his people could see that duty demanded this constant and ardent utterance. Just then the Rebellion, terrible in its suffering and bloodshed, but glorious in the reward of justice and liberty it won, was urged on by the sadly mistaken South. Mr. Whitney's heart and mind could then rest only in active

> service. He had spoken for liberty; he now wanted to work for liberty.

An article in the Keokuk paper, 1887, states: *Mr. Whitney remained with the society until March 1861 when owing to a division in the church on the slavery question, he resigned.*

From Harwood's "Recollections" (see previous "Early Recollections of the First Unitarian Society of Keokuk" p.21) his father, Rev. Leonard, resigned from the church on January 7, 1861, whether lack of funds to pay him or the controversy over his political ideals had anything to do with this, I do not know. Geo McCrary, in the letter to the Iowa Historical Record article, says he had trouble obtaining an appointment as a chaplain because he was of a liberal religion. It was not until November 29, 1861, that Rev. Leonard received the letter from Col. Ingersoll asking Rev. Leonard to join him as a chaplain. The following is a letter written for the Iowa Historical Record (p.62) by Geo. McCrary. This letter gives more insight into the early days and the character of Leonard Whitney.

> He was installed, I believe, over the Keokuk church in 1853. When I went to that place to commence the study of law in the fall of 1854, he was preaching to a small congregation of exceptionally strong people, in a hall near the corner of Main and Fourth streets. The Keokuk church at that time numbered among its supporters such men as Samuel F. Miller, now senior justice of the Supreme Court of the United States, Col. C.H. Perry, Dr. Freeman Knowles, Wm. Leighton, E.H. Harrison, J.M. Hiatt, and others of scarcely less prominence, all of whom were much devoted to Mr. Whitney. As a preacher Mr. Whitney was chiefly distinguished for the force and power of his logic. It was an education to hear him from

Sunday to Sunday. His was for a long time the only Unitarian Pulpit in Iowa. He stood at his post, surrounded by his little band of devoted followers, and right manfully defended the Liberal Faith. In his day controversial preaching by the liberal clergy was necessary. It is, happily, not so now. Mr. Whitney and his church were a target for many sharp shots from all the surrounding pulpits. I knew and admired the orthodox clergy of Keokuk of that day, and I do them no injustice when I say that Mr. Whitney was more than a match for them all. On one occasion I remember he had mercilessly exposed the unreasonableness of certain popular theological doctrines, and a neighboring minister had replied soundly berating him for speaking so of sacred things and insisting that the doctrines in question only seemed unreasonable because finite minds can not understand the reasoning of the infinite. In reply, Mr. Whitney exclaimed with great force: "I can not accept these things on the ground that I do not understand them, for as an honest man, I am bound to reject them because I DO understand them."

But he did not always debate in his pulpit. In spirit he was gentle and charitable, and preached much upon topics of duty and practical living. Once, I remember a curious circumstance happened which will illustrate something of his deep religious faith as well as his readiness as a speaker. He was preaching in the evening and his subject was immortality. Suddenly the gas went almost out, so that for a time the church became dark. He stopped his discourse while the darkness continued, which was several moments, and when the light returned, as it did very suddenly, he said, "So, my friends, I believe it will be with all of us. For a moment, at the end of life's journey, darkness may come over us, but it will be but for a moment, and will be followed by the glorious light and joy of eternity."

As a preacher he was far above the average. His power was the result of great ability coupled with evident sincerity. He never descended to hair splitting niceties, but always grasped the vital questions touching the subject in hand. He had no patience with arguments founded on isolated passages of scripture. He adopted a very different method of argument. The attributes of God as understood by all Christians were taken as his premises, and from these he went with unerring certainty to his conclusions. God is love, therefore, nothing can proceed from him that is not prompted by love. God is justice, therefore no punishment that is not just can proceed from him. God's mercy endures forever, and therefore will always be with every child. God is wisdom, therefore his chastisements must be wise, hence can not be aimless nor endless. These are samples of his inexorable logic. Many others might be added. His sermons cast in this mold and delivered with a fervent eloquence not often seen, produced a marked effect upon his hearers. They appealed with equal power to the head and heart, to the intellect and the affections.

Mr. Whitney was deeply interested in the anti-slavery cause and could not see it to be his duty to keep silent upon that subject. He was one of the few ministers in southern Iowa who preached openly and boldly against slavery from 1854 until the war. I remember well one of his sermons, preached I think in 1856, in which he arraigned the slave power as hostile to the Union and predicted that war would come if they persisted in their course, and that the result of war would be the destruction of slavery and the establishment of the Union founded upon liberty and justice, and therefore destined to be perpetual. Having preached thus for many years, he naturally felt, when the war came, that he ought to do something more than just preach for the cause he loved so well. He doubted whether a Unitarian minister could get a place as chaplain, and this gave him some trouble. Hearing, however, that the famous Col. Robert G. Ingersoll had raised a regiment of Illinois cavalry, he very naturally surmised that Mr. Ingersoll would not object to him on account of his heterodoxy. He accordingly wrote Col. Ingersoll a letter applying for the chaplaincy of the regiment and saying, "If appointed I promise to take care of the sick and wounded half of the time, to fight half the time, and preach the remainder." He got the place, and he had the reputation among the officers and soldiers who knew him, of being one of the best chaplains in the army.

Col. Robert Ingersoll wrote:

Peoria, Nov. 29, 1861 - Leonard Whitney, Keokuk

Dear Sir, I am informed by Mr. Palsifer that you would be willing, if appointed Chaplain, to accompany the Eleventh Illinois to the wars. Mr. Williams and the Rev'd Mr. Ried have also spoken or written to me of you. If you will accept, you shall have the office. You had better be here by Wednesday next so as to be mustered into service. The mustering officer will be here next week. You will forgive my leaving the "Rev'd" off your name. I pledged my honor to put it on the envelope.

I am forever, Robert G Ingersol

> N.B. If you are here on Wednesday next your salary will commence. If you delay you may lose a hundred or two.

From an article in a pamphlet, "The Month at Goodspeed's" March, 1936, published by the Boston Bookstore, the following article is about finding piles of Ingersoll's old manuscripts.

> Col. Robert Ingersoll was one of the greatest orators and his speeches made him a national figure. He was later known as "The Great Agnostic" and championed the new ideas of Darwin and Huxley. After the Civil War he was the Attorney General of Illinois, and it was believed if he had not taken on the task of correcting the "Mistakes of Moses" and applying the new word agnostic to himself, he would have gone far in politics, at least to the governor's chair. Although his unorthodox notions made him bad political timber, it is said that his fine character saved him from an ostracism that would have been the lot of any man of less positive integrity who had had the temerity to speak as Ingersol spoke in the America of his day.

We also have an old book containing 44 complete lectures by Ingersol. (For more information about Col. Robert G. Ingersoll see Appendix D)

From the Iowa Historical Record, p.55:

> For this work he (Whitney) was peculiarly fitted. He was genial in spirit; he met all men in a happy way. He had an appreciation of man; he could detect the divine-human through the lowliest and most sinful guise. He was unselfish; he gave gladly his last crust to the suffering. He was entirely without sanctimonious pretense; he went among the men as

> a brother, a friend, a sympathetic helper. The officers and men were drawn to him at once. The relations between him and them were cordial and brotherly. He was their minister in the true sense - their helper, their leader in the best things.

And so, Rev. Leonard Whitney left for the Civil War.

# PART 2 - LETTERS

*"How to meet your death and overcome its fears"*

*[His last sermon, see Letter 21]*

*Rev. Leonard Whitney*

Following are letters written by Leonard Whitney to his wife and son Harwood, who was also in the army's 3rd Iowa Cavalry Co. C. I have retyped them all completely, however they are very hard to read as some are in faded pencil, and his writing was not the clearest. Consequently, some words are missing and there are blanks where this occurs.

At the time Rev. Leonard left for the war, those he left at home were Carlton Perry, age 1 year; Leonard Bennison, age 11 years; Charles Edmund, age 15 years; Harwood Otis was 17 and enlisted in August 1861; and his beloved wife, Ann Jenette, age 36 years. Rev. Leonard was 50 years old. Of particular note is the letter detailing the Battle of Shiloh, April 1862, to his wife, and the tin-type picture of Harwood in his uniform, age 17. A strange coincidence is another picture we have of Harwood, full length, in his uniform taken by Enoch Long, a photographer, in St. Louis, Missouri. Enoch Long was my Great Grandfather, my grandmother's father, and grandmother would have been around 4 years old at the time of the picture. Harwood, 44 years later, married my grandmother's sister-in-law. At the time they were not acquainted with each other.

Harwood Otis Whitney, age 17

## Letter #1

Peoria, Dec. 12, 1862

My Dear Wife - Failing to make legible marks with a steel pen I sit down with Charley's stub of a pencil to give you some account of my progress thus far. I had a very pleasant trip to Burlington, arrived at Galesburg the same nite and here the next day (Tuesday) before dinner. I put up at my old Hotel the "Peoria House" & found on inquiry our cousin Sidney just gone up to Hennepin to spend the week. In the afternoon I visited Col. Ingersoll at "Camp Lyon." He and his regiment were all gone some two miles to the drill ground and did not return 'till about dark. I spent the intervening time toasting my feet at the campfire and chatting with the privates. When the regiment returned, supper was announced at the officers' quarters by a large dignified Col. Quarterman and I was invited by one of the staff to partake. Col. Ingersoll was at the head of the table and after introduction gave me a seat opposite him. He is a man of mark in any crowd. He is of large full proportions, fine hew & forbearance, the picture of good living, good nature, and good sense. His weak side has been, I am told, the love of good liquor and hard profane and rough language. Our supper was excellent save the adulterated army coffee, three fourth Rye which I as an officer will reform. After a service from the Col. Pike and a chat with him and some of the other officers, I returned to the Hotel as they have not any camp quarters ready. Yesterday I called upon Rev. Mr. Reid who took me over and introduced me to the present Mrs. Palsifer. She is quite out of health and this morning my eyes were open to the fact that she is preparing for another baby. She is quite tall, light complexion & hair and eyes, & quite deaf for the last year & as prim and precise as a schoolmarm, which she had been. All Jane's children were at school, so you see they have grown some tho none of them are ..?.. than Leonard. I had a good visit with them last night about the Hennepin people. Lyman's health is very poor, Rollin is with him, came there sick from Cairo last spring. Edward's boy is married & has a baby. The rest of the news I will tell you when I see Sidney. I expect to be mustered in tomorrow and go into Camp. My throat is not well and I cannot bear much exposure for awhile. The officers' quarters are not the nice parlour my fine wife supposed them. Our dining room has no floor and the finish of the best room is rough board. The best chair I saw was the head of a nail keg and the best bed a soldier's bunk of rough boards. But they say the officers have plenty of blankets and straw, so I presume we shall sleep, if not like 'Pigs in the Clover' at least like hogs in straw. I don't suppose the boards can be much harder than our bed so the softness of the straw will be extra above my own bed & board at home. I hope whatever the fare may be I shall have health enough to stand it, as it seems at present my only chance to serve either my God, my Country, or my family. I see by Gen. McLellan's last order that the uniform of a Chaplain is very simple, a black frock coat with standing collar and 9 black buttons, blk pants, plain, and blk felt hat. I have it, you see, all but the standing collar and hope the old coat will do till I need a new one. I am not yet informed anything about my horses, script or wages. I suppose there is no prospect of pay very soon at least until I earn some. They say there is no danger of the Regt. being broken up and when or where they will march us no one can now tell. The Col thinks the destination will not be St. Louis but Ky.

I hope the boys are all well, kiss them all for me and tell Leonard if he ever hopes to make an officer he must go to school and try "for to learn." I hope you will try to ..?.. yourself, live well and ..?.. as I ..?..

above means will warrant it. And now goodbye till I hear from you. Direct me as follows, Rev. L. Whitney, Chaplain 11 Ill. Cavalry, Camp Lyon, Peoria, Ill.

P.S. I shall write to Harwood soon perhaps today L.W.

## Letter #2

Camp Lyon, Peoria Ill. Jan. 12, 1862

My dear son - On my return to Camp last Friday I found a letter from you which I have not found time to answer before. You may dismiss your fear about my sore throat - at least it has not troubled me much and seems to get better rather than worse since I enter upon the duties of Camp life. But the tug of war has not come yet, and by this I do mean ...?... & ...?... but the exposure of the march, camping out and the dreadful jolting on horseback. I wish I had your old horse to practice up on and then I could stand any jolt in creation. Do you keep him yet, or has Capt. Hendriksen given you a better?

I suppose Mother wrote you of my long visit at home & how we wished you were there to enjoy it with us. She thought from the tone of your last letter you were a little homesick. You spoke of Mr. Stone and of gain leaving the mess in consequence. Who are those officers, so stirred up by a little brief authority you cannot live with them? Sit down every such man as wanting in common sense and get along with his vanity as easily as possible, especially do not give a fool the power to disturb your temper or your digestion. I wrote you a long letter on my way home from Burlington which I hope you got and could read. In that I gave you some advice which I will not repeat here. Indeed, it may be you should be my instructor in the Art of Camp Life. But I suppose there are no secrets about Camp Life more than thru life - to observe the laws of cleanliness and health as well as circumstances will admit, to keep the mind well employed and the temper even and cheerful are the basics of the whole thing, but I suppose we shall both have occasion to acclaim with the apostle, "how to perform, I find not."

The stay at home was longer than I intended, chiefly because some winter clothing I ordered was not done when promised. I got the new chaplain uniform - a black frock with standing collar and 9 black buttons, blk pants and calf haired lined cav'y boots. I got them on credit of my office and hope when I get my horse and trappings, my outgoes will end for a while. I can collect nothing on the Rudick note and have put it in Miller's hands to be served. He thinks he can collect it in the course of one or two years. I have borrowed $50 of Sidney P. for current expenses here and at home. I believe I expressed my thanks in my other letter for the $10 you sent your mother. It was as welcome and generous as unexpected. I hope we shall both be able to save enough to settle us in some independent business at the close of the war and both live to enjoy it.

Our quarters here are very roomy and good and our Reg't enjoys remarkable health. We have now 6 in the hospital, none of them dangerously ill and were it not for 2 cases of measles I should have no fear of our continued exemption of disease. We hope to limit the disease to the cases on hand. I do not preach today as it is too cold outdoors, and we have no other place fitted up yet. I brought a big trunk of books and tracts from home and have distributed to the men. All seemed to receive them kindly. Some I suppose will read them and some not. I think we have a rougher set of men than yours and my great trouble is to keep up Faith that anything I can do will do them much good. But there is a script- "Cast thy Bread upon the water and thou shall find it after many days"- and though some seed may fall by the wayside some may fall into your ground. I do not see much chance to Preach to any advantage during this cold stormy winter weather. All I can do is to introduce reading matter and by personal intercourse and kindly words try to keep men from evil habits and will them to a better life. How does Br. Ingalls get along and what means does he use to help you? Do the men like him and is he doing any good? The prominent evils of the camp are swearing, drinking and general rowdyism. Can you tell me how to make a change upon them with a ...?... hope of success?

I know of course the cure of all these evils does not make a man much less a Christian man. A man might not swear or get drunk or steal and yet be a very poor, mean specimen of humanity, destitute of all those noble positive virtues that make the character of the good man a glory and a joy. Let it be our daily effort and prayer not merely to break off evil habits that degrade us, but to put on the beautiful garment of a higher virtue- to become more true, more generous and unselfish. More kind, more noble, braver and more devoted to every good word and work. It is getting too dark to write and I fear I have written more than you can make out. I will try to direct this right and hope you may get it soon and reply soon.

Your Father

## Letter #3

Camp Lyon, Peoria Jan 13/62

My Dear Wife, - I wrote Harwood yesterday and should have written to you had not darkness overtaken me unawares. It is awful cold, and the only stove is surrounded so I must rub my fingers and just let you know how I am. I got here last Friday and came at once to camp. I have hardly been warm since and last night froze out, got up and built a fire and like Paul "waited for the day." I did not preach yesterday as it was too cold outdoors, and we have no room fit. I spent the day distributing the contents of the big trunk and in a small social meeting in the eve'n. It was in the Methodist Capt's tent, and we sang the good old Meth't tunes.

Young Perkins is in camp and I made him a call. He is well and likes soldiering. We have got the Measles in camp (8 cases) but we do not mean they shall spread. I have not seen Sidney yet but mean to go and stay with them tonight and see if I can sleep warm. The Col. is gone to St. Louis and when he comes we expect marching orders, but we "don't know where"- I believe I told you not to have the Rudick note served yet? Miller could make it perfectly secure. I think they would at least give a Mortgage on the farm they offered me until I can get home in the Spring to go up and see it.

I hope you got your woodpile and will keep warm without shortage of fuel. I have not shown my new uniform yet, nor got a horse nor done anything to distinguish me as a soldier. I must close as all my ideas are froze up and my hands are stiff with cold. I hope you are all well and the boys are obedient to Mother, attentive to their lessons and above all kind to each other. Do write soon and let me know all about home.

Your husband, L.

## Letter #4

Camp Lyon, Jan. 20, 1862

My dear wife - I got your letter in due time and was glad, as I always am, to hear from you and know that you are all well. About that note, I presume you will secure or collect it better than I can so I shall leave it to you and your attorney, Mr. Miller. I received a letter from Ed, who offered to take my note instead of Ruddick's. I shall send it today. Mother and all the rest are well. I went over to Sidney's and lodged Saturday night (a great treat is a good bed) and preached in their fine church for Rev. Mr. Reid yesterday. It was a rainy day, and the church was not full- but the cong's was good and Sidney said he knew they were well pleased with the sermon. I went home to dine in a sleigh with Mr. & Mrs. Borland and after dinner they carried me up to camp. They visited our hospital with me, and Mrs. Borland refreshed the sick with the Light of her countenance, some current jellies and cordials. Her curls have grown a little grey, but she still is Ladylike as ever and presume thinks herself as charming. Sidney says she is really a good woman and only repels some people by an apparent assumption of superiority. They both treated me very cordially and invited me to come and stay with them as much as I could. I found the measles in our camp when I returned, and we have lost 2 men by the disease. It has not spread far yet but seems to be very fatal. I have distributed most of the reading I brot from home and more sent me from Boston. That, with visiting the sick, attending funerals and personal intercourse with men at their quarters, is about all I shall be able to do for them until the weather is warm enough to preach outdoors. The rumor now is that we shall soon move with our tents across the country to Quincy, and on our way to join the Jim Lane expedition from Ft. Leavenworth south to Texas. If we should go and stop sometime at Q I may come home a few days - if you will let me. I have no horse yet and I don't know as I shall try to get one till I get to Q or come home. I would not venture the march across the …?.. and camping out on this cold snow when I can go so easily by cars. I have tried horse-back riding several times and stand it much better than I expected. Indeed, I think I shall like it if I get a good horse. We have expected the paymaster for some days to pay us all off to the 1st of Jan. My pay will be only part of a month. Had I not better pay the $50 to Sidney and keep the rest (unless you need some) to meet my current expenses? I am told our board is costing us about 4 or 5 dol. for a week. You may think this high, but it is not worth changing if we are to move so soon.

I found a letter from Harwood when I came back to Camp and replied to it. I wish I knew whether he were still in St. Louis. It is now impossible his Reg't may go with Jim Lane. I hope your health is improving with less work and care, plenty of good things to eat and drink and the prospect before you of a brighter and happier future. The boys must learn to obey you at once and in good temper and put in their time at school. The baby I know will be well governed as you have his exclusive training. Remember me to all the neighbors, especially Mr. Fletcher and William's people. I would write you something interesting from camp if I could to fill up my sheet as you know I cannot write a short letter. For instance, we had a man stabbed at a show in the city Saturday night, and the Col. knocked down a Sandy Soldier. "Channing Works" which I presented to the Officer for the most part lie about in heaps unread, and only two or 3 thot to put their names in them or ask me to do so. What Channing wrote about slavery, by the most of them would be called "Damned Abolitionism." And this is all explained by them almost all being Democrats of that pro-slavery stripe who charges all the blame of this Rebellion upon the Republican Party. Who had rather shoot an Abolitionist than a Rebel and want like to catch a Nigger when we get down South for their own use. Well, I will try to do them all the good

I can, but to know where to begin to civilize and Christianize some human beings is more than I know. Blessed be the Faith that can make something of all souls in the Infinite Future. Write soon and as often as you can.

Your dear husband, Leonard Whitney

## Letter #5

Camp Lyon, Peoria, Jan 24, 1862

My Dear Wife - Supposing you may be as glad to hear from me as I always am from you. I improve a little leisure to write, for once a short letter. I have just finished a little puff for one of our daily papers, dedicated to Mrs. Palsifer & Forland for nice things sent to our hospital. Sidney came up with me last ev'g and brot me and them, and the clean sheets and pillowcases on the bunks this morning make our Hosp'l look like a new place and something like home. Another home feature I propose tonight is the commencement of evening Prayer in the room occupied by the sick. You may think this is a new fit for Devotion on my part, but I think I told you before, that to dwell in the tents or wickiups only increases my interest in Spiritual things. I hope the Voice of Prayer in the sick room may touch hearts that would be cold and callus in the riot and excitement of Camp Life.

Do not be surprised or vexed when I tell you I am trying to have Harwood transferred to our Reg't. I have done it at the suggestion of the Col. who says he and I may dwell in a tent together and he will save me the expense of a servant. He will be under my eye and I trust under my control. I have had a good letter from him lately in which he spoke of being transferred and thot it might be done if I desire it. I don't know if his petition will be granted. If it is he will be with me soon; if not, I will tell him not to be disappointed. The Paymaster has not come yet and we don't know when he will and the order to Quincy is revoked. We know not where or when we shall march but the arrival of our Mule Trains came last night smacks of the Plains and Jim Land. Our Mess is getting economical having dropped suddenly down to Soldiers rations, to go up again I presume as we get starved out. I am getting more reconciled to the bunk and as the weather grows warmer, I presume I shall thaw out and sleep more comfortably. Harwood's mess is in tents and he says they are much warmer and better and healthier than this Duenten. I hope you are all well and try always to think you are when I do not know to the contrary and hope you think so of me. Kiss all the children for me and tell them how happy I am to hear they are good, obedient, affectionate boys. I know they will try to be good to you for my sake as well as yours. Write as soon and as often as you can and tell me everything about Home.

From your Husband

## Letter #6

Camp Lyon, Jan 30, 1862

I enclose the half sheet about Harwood's transfer, so that you may see what they say about him. (not in letter)

I got your welcomed letter this morning and I should have replied to it at once had not our sick soldiers in the hospital needed my services more than you. They complained they had nothing to eat but poor, burnt bread for toast and poor fried pork. Poor enough certainly for men in battle and not much of a relish for the delicate appetite of the convalescent. So I told the Doctor this morning if he would give me a list of the articles most needed in his department I would go out begging among my friends. The list was as follows: 1- chicken cooked & chicken broth, 2- dressing gowns & slippers, 3- flat iron & strips of old carpeting.

I accomplished my mission in time to go home with Sidney to dinner and get his horse & buggy to take my traps to camp before night. Mrs. Palsifer and the Baby are not well but so as to be about. I told her that you wrote about learning to make her puff crust, and that I could not tell whether you desired written instruction or whether it was a sly hint for an invitation to visit Peoria that you might see the thing done with your own eyes and look in upon my quarters at Camp Lyon. I should with ..?.. heart assume the latter construed the true one. If it were only warm weather or we only knew anything about how long we would stay here. As it is I suppose I must content myself with hearing from you often and feeling that you and the children are better off at home for my absence in camp. Do make yourself as comfortable as you can and if Old Meesy won't do make a change as soon as you are sure you can do better. But I don't see why you have grown so suddenly aristocratic that "Come on" won't do as a good call to dinner. To me as you know, the dinner itself is the chief thing and whether the call be "come on" or "charge" or "fill up your bread basket," so the dinner was good and up to time. I shouldn't find it in my heart to complain. But folks is different, especially about women folks, so you must make Old Meesy toe the mark.

I suppose by this time you must have got my letter about Harwood's transfer to our Reg't. Before you protest let me tell you I have just got a letter from Maj. Berry, written by Kate, which informs me it is not probable it will be done. He says Gen. Halleck, to save himself annoyance, has proclaimed that no more transfers will be granted.

He also says Capt. Huelerson does not like to lose such a boy as Harwood and speaks in the highest terms of his personal appearance and habits and soldierly learning. I am not much sorry at this result, tho I should like to have him with me and could save some money by it. About Rudick note, I suppose it is too late to advise, if it is served. If it could be made perfectly sure, I would not mind waiting one or even two years at 10%. But let there be no doubt but the security is good for the money.

My health is quite as good as usual, and my only real discomfort the want of a good warm room for my own use and a bed. I have partly negotiated for one in a private home near our Camp, and if Harwood doesn't come shall take it soon. I think I told you we were living on rations at 16 cents a piece; and the only trouble is our mess will not stick to it more than 2 days at a time. This morning the pure old Java and hot rolls were restored from their temporary banishment. I think however, we are all growing economical, and if my living costs too much I shall either take private board nearby or get a servant and pitch my tent alone.

I yet find it impossible to preach out of doors and do what I can to make the sick comfortable at the hospital and furnish reading to the boys in their quarters. I cannot boast of the good and yet I console myself with the tho't that nobody else under the cir's could do much more. I hope the boys are doing well in all things, tho you only told me they were attending school. Yes, you did tell how fond Leonard was becoming of his reading. I am so glad. Does he get any better of his temper? Charlie I know will do well, if you can wait for him. Kiss the Baby for me and take all the Love for yourself this big sheet will hold. Don't forget to answer.

Your Husband

## Letter #7

Feb. 7, 1862

My dear wife - I'm sorry I was so careless about the Letter. I don't know anything to match it but your carelessness in sending Leonard to lose it. So we will balance the account. There was nothing of value in it except some Love for you and the children. I have just returned from a trip to Pekin (10 miles on horseback) went one day and back the next. Isn't that pretty well for me. I don't feel lame this morning and enjoyed the ride much. I went with our Major to a Sunday School Exhibition and to see the Universalist Minister, Mr. Chapin. I had a good visit but was bored to death with the exhibition. The dramatic part was performed by Mrs. Chapin.

Our paymaster doesn't come yet but we hope to see him soon. I have no horse and shall not till we are paid off.

I hope you take the Arm of Life as easy as you can so as to get fat by the time I drop in on you some dark night. I can't tell how soon this will be but hope not many weeks. One of our men broke his leg on the ..?.. yest'y. Our Measles are going pretty easy. I hope it will be warm enough for a sermon outdoors on Sunday. The sun looks out warm this morn'g. I hope it looks in upon happy faces at Home. This song sent from Boston will explain itself,

Your husband, Leonard

(This letter is written on the back of a printed song- words and music "The Triumph of Liberty"- the words of this song were written in 1843 by the late Henry Ware, Jr; the tune, familiar to many, is said to have been first played on the entrance of the allies into Paris.)

## Letter #8

Camp Lyon, Peoria, Feb.19, 1862

My dear wife - You can't tell how uneasy I had become before I got your letter today. I suppose your excuse that "you are about sick" must do. But don't delay so long again when you know how ready I am to imagine something is the matter with you or the children. I am glad there is nothing the matter with you but overwork and hope you will soon relieve that by getting over your hurry, you must somehow learn to take life easier in Body and Mind. I know you will try for my sake if not your own; but it is hard at once to throw off care and break up old habits. O, that to do were as easy as to will.

I thot from what I saw in the papers Harwood's Reg't must be after Price and hope nothing will befall him in this new and exciting service. Our Reg't is ordered to St Louis and will probably get ready to start next week. If they move by land with their tents and train as the order now is, it will take them some 3 or 4 weeks and I shall try to come home by Burlington and join them when they reach St. Louis. So you will not be taken by surprise if I come home next week, if I can raise the money. We have not rec'd our Dinn and I think shall not 'till we move, but we hope to get two payments when it comes.

The Col. is still absent with his bride but is daily expected. Sidney and his son Eddy started on Monday for the battlefield of Ft. Donelson. They hope to see the battles and help the wounded. They were too late for the first, but as they have not returned, they must have gone on to see and do what they can and perhaps wait for the next Battle which must come off soon. Several have gone from here among them Rev. Mr. Ried whose desk I have agreed to supply next Sunday. Edwin Pulsifer was down from Hennepin on Monday. The folks are as well as usual and he and Oaks Turner are Cordial Enemies and about to engage in a lawsuit.

I think I wrote you I had borrowed a feather bed and I only need you and the Baby to sleep very comfortable and be very happy. As it is, I sit up very late and then turn in and do as well as I can. You will not be alarmed about my health when I tell you I manage to eat and digest 3 to 5 hearty meals a day. The last is a lunch from 10 to 12 o'clock at night. I suppose we eat more because we have so little to do. I don't ..?.. but I can find enough to employ my time if the men are to be got at, but there are only certain times of the day they are at home to callers. I improve them as well as I can and hope not quite in vain.

Your Husband, Leonard Whitney

## Letter # 9

Burlington, Iowa, Feb. 21, 1862

My Dear Son, Your Mother tells me you never got the other letter I wrote from this horrible place. Horrible because you can never get out of it when you expect to and am so anxious to get home. I believe you were imprisoned here a day when you came home from the 'sea voyage.' I got in from Peoria at 2 and when I was here last the stage left for Madison at 3 P.M. Now I have to lie over for it 'till 9 tomorrow morning and get home at 4 P.M. I suppose they have arranged it for my benefit. Well, I will fill up a part of the time in writing you. You will ask why I am going home? Because our Reg't is ordered to St. Louis and to make the march with the horses and tents across the country it will take them at least 2 weeks and why should I not come home and meet them in St. Louis? I have no horse yet and could hold no services on the march and I do not like the camping out in the snow and ice for nothing. I only wish I could meet you at home to enjoy the visit with us and our joy would be full. Don't you think if we are all spared to get home alive and well when the war is over, we shall prize it a little more than we did before? I know I shall. And it now looks as if the war would be over this year and I hope we shall both live to return safe and sound.

I suppose from what Mother wrote me you are up with Carter after old Price. I wish I knew how you stood the forced marches and prospect of Battle. I hope your health and strength hold you and your courage is equal to a retreating foe.

I do not see why we should be all our life time in Bondage to the fear of Death. If the old Pagans could say "It is sweet to die for one's country" how much more should we with "Life and Immortality bro't to light by the Gospel." But then as I have told you and as this and all wars prove, the danger of Death upon the Battlefield does not equal that from Disease and exposure, neglect and dissipation.

The Reg't that lost the most in the charge at Ft. Donelson only had about 5 killed a co. I believe you read of the noble charge of the 2nd Iowa. They met the storm of Lead and Grape at double quick without firing a gun and never stopped 'till they pitched the Rebels from the entrenchments on the pointing their dipping bayonets. They lost 38 killed. I have not heard whether any of the Keokuk boys are among the number. We have not yet got a full list of the killed and wounded. I don't suppose Price will favor you with any such hand fighting as they had there. If he does, let every nerve welcome Death rather than defeat, and then there will be no danger of defeat. (This is all there is of the letter- the rest must be lost or else he never finished it.)

## Letter #10

Keokuk, Tuesday Feb. 25, 1862

Dear Harwood - We learned from Mrs. Perry yesterday that you were taken sick on the march to Springfield, Mo. and that her husband laid over at Lebanon to take care of you. We can never repay the kindness of our old fast friend, Col. Perry, for their attention to our son, when you stood in such need of sympathy and help, but we will do what we can toward it if he lives to get home or to his family if he does not. Of course, we are all still anxious about you and shall be 'till we know you are well but as he writes his wife "you are better and will be well in a day or two" we will try to think so until we hear from you again. Don't give up to slight ailments - don't get discouraged, don't yield to the fear of battle or dread the deadly charge. It is in the post of honor, almost of safety.

We have Letters this morning from the glorious Iowa 2nd Infantry, who first planted our old Flag on the Rebel entrenchment of Ft. Donelson. They charged up a bare, steep hill, right in the face of a storm of grape and lead, gave the Rebel lines a sheet of fire, in their faces from the top of their works and then pitched them back with the cold steel. It was the bravest charge of the war, one of the best on record. And yet, facing such a fire and storming such a strong hold the Keokuk Co. lost but 1 killed and had some 15 wounded, none mortally. And their whole Reg't which lead the charge and met the whole fire of the Rebels lost only 36 killed and some 100 wounded. There is no way to face Danger or cheat Death of his prey in war but quick movement and sudden blows. There is not one Reg't in 100 that will stand a sudden united, bold charge of saber or bayonet. I suppose you may not have the honor of trying it, but if you do, go into it with the speed of Lightning and the force of an avalanche.

I arrived home last Saturday. I shall remain while our Reg't marches across the country to St. Louis. I could be of no use to them on the march and as I have no horse yet, had no way to move but the cars. They will be some 15 days on the road, so I hope the River will break up and I go down on the Packet. I don't know what our destination is beyond St. Louis. I hope we shall remain there 'till I see you- at least till we are ..?.. and paid off. We have no pay yet tho' some served over 5 mos. Sidney and his son Eddy started for Ft. Donelson the day after the surrender to see the sights and help care for the wounded- but not returned when I left Peoria. Our little family are all about as you left us only the Baby grows cunning every day and tries to talk. Mrs. Perry bro't him a fine Photograph of Maj. Carlton Perry senior the other day. Charlie and Leonard go to Obey and Dancing School and put up in your old cloth and ..?.. make a very creditable appearance. You must write often, especially if any thing is the matter.

Your Father

Rev. Leonard had gone home by Rail on February 21 and joined his Regiment in St. Louis on March 23 or there about. Harwood had been left sick in a field near Lebanon, Mo. on a forced march from Rolla to Springfield, Mo. with a severe case of hemorrhoids and piles caused by the march on horseback - not too glamorous - around February 15th or so. Later he went on to join his Regiment to be in the Battle of Pea Ridge, March 7th and 8th, 1862. They evidently did not hear from Harwood again until after Rev. Leonard arrived in St. Louis on March 24.

The following letter to Rev. Leonard from Col. Ingersoll is very interesting, but very hard to read. I have typed as much as I can make out. Rev. Leonard and Col. Ingersoll had evidently become good friends.

## Letter #11

Everett House, 4th St. between Olive & Locust, St. Louis

Mar. 14, 1862

Rev. Leonard Whitney -

Dear Friend - Both of your letters were rec'd and both should long ago have been answered - accept my sincere thanks for the good advice given and the friendship manifested in final - the advice was rec'd in the same spirit you gave it - one of kindness - and I sincerely hope that at some time - though far in the future - I may be as deserving of praise as I now am of just and friendly censure.

Since the death of adored father you are the only man I have met - friend enough to tell me my faults - I shall remember you with kindness for it - you are to a great degree by your profession, removed from a thousand temptations that continually beset me - standing as you do, as it were, on the verge of the human - appealing to the divine - lifting the heart from the grave to immortal life - The great things of the world are small to you - the baubles striven for by the ambitious and falsely great, are baubles to you. You inhabit a purer and higher atmosphere - the improprieties of life, so to speak. Your own creations are cool and calculating to keep you there, mine to draw me down. You are above - I am beneath in the birth scramble her soil and dust - "The statue of Jupiter upon the great temple looks and acts like a God"- remarked an Athenian - "Why?"- Because it is never agitated by the convulsions beneath. Well enough of that - I am anxious to see you & have missed you much.

You had better come as soon as convenient - I presume the reg't will be ordered away in a short time - we have 1100 sabers - 694 seven shooters, 120 short rifles and will be fully armed in a day or two - we will I presume be paid off this week - likely by the time you could arrive - Do as you please about a horse - I can furnish you one if you wish - There is great activity among the military now - steamer after steamer bears reg't after reg't down the Great River - nothing but march, march- the Splendid ..?.. of ..?.. ..?.., ..?.. ..?.. and then crowning all as with a glory - Fort Donelson- The evaluation of ..?..- thus ..?.. The flight from New Madrid have made invincible the Grand Army of the Great West.

I am yours truly,

Robert G. Ingersoll

Rev. Leonard was finally paid in St. Louis, the first time since he went in on Dec. 21, 1861. He had borrowed money for his clothing, food, etc. and also $50 for the family at home. The soldiers had to pay for their own food, buy their own clothes, horses, saddles, etc. It seems the officers were given extra for a "servant" which Lenard did not have, but he finally bought a horse in St. Louis. He received $360 for 3 months.

The Battle of Pea Ridge was March 7 & 8, 1862. The family finally heard from Harwood on March 23.

## Letter # 12

Camp Benton, St Louis - March 24, 1862

My Dear Son, I heard from you yesterday for the first time since you were sick at Lebanon, (Feb. 25). You little know the anxiety we have felt for you, especially since Col. Bussy's Dispatch home that he lost 50 men in the late battle. I remained home until last Thurs. hoping somebody would send home the names of the killed & wounded from Keokuk. But I only met Col. B's Report on the boat in a St. Louis paper. Since I left your Mother has seen Lieut. Leech & sent me word you are safe & well. I do hope soon to meet you, for our Reg't was under orders to join Carter, but today our destination has been changed to Tennessee. But don't be discouraged for I trust we shall both be spared to meet before many months when the war is over & we can enjoy the quiet and comforts of home. I have just come to their camp from a good long visit at home. Our Reg't was ordered to march here across the country and as I could be no use on the march, I went home by Rail to meet them here when I was needed.

I came on the Packet last Thursday. It is a scene of constant change and excitement here. Almost every boat brings or carries off troops. Today I saw for the first time an installment of your Sesesh Prisoners. Can it be possible that God will permit such a set of human Animals to succeed in anything? - especially such a thing as a Slave Confederacy? Tell about the Negroes as an inferior Race. If they are not superior to these scamps God pity them. And I pitied more than blamed these poor scallywags. They are hardly responsible for their acts.

Harwood, we never can be thankful enough to our old friend Major Perry for stopping to take care of you in your sickness on the road. I hope you will feel this and convey to him from your Mother and I warmest gratitude. I left your Mother & the Boys all well. They all often speak of you and you may be sure you will be the Idol when you get home. The Baby begins to talk. Now keep up your heart & may the Good Father preserve you and make you a happy, good man. Remember me to Major Perry & Kate.

Your Father

## Letter #13

Camp Benton, St Louis - March 24/62

My dear Wife - I was much rejoiced yest'y to hear from you that our Dear Boy Harwood is alive and well. I did not see Janings but he met Lieut. Reynolds of the 1st Iowa Cav. who told me I shall start this week to see our Boy as our Reg't is ordered to join Curtis immediately. We were paid yest'y & I will send you some pay before I go. I send this by Mrs. Maguire who will call upon you. We couldn't get her boy discharged but I guess he will help her more to go with us. He has paid her $25 and will send her more at the next pay day. I must pay my debts in Peoria, get my outfit & save some to buy my grub 'til next pay day & will send you the rest. I hope I shall hear from you before we leave. If not, a letter would reach me at Rolla where we go by Rail. I want to hear all you know of Harwood. I have not yet got a horse, blankets or overcoat, but should have some days before we start. Hope you and the Boys are well and will keep well. Don't worry about me and I will try not about you.

Your Husband

## Letter #14

Camp Benton, St. Louis, Mo. March 25, 1862

My Dear Wife - War is proverbially an uncertain business. When I sent the line to you by Mrs. Meguire yesterday we were under marching orders to report to Gen. Curtis in Arkansas. Today at this hour 8 PM our 1st Battalion is to take the boat for Tennessee. We shall all probably follow in a day or two, or as soon as we can get a Boat. I suppose I am about the only one in the Reg't who feels disappointed in our change of destination. And how much I feel it you, who have shared my anxiety during his long absence and late peril, may well imagine. But as all came out well in his late sickness & peril (so very different from our dark forebodings) let us hope it is all for the best & that the Good Father of us all will still take care of his life and health, tho we are not present to watch over him or even do not know where or how he is. I wrote a letter last ev'g directed to Rolla, told him we had heard of his safety, how you all were at home and where I was going. I hope you will write him soon & learn of Mrs. Perry how to direct. I sent my overcoat by Lieut. Reynolds last night & am sorry I did not send the 4 pound Boots as we are going South. We were paid up to the 1st of March last Sunday & I presume no Gospel of mine was ever so welcome to the Poor Sinners of my parish. I had an appointment to preach in the ev'g but as the officers were to be paid off in the ev'g, I had to be present and instead of my manuscripts, count over $360 of Uncle Samuels Script which was to come into my own pocket. I have paid 25 for a saddle, sent $61 to Peoria and intend to send you 200 if I can get a horse on credit. I have still my bank loan Bill to pay, besides getting me a Revolver & some other outfit and saving some to pay my way 'till next pay day. The Paymaster was very easy with me. I told him I had no serv't. He told the man who counted us the money, to put down "John Jones" as my serv't, and paid me the full amount. It seems to be the custom only the Officer generally give the fictitious names themselves. If I do not send money enough to pay all we have promised to pay soon you must pay each a part 'till I send more. Be sure and keep your credit good with those who have trusted and fed and clothed us when we most needed credit. Save enough to use 'till the next pay day which ought to be 1st of May. I think I may depend upon the next payment to meet the Bank Note of $50 Miller signed with me. It runs 90 days and I paid the Interest for that time.

It has been rough weather since we came here 'till now but I am writing this in my shirt sleeves and suppose we shall find the corn up in Dixie when we get to the end of our present trip. I have been well since I left home and will try to keep so. All is hurry and excitement here and what I miss most is the quiet of home or at least room to sit down and sleep. But I hope it will be better when we have a small ..?.. in our own tent. I think of messing with the 2 surgeons. I have today looked at a fine horse & partly engaged a serv't- a boy about Harwood's size who wants to go and see the war. If I must have a horse, I cannot do without someone to take care of him. I hope you will take life as easy as you can and not keep lean with over much worry and care. And now may the Good Father keep & cherish you all as tenderly as I do in my heart of Hearts. Write often & I trust your letters will be forwarded to wherever I go. Kiss all the boys for me & tell them to be good and start quick to your orders and wishes.

Your Husband - L. Whitney

P.S. March 26- Direct your letters to Rev. L. Whitney 11th Ill. Cavalry, Gen'l Grants Division, West Tennessee. I got your letter last night and was so glad to have one from you before we start. I read and reread it with mingled tears of Joy and sorrow, joy that our Dear Boy was spared, sorrow that so many other anxious hearts were stricken. The more I hear of that 3 days struggle, the more I wonder our Army was not cut off or captured. I shall get the picture for you if I have time with all the preparations I have to make before we start. What a shock the death of Tom Estes must have been, not only to his Family but to his associates. If the Baby takes measles be sure he does not take cold and I don't think there is much danger. I know you will watch him well. I slept last night in my blankets on a hard board and slept well. And now again- good bye. You know your weakness of indulging in too much anxiety about everything. Let the past give you trust. Harwood has so far been preserved and as to my safety, I have heard of but one chaplain killed in Battle since the war commenced. If anything special is the matter, I presume a Dispatch by Telegraph would reach our Camp. Trust the Lord, be of good courage, and hope we shall all meet in safety when the war is over. - Your Husband

## Letter #15

St. Louis, March 28, 1962

My Dear Son - I wrote you a day or two since from Benton Barracks and directed my letter to Rolla. I don't know whether it will reach you so I will direct this farther on. I got a letter from your Mother since Lieut. Leech got home. You never can tell how much good it did me to hear of your safety and your conduct. She wrote Leech couldn't speak of "the Boys" (as he called them) without tears - said all fought well - they never had to speak a cross word to them after they left Benton Barracks. I wrote how near I came to seeing you when the Order was revoked and we are sent to join Gen'l Grant in Tennessee. Half of our Reg't has gone and the Big Steamer "Imperial" is now at the Levee taking on the rest of us. I have sent home overcoat, heavy boots, fur gloves and am preparing for "Dixie Land" and hot weather. We got our first payment here i.e. up to the first of March. I rec'd $360 and sent most of it home to pay Debts. I have so far, no horse or sev't tho' they would give me full pay. If I can I want to get everything paid up with the next payment I receive and then with your pay and mine, we may hope when the war is ended to secure each of us a good home. For I suppose, to pay for your hardships and self-denials and honorable ..?.. some girl may want you for a husband some of these days.

Your Mother wanted I should get some photograph of my Rev'd self in Chaplains coat and send her. I have ordered 4 today and shall endorse one to you if they are finished before the boat goes. I saw them this morning and feel quite discouraged all my pictures are getting to look so old and ugly. I got many compliments when I was home for my young appearance, but alas, the too faithful reflection of the Instrument tells me there is no dogging the fact that I am nearly 50 so I remember when my Father was 50 I use to think him an old man. And O, we think, if we could only go back and live our lives over again how we could improve them. How much less we would worry and first, how we would try to make the best of every day, and every place and circumstance, how contented we would be with the joys and friends and comforts within our reach and the quiet of home and leave fools to roam and misers to grasp for more.

You have never yet told me how you like the life you are in or how you get along with your officers and mess-mates. I hope at any rate you have resolved to make the best of it 'till it is over, and this is all many of us can do. Remember me to our old friend Maj. Perry and repeat my thanks for his kindness to you in the hour of need. That the lord may keep and bless you is the constant Prayer of

Your Father

## Letter #16

Gen. Grants Division, West Tennessee - April 4, 1862

My Dear Wife - Here we are then safe and sound at the "Seat of War". Our good Col. whose face I hope you have seen ere this, expressed some doubt to Gen. Hallack when we left St. Louis, whether we could find the "seat" on so large a surface. How large it is we don't know tho' I suppose we are on it, it is said, with some 150,000 others. Our camps extend some 10 miles along the river and about 5 miles into the country. As the country about here is hilly and wooded the eye can take in best but a small part of the vast encampment and I have seen but a tithe of this countless host. We see almost every day separate Divisions on the march to some open field for review. These Divisions turn out from 10 to 20,000. And as you gaze upon the endless stream of glistening bayonets with streaming Banners and soul-stirring music and think this is but a small part of our "Grand Army of the West" now encamped in these old woods, you feel that it is invincible and must be victorious. The Enemy are said to be in force at Corinth about 20 miles from us and our Pickets are so near each as to sometimes exchange shots with fatal effect. Beauregard, Bregg and several of the ablest Rebel Gen's are said to be ready to receive us with an army of 100,000 constantly increasing. How soon the Great Battle will be fought we don't know, tho all look for it soon. But Gen Halleck says it will not be 'till he has a force concentrated that will ensure success - that he has men enough to whip them and means to use them. There seem to be very fine Cavalry and I presume the chief service will be scouting and Picket duty, the worst in the service, especially in such rough wooded country as this. We have not yet been assigned our Division or put into active service. We are encamped in our tents on a wooded hill about two miles from the river (The Tennessee) surrounded by Battery and Reg'ts of Infantry encamped on every side of us. And you may want to know how I like Camp Life in the woods and on the "Tent in Field" and how I manage Housekeeping? I am at present quartered in the surgeon's tent both of us destitute of serv'ts. We get the women of the Hospital to cook for us and groom our own horses and keep our own house. The tent is about 10 feet square in which we have 2 cot beds, our trunks, saddles and on a box of medicine at the head of my cot I stick a sten candle and keep up my old habit of reading in bed and feel quite at home. Our common fare at table is hard bread and ham, and luxurious potatoes, cracklin, coffee and tea. We have got beyond the region of milk, butter and all such non-essentials. Indeed, were it not for the fleet of Steamboats that the gov't sends with supplies we should eat up this whole country at a single meal. There seems to be few inhabitants and they have fled leaving nothing behind. The weather has been very warm since we arrived and we have to strip to it under the hot sun. I have wished more of my woolens at home and may send more by Express. The nights are cool and damp and we have to tuck up the blankets before morning to keep off chills. Many of our boys are sick from the sudden change of climate and water and last night we lowered the first one into his rough grave in this strange Rebel soil. If we do not hurry up our Fight, I fear disease will prove our worst enemy. My own health has been good, and I think as usual I shall continue pross against any form of Diarrhea. I yesterday met for the first time old neighbor, Col. Parrot, Dan Tisdale

& Cap Huston. Their Reg'ts are encamped not far from us and we promised mutual visits. They seemed in good health and spirits, but I think all who have been in a fight look upon war as a more serious business than raw troops.

I sent home by Express $200 and my Boots, gloves and slippers and by Lieut. Reynolds my overcoat. If you get them let me know by letter and I may trouble you with more express goods. I hope you and the Baby are better than when you wrote me at St. Louis and that Leonard and Charley are well and working up to time. I wish they could know the happiness of instant and cheerful obedience. They would find the work somewhat lighter and why won't they do it for my sake? I have sometimes wished Charley had come with me, as I find no boy I can trust and I think he would have enjoyed it, but you need him at home where I hope we may all be soon in health and happiness. Write the last news from Harwood as often as you get any. I sent him my picture from St. Louis and hope you got those I sent you. Take good care of yourself and of all 'till I come home but let not care or anxiety weigh down your spirits or destroy the even flow of life, if it ever flows even.

Your Husband - L. Whitney - Again good bye. God Bless You.

The following are the letters written after The Battle of Shiloh, which was fought April 6th - 7th, 1862- 2 days after the previous letter was written to his wife.

## Letter #17

Pittsburg Landing, Tennessee - Thurs. April 10, 1862

My Dear Wife, I suppose 'ere this reaches you the papers will have informed you of the terrible Battle which raged here on Sunday and Monday. I did not Telegraph you, both because I wished to wait until the conflict was fairly over & because our neighbor Mr. Walker said he was going home and would tell you I was well. He was wounded in the hand and hopes for leave to go home until he was well. I have seen Col. Parrot and most of our Keokuk Friends, and think they are all safe, tho some are slightly wounded.

The Battle was opened very early Sunday morning by the breaking into our lines in great number and fury, by an enemy who had crept upon us by stealth and took our camp and I think our Generals by surprise. The thot had occurred to me and I'd thot, what if our enemy should not wait for us to get ready and attack him, but wake us up some fine morning by a sudden attack upon our mob of a camp? If he is as wily as Beauregard is said to be he will do it! So, on Sunday morning he did it with a rush and roar that might have put to flight veteran troops. But he knew enough to break in upon our weakest point and attack our greenest Reg'ts. Some of them had but just got into Camp and had not rec'd their cartridges. They stood a few rounds and when ordered to fall back retired very much in the order of a flock of frightened sheep. This first terrible onset of the enemy was made upon our left wing - Gen Prentiss Div. to which we are attached. Our camp was about a mile in the rear of the first charge, but our boys only had time to mount and reach the field before our killed and wounded began to be brot into camp. Several men killed with shells. One Lieut. had his bowels torn open and lived but an hour or two. No other officer was hurt and our Reg't. only lost 10 or 12 killed and wounded. But this was because they were ordered to the rear and only exposed themselves to the first fire of the enemy. All of the fighting was done by Infantry and Artillery and for two long days, last Sunday and Monday, the roar of cannon and the rattle of Musketry was almost incessant. And when you know these were not less than 400 pieces of ordinance and 150,000 muskets engaged, you may imagine as well as you can the awful grandeur of the scene. But alas, the grandeur all fades away before the awful reality of the forsaken Battlefield. I have read fearful descriptions of its horror but not the most graphic pen or vivid imagination can begin to paint the scene. I have passed over but a small part of the ground fought over (for it extends for miles) but I have seen sights which I would not describe to you if I could - sights of mangling and horror and death which I fear will never fade from my mind. Most of the fighting was done in the woods over a hilly country and hence the difficulty of seeing the whole field or finding all the dead and wounded. I went out yesterday and saw heaps of the blackened corpses unburied and fear all the wounded are not yet found, tho it is now the 3rd day since the battle. I hear various estimates of the loss on both sides, from 5,000 to 40,000. My own is perhaps 5,000 killed and wounded on our side but it is merely guesswork until we get the official report. I suppose you will be interested to know what I did with myself in the fight. As I told you, our tents were near the line of the first onset of the enemy. I suppose it was not over 20 minutes after the first roar of battle reached us before we were ordered to pack the hospital stores and remove with the sick and wounded to the Landing at the river. There were all our Army Stores and fleet of Steamboats to receive our wounded. Before we got out, the shot and shell fell thick in our camp and near the tent where we were ministering to the wounded and dying. After the teams had started, I mounted my horse to follow to the Landing but soon overtook a poor fellow with his leg broken by a shot who begged so hard for my horse I couldn't refuse - so I mounted him and told him to hitch at the river. I haven't seen my horse since. He was and is probably lost in the mud ..?.. to be found when the confusion is over. I then went on to the field to see our Reg't. then back to our tents to lift a wounded stranger into a tent and give him water. Then the Cav'y were ordered back to the river to wait 'till they were needed. And there in the low bottom in the mud and rain we spent the night. I shared a blanket with a solder and slept until the rain soaked under me, then leaned against a tree and waited for the day. During the night Gen. Pouals force began to arrive and early in the morning our forces opened fire upon the enemy and drove him back with great slaughter. The next day we moved back to our tents and buried our dead and prepared for an advance. But it has rained and rained ever since, the roads are impassable, and we can only wait and attend to our sick and try to keep ourselves from getting sick. And to close, I am sick of the whole thing in camp and field. There is no comfort or decency in it. It is all hard and bad, too bad to describe.

Your Husband

## Letter #18

Battleground, Pittsburg, Tenn, April 20, 1862

My Dear Wife. I hope if you have been as anxious about me as we were about Harwood after we heard of the Battle he was in, that the suspense is over. I supposed I could send you a dispatch at once but found on inquiry that nothing was permitted to go for some days after the Battle. I presume it was to prevent exaggerated reports from going to the country. I knew one lad could not get a line through to his wife that he was safe and well. I believe we both resolved after we found our Dear Boy was safe, that we would always presume all was well until we knew the contrary. But alas, for good resolutions, when the hour of danger comes to those dear to us as our own lives. I only hope you did not consider me in much danger, or else that someone who went to K after the Battle told you of my safety. I wrote you something of my doings during the long fight and tho I escaped all harm, the shot and shell fell so near me and several times as to destroy all the sweetness of the music. Indeed, I have not met one who desires to witness the sublimity or hear the grand music of another battle. Their curiosity is perfectly satisfied. It is quite the reverse of what I expected. I supposed those who had seen the worst fight would be most anxious for another, but it is only those who have never seen one, or walked over the torn, blackened corpses of a Battlefield, that have any such ambition. To us it was a hard bought victory. How could it be otherwise when the same ground was contested inch by inch for two long days by at least 100,000 men, equipped with the best firearms and artillery which modern ingenuity has invented. There is no conceivable form of mangled and torn and swollen and blackened humanity that might not be found upon that terrible field of strife, and it is hard by exaggeration to say that the collected dead and wounded have covered acres of ground. We have had a long and gloomy time burying the Dead. The weather has been dark and rainy, and our men were so worn with fatigue and exposure it was about all they could do to muster strength to bury our dead. And yet, as the enemy sent no flag of truce to do this last duty to their friends, we have had to search the roads and woods for miles around and gather up and bury their torn and ..?.. remains, sometimes hundreds in one common grave. One pit, I am told, received over 500. 13 of our own men were buried behind a log in our own camp. We have left it now and moved forward, as have most of the other Reg'ts. The stench of the old battlefield from dead men and horses was getting intolerable. And now enough of the Dead. Peace to the slumbering dust, and may God have mercy on their souls, and comfort the tens of thousands at home who will never know the spot where their loved ones are laid. Most of our members have to go thro an acclimation. Nearly half of them are ailing now and few escape what they call the "Tenn. Quickstep." It is in this emergency I find my habitual costiveness really valuable and invulnerable. I can say with the Apostle of Tenn. water, hot sun, and worse of these things never me. But then, I can say too with Prest. VanBuren "Our suffering is intolerable." I am Dyspeptic and salt pork and hard bread almost kills me. I am Rheumatic, and the wet ground is the worst possible bed for me. What do you think of laying that fine Chaplains coat on a Blanket in the soft mud of Tennessee and sleeping under the "open canopy" with the rain pouring? I wished it snug at home, with my aching bones in it. How I hope I will be there soon. I have asked leave of absence for 20 days to attend to my temporal affairs, and if it is granted shall be home in the course of a few days. I can't be of much use now we are moving so much, and nothing will be done at Corinth to reduce the enemy until we get them cut off from the R Roads. And that will be slow work if it always continues to rain. We cannot move ..?.. our Ailge guns without hard roads. The rain is now pouring again after a few good days. The ground of our tent is so wet we had to sleep on boxes last night and should have slept well only that we slid off every few minutes. I have a gun, shot from the hand of a 'sesish' which I mean to bring the Boys. I meant to have paid Kellogg and Birg and Negel all up, which I hope you will do if you can spare the money. I promised to pay them long ago and we must deny ourselves a little 'till these debts of honor are paid. I did not think Henilly's bill so large. I only put $3 on the overcoat. I know you will mean to do just right, but you must not ..?..

I can stand this hard life in the woods very long. Even now they talk of moving us without our tents and won't that be nice in this Spring rain?

Your husband L. Whitney

## Letter #19

Battleground near Pittsburg Landing, West Tennessee, April 23, 1862

My Dear Son - I don't know whether I have written you since the Great Battle here or not. I think not, so must let you know I am safe and well, remembering how anxious your Mother and I were to hear from you after your long hard fight at "Pea Ridge". The Rebel Army entrenched at Corinth about 20 miles from our camp, 80 or 100,000 strong, broke into our Camp on a fine Sunday morning (6th) while our men were asleep or at breakfast. Tho some had been seen near our lines on Saturday, I think the attack was as much a surprise to our General as I know it was to our Army! We had been in Camp for only about a week and were placed on the left wing composed mostly of green Reg'ts, just the weak point Johnson and Beauregard selected for the onslaught. They came thundering down with heavy masses of Infantry and Artillery and of course after a brief resistance drove our scattered Reg'ts before them. Our Camp was about a mile from where they broke in but our Boys hastened to the rescue and it was not 20 minutes after we heard the first firing before our killed and wounded were brot into Camp and we were ordered to move them and the sick in our hospital to the landing some 2 miles off. Our Camps were soon all in array and the roar of cannon and musketry was heard all around our lines of 4 or 5 miles. But it had recovered from a surprise or turned back in a retreat. And so slowly but surely the Rebel host pressed on, and our lines fell back until it looked very much as if we were all to be forced into the river behind us or surrender. A vast crowd of retreating cowards and stragglers lining the banks of the River increased the panic and confusion. But still the field was persistently contested by our boys who knew no such words as fear or fail and the last circle of Battery, armed with some heavy siege guns was well supported for a last desperate stand. On the River too, we had 2 gunboats which plowed the Rebel Ranks with shell. Just at this critical moment too the advance of Buel's Army (all day looked for to reinforce us) appeared on the opposite bank of the River. The Boats soon began to ferry them over and as Reg't after Reg't marched to the lines and all our hundred guns opened upon the sanguine Rebels the roar was terrible and before dark they concluded it was best to fall back and sleep upon their victory, before taking possession of our Army and its spoils. But their slumbers were all night long disturbed by the 84 pounders of the gunboats and the solid shot of our siege guns. And alas, for all human calculations, instead of waiting to receive their call in the morning our men were up and at them as soon as the day dawned. They struggled hard to keep the field they had won on Sunday but could not withstand the fire of musketry and artillery that on some parts of the line cut every tree and bush to the ground and left it covered with the mangled bodies. If it was almost a rout to us on Sunday, it was quite so to them on Monday. Their force is said to have been 80 or 100,000 and about 40,000 on Sunday and 60,000 on Monday. I know not if this is correct. I estimate the loss in killed and wounded at almost 10,000 on a side and about equal. I went over but a small portion of the field for it covered ..?.. of ground and I need not tell you Harwood, who have witnessed this sight, that this only reveals to us the horrors of war and the worst of wickedness of those, who without Guns, have brot its terrible woes upon us. You too have seen the human form blackened, torn, deformed, obliterated and tumbled into a ditch like the Druid to be forgotten, while their loved ones at Home shall never know even the spot where it was laid. I think we shall both have seen enough of war to make home and quiet and peace dear when it ..?.. kind Father preserve us for such a meeting. Your Mother sent me your last letter to here. She says Dr. McGugan says you are a "noble brave boy", which you know rejoices both our hearts. Write soon. Direct Rev. L. Whitney, Chaplain 11 Ill. Cav'y, Pittsburg Landing, Tenn.

Your Father L. Whitney

## Letter #20

In the woods near Pittsburg Landing, Tennessee - April 23, 1862

My Dear Wife - I wrote you the other day I hoped to visit home soon. But my furlough was "not allowed" so I must submit to this wretched life or resign. I would be sufficiently "desolate" in pleasant weather and your company. For a poor Dyspeptic to diet on hard army Bread and salt Bacon and sleep upon the cold wet ground is not the most comfortable fare. But when you add to this almost constant rain and wind and not much as one really congenial associate or association it is getting about as near the "wrath of war" as I ever expect to go. And not much to increase my misery, I was taken a few days ago with the Camp Flux. It is better however this morning and I fear will not hold out long enough to give me a Furlough on the ground of sickness - the only ground on which they are now given. But there is one consolation I constantly have in the darkest and rainiest day. It is that there are loved ones at home for whom I am toiling and suffering and that every day I remain in the Army may afford the means of increasing their comfort and happiness. Today the sun shines and if you were only here to lean upon my arm and wander over these old woods and view the wonders of the recent Battle Field, I feel as if I could really enjoy it. But still, I do not want you here even for my gratification. It is the last place for a woman to be and the few that are here only enjoy it as they are not in the true, refined sense, woman. We are only waiting better roads to move upon the enemy at Corinth, i.e. if he does not surprise us again in Camp. We are getting a very large force and we are told the Rebels are very strong. It is thot the next Battle will be much harder than the last. How soon it will come none of us can tell. I hope you and the Boys are well. I wrote you about paying some more debts. If you have not yet disposed of your money will you see Miller and inquire how long our $50 Bank Note runs and if only 60 days pay it if you can. I fear we will not get our pay on the 1st of May. If we could I would meet the Note. If not, and you have no money to meet it ask Miller if he can get it renewed for 60 or 90 days.

Have Curtis' folks come with your Dr. Parker, of Philia.? If so, write me and all the news. Remember I am in the woods and everything from home will be a feast. Our Currier is ready to start and I must close. May God keep and bless you all 'till I see you again.

Your husband - L. Whitney

## Letter #21

Direct to Pittsburg Landing, Tenn. In Camp near Pittsburg Landing, Tenn. April 29, 1862

My ever Dear Wife - I am not among the "Prisoners," killed, wounded or missing, nor do I expect to be. I have just got yours of the 20th to the care of Col. Parrot and was never more surprised and grieved that you had got none of the three letters I have written you since the Battle, besides sending word by some half dozen of your neighbors who said they were going home to K and would tell you I was safe and well. I trust you know by this time and that you will not think I was negligent in trying to relieve your anxiety. No letters of Dispatch were allowed to be sent off for some days after the Battle, so I did not write 'till my letter could go. But where has it been so long delayed? I see your letter (to be sent if need be open, to me, a poor Captive of Rebellion), is dated 14 days after the Fight. The Chap who told you the 11th Ill. Cav'y were all Prisoners must have been green battle about its Fighting and Retreating qualities. It is true we lost a few men killed and wounded in the morning, when we were placed in front where Cav'y have no business, to support Battery, but were soon ordered to fall back and keep safe in the rear until our services were needed when the lines of the Rebels were broken. This order was executed so promptly and in such good order that Col. Rob. boasts there were no Reg't on the field so good at a retreat as the 11th and says, if the Army had surrendered, they would have been the only Reg't that would have got away, as he had taken the precaution to look out the only road. As I had put a poor wounded soldier on my horse and had to foot it the rest of the day, I was to join our Boys on the other side of the Jordan on a Raft of Rail rather than ride a rail as an Abolition Prisoner in the Kingdom of Serfdom. No, do not distress yourself about the 11th. They have no idea of being made Prisoners, while they have good horses and there is a "hole out." Whether they will Fight as well as they can retreat has not yet been proved, as our battle was in the woods there is little chance for charge or cav'y.

But this feeling I find almost universal - Those who have been in a fight and witnessed the horrors of the Battlefield are not half as anxious for another as green troops. They may stand and fight better, but to them it is no pastime, but the most serious and dreadful work. I wrote you about coming home soon on leave; and again, that my Furlough was not granted. But still the Col. thinks he can get one for me before long and says I must not think of Resigning. I do not like to plead ill health when so many are making that an excuse to get away. Indeed I have been among the most fortunate in our sudden change of water and climate. Diarrhea, chills, and Flux have been about universal, and I have escaped all except a short spell of the latter, which readily yielded to Blue Mass and opium. I am almost alone a model of the healthfulness of this "Beautiful Tenn. Climate" and when all are complaining, it does well and I think them good to say "I am well." It is true our eating is so abominably dry I have to drink a good deal of Whiskey and use just a little tobacco, but I know you will forgive me the sin when I declare to you it is mostly on your account. It is hard enough to drink to drown trouble, but what shall we say of it when men resort to it to drown the voice of Affection that calls them home, to blunt the sensibility which unfits them for this rough toil and coarse aspirations and nerve them to the hard but pressing duties of the hour? I know you will say, I Forgive, if it keeps off Home Sickness for you and the Dear Ones there and makes me more useful and contented in my present lot. We are having a good deal of sickness now, some very serious, and I hope my labors are not in vain. Last Sunday I preached in these old woods, subject "How to Meet Death and Overcome its Fears." I am Tented with Dr. Stratton our Asst. Surgeon. I do some cooking for ourselves and the sick and my own washing so far. My socks and towels are now on the line in front of our tent to dry. I keep no Boy, they all say it is so much work to take care of them, so I think I will stick to "John Jones," my old and faithful serv't on the Pay Roll. I have no horse, saddle, quilt blanket or encumbrance of any sort or kind. I gave them all up to the wounded on the Battlefield and have not seen them since. The horse is not a loss nor mine. The rest, some $40, have helped those in sad need and they are welcome. No one thinks of looking for any lost things in this vast multitude. Do write as often as once a week and I will try to do so. Kiss the Dear Boys for me and consider yourself hugged and kissed to death by me. Yours till we meet at Home.

Leonard Whitney

## Letter #22

In the woods 5 miles from Pittsburg Landing, Tennessee. - May 6, 1862

My Very Dear Wife - Your resolution to write me every week was a good one tho by some unaccountable bungling in the mails I have only rec'd two brief notes from you, one of the 17th ult. with Curtis, the other of the 20th presuming me a Prisoner of War in the Kingdom of Sesished. It seemed when you wrote you had not been more successful; for I have certainly written you 4 or 5 times since I arrived here, none of which you have gotten by the 20th. I hope by this time you have learned from my own hand that I am neither killed nor a Prisoner. If you have got all my letters, you may infer too that I am not exactly in Paradise, tho in the "Sunny South" provided with all the conveniences and Luxuries which Uncle Samuel provides his faithful soldiers in the field. But when I think of our Dear Harwood, living on parched corn and for days without food, sleeping in the cold snow without tents, I am ashamed to say one word about our discomfort. We always have plenty to eat and waste such as it is, and I have only one night on the ground in the open air, and that was the Sunday night the Rebels occupied our tents. They moved out so soon we have no reason to complain. But this "sunny south" has been very overcast and gloomy since we arrived on the 1st of April. Some who have counted say the rainy days have exceeded the fair ones. And the storms are a great drawback upon Camp life. Indeed it is not much better than a Picnic in the rain. True, the tent doesn't leak much, but then the floor is the ground and that is all wet and since we move so often it is our bed too. If we have a Poncho we spread that under our Blankets so the water only works in a little at the sides of our Bed, seldom wetting more than one side at a time. How do you think I have stood 20 such rainy nights in a tent 10 feet square with the sick purging and spewing all around me and the wind and rain roaring without? Pretty well, I thank you - I haven't taken cold and scarcely one night omitted my usual Luxury of reading myself to sleep in bed. I stick my candle in the socket of the Bayonet and the Bayonet in the ground and I am nicely fixed for a Light Stand. And in the fair weather in some places open by a fine Spring I sometimes think had I my Jenny by my side I would be about as snug and happy as I could be. But alas, I have not her so much as one that I care a fig about only to try to do my Duty by them, and not hate them. It is so hard to love everybody, or to care much about the selfish mass around you. I suppose you must have rec'd the Business Items I wrote you. Do meet the Bank Note I got Miler to sign with me if you have the funds. If not get him to renew it 60 or 90 days. Our next Payment was due the 1st of this month and as the Paymaster was here paying off some Div's - we hope to get ours when our turn comes. I hope to get a Furlough when we get thro' to Memphis, if we ever do; but at present we know not what a day may bring forth. We are moving upon the

Rebel Army slowly, but in time we hope surely. I will remember your advice and try to 'take good care of myself' and leave the home ones to your care and the care of Him who will never leave or forsake us.

You mention the happy meeting at home if we are all spared to meet again there. I hope we shall all prize it more than we have and by mutual forbearance and forgiveness and what is more and better of mutual Love and good will make it all that a Home can and should be. May God keep and bless you all.

Your husband, L. Whitney

### Letter #23

Pittsburg Landing, May 8th, 1862

My Dear Wife - Don't think I am dead because my trunk has come, I send it because I can't carry it on our forced marches in the woods and I don't want Sessish to get hold of my sermons if I should happen to be nabbed. I dated my last letter the 6th tho' written the 5th. I only told you how well I was and how the wet ground agreed with me. It was only that night I was attacked with Bilious Charlie and thot I should die sure but did not. I got relief before morning and I am all right except some soreness of the bowels. Hope to come home and see you before long. Love to all and God bless you.

Your Husband L. Whitney

Included as Appendix B is "The Battle of Shiloh," an article written for The American Heritage magazine by Bruce Catton (Vol II, Issue 2, Grant At Shiloh) which contains much more of the background about this particular battle.

# PART 3 --AFTER THE WAR

*In Flanders fields the poppies blow*
*Between the crosses, row on row.*
*John McCrae*

Rev. Leonard Whitney died June 12, 1862, one month after his last letter from Tennessee. I have no information as to what happened to him other than what was written in the Iowa Historical Record. I feel he was a disillusioned, broken man - mentally and physically.

Following are two letters taken from the Iowa Historical Record, Pages 55 & 56, which give an insight into his "War Days." The first is from Col. Ingersoll to Rev. O. Clute:

> New York, Jan. 6th, 1888
>
> Rev. O. Clute -
>
> My Dear Sir - It gives me great pleasure to write a few words in reference to Rev. Leonard Whitney. He was one of the purest, one of the noblest men I ever knew. He was in the highest sense a deeply religious man - that is to say he lived in accordance with his ideal. There was about him neither can't nor hypocrisy. He did not pretend to be better than others - he wished only to make others better.
>
> While I knew him, his entire time was occupied in doing good to others. He was a perpetual consolation to the sick and wounded - an example for all. He won the respect of every man who knew him, and his influence was only good.

He was a thorough believer in the religion of good works, and he lived in exact accordance with his belief.

He as truly gave his life for his country, as though he had died on the field of battle.

Yours truly, R. G. Ingersoll

The other letter is a rather lengthy one from Samuel F. Miller, who was a Judge on the Supreme Court appointed by Lincoln in 1862. He was Rev. Leonard's friend in Keokuk in 1853 and one of the founders of the Unitarian Church there. His home in Keokuk is now the home for Lee Co. Historical Society.

Washington, D.C.

Dec. 21, 1887

Rev. Oscar Clute - My Dear Friend -

Your letter of the 15th inst. was received by me about the 20th, when I was so busy in disposing of the business of the court, preparatory to the recess of the Christmas holidays, that I had no time to make any response, so that it has been delayed until now. I hope it is not too late, for it gives me great pleasure to speak of the Rev. Leonard Whitney, with whom my relations were of the most intimate character. Indeed, I fear that what I may say about him will be rather the result of the most affectionate remembrance of a devoted personal friend, than a critical historical statement.

I do not know precisely in what year Mr. Whitney came to Keokuk; somewhere I should think between 1852 and 1854. There was no organized congregation of Unitarians there when he came, but a number of the most intelligent citizens of the place had been Unitarians in other localities or were incited to some more liberal form of Christian doctrine than was taught in any of the orthodox churches. A room was rented, and Mr. Whitney preached to these persons and to all others who came to hear him. This continued for several years, the place of worship changing as the exigencies of the case required.

Mr. Whitney was, I think, a native of Vermont, where families of Whitneys are numerous, and I have since met more than one person bearing his full name of Leonard Whitney. He was, I should think, forty years of age when he came to Keokuk, and as I understood had been a Baptist minister, but had left the ministry of that church because he could no longer hold to its principles. This change of conviction may have led to his over-estimate of the evils incident to creeds. Certainly, he was an aggressive preacher, and gave much of his time and energy in the pulpit to showing the untruthfulness of popular doctrines. And if there was in the character of his preaching anything which to me seemed objectionable it was the vigor with which he denounced what he thought to be the erroneous principles of the prevailing creeds of the Christian churches generally.

This developed a seeming inconsistency in his character, for his social relations not only with the members of the other churches of Keokuk, but with their clergymen, were of the most cordial character. He was respected and beloved by all of them, and in his intercourse with the world at large, with his friends and with his family he was the kindest and tenderest friend and the most affectionate father and husband. But he seemed impelled by a solemn sense of the duty which had fallen to his lot to expose those errors in the orthodox creeds which he believed led to contention and evil in the Christian churches, and in accordance with the energy of his nature and the strength of his convictions he was not choice in the selection of the words by which he denounced those errors.

He was a man of very vigorous thought, and still more vigorous language. Some of the illustrations of his arguments have remained with me through long years and absence from the theatre of his services. Perhaps I cannot better show the man than by reproducing one of these.

The years 1857 and 1858 found the people of the city of Keokuk utterly prostrated by the financial crisis which pervaded the United States, but which fell with peculiar force upon that place, because it had been a prosperous town, and its citizens venturesome in their desire to make money by speculation, and particularly in real estate. The result of this crisis was to leave many persons who believed that they had accumulated fortunes, struggling with absolute poverty and in debt beyond any hope of relief. This condition of things was accompanied or followed, as is very often the case, by a great religious revival in which under the influence of religious zeal the occasion was improved to turn the attention of those who had been thus unfortunate, to a land where sorrows never come. The interest awakened was very extended, and the number who joined the different churches during this revival was quite remarkable. As Mr. Whitney did not believe in this mode of adding to the church, nor in a permanent good influenced on persons who professed a change of life and heart under this kind of teaching, he took occasion to preach a sermon upon the subject of revivals, in which he, with his usual force, pointed out his belief that such motives as had induced the additions to the churches under the circumstances then existing were not of a character to prove lasting with the individual nor creditable to those bodies in the end. In illustration of his view of the matter he said: "Those who have thus been seriously distressed by losses of corner lots in Keokuk have only transferred the same earthly affection to their faith in the corner lots which they desire to secure in the New Jerusalem."

I do not know that this illustration was original with Mr. Whitney. I am very sure I never heard it before or since, and its force as a mental photograph of what he supposed to be the moving principle in such revivals of religion can hardly be equaled.

It is with more pleasure, however, that I give illustrations of his warmth of heart, showing the practical benevolence of his nature. On a Sabbath in mid-winter when he was expected to preach to his congregation, not then very large, he failed to appear, so that after some singing and reading from the book of prayers the people dispersed. During the succeeding week it was ascertained that Mr. Whitney had that morning started in a snowstorm from his home, which was some distance from the place of worship. On his way he had to pass the house of a widow, who was in very poor circumstances, and it occurred to him to drop into the house and inquire into her situation. He found her with a family of children, without fire, without wood to make one, and if she had anything to eat no means of cooking it. He instantly set himself to work, went to some neighboring house and got a few sticks of wood, sawed them into the requisite lengths, split them up, started a fire in the widow's stove, and saw that she had something to eat. With his attention to her the time passed so quickly that before he finished, it was too late for him to preach. Of course, this became known to a few of his congregation, and the next Sunday, when he addressed the members who attended, in a short and modest way he stated the cause of his detention and said that he had no regrets for himself and no apology to make for his failure to attend the previous Sabbath.

The circumstances attending Mr. Whitney's death constitute a tribute to the tenderness of his heart and the nobility of his character which must endear him to the memory of his friends as long as they live to remember anything. In the early part of the late Civil War he was appointed by Col. Robt. G. Ingersoll as chaplain of his Regt., the 11th Ill. Cav'y. I do no stop here to make any criticism upon Col. Ingersoll's religious principles, either then or now, but it seems probable that the friendship between them may have been strengthened by the fact that at that day, over thirty years ago, each of them was aware that the other was struggling for light on the great subject of religious thought.

He accepted the place – joined the Regt – and soon found himself at the Battle of Pittsburg Landing. It will be remembered that after a hard day's fight our soldiers laid down on the ground, where darkness had overtaken them, and that rain fell during a large part of the night. Notwithstanding the bad weather and his fatigued condition, Mr. Whitney occupied the entire night in going around over the field looking after the sick, the wounded and the dying, and in doing all that he was capable of in the way of relieving their sufferings.

I do not desire to harass the feelings of your readers by descriptions of the sufferings which he attempted to relieve, nor of those which he must himself have encountered in this first essay of his duties as chaplain, nor in recalling the unfortunate result to Mr. Whitney, and his congregation in Keokuk. I can only add that during that night he contracted a disease from which he died within 2 or 3 weeks, and indeed was hardly able to be brought home before the event occurred.

His grave lies in the most beautiful part of the cemetery of Keokuk, among those of other citizens who have died and been buried there. Adjoining this is a National Cemetery, where the bodies of those who died in the Army have been interred. On Decoration Day once a year, the People of that city, as of other sections, meet and scatter roses on the graves of their friends and heroes. For many years after his death, and as long a I was personally able to attend those decoration services, I never failed to visit the grave of my departed friend and contribute my floral offering to his memory.

Mr. Whitney died in the prime of his life, died regretted and mourned by the population of an entire city, died without an enemy, and his loss was an irreparable one. He left a widow and four children. Through the kindness of Col. Perry and some others, he had secured a comfortable house in a pleasant part of the city. He was indifferent to making money, perhaps too much so, and his wife and young children were left in struggling circumstances. Perhaps the pervading influence of his earnest example, of his devotion to duty, of his generous character, and of his self-denying consecration to the cause of humanity and the Christian religion, as he understood them, were worth more to those he left behind than any money would have been.

He was a true man, with a noble heart and a commanding intellect. He died a martyr to his sense of duty, "of such is the Kingdom of Heaven."

Sam F. Miller

Samuel F. Miller is buried across the road from Rev. Leonard's grave. Samuel Miller's funeral in 1890 was at the Unitarian Church in Keokuk. I have a booklet written in 1990 on S. F. Miller and his life in Keokuk in the 1860's and mentions some history of the church and Rev. Leonard.

When Rev. Leonard died, he left Harwood, still in the army; Charles Edmund, 15 years old (who died 2 years later at 18 years); Leonard Denison, 11 years old (who died in 1899 at age 39); and Carlton Perry, then 1 ½ years old. Harwood and his Army pay were their main means of support.

Ann Jenette tried to get a widow's pension and Mr. Miller tried to get Harwood raised to a Lieut. in order to be of more help financially. She did not receive her pension until 1873 as far as I can tell.

The following letter from Col. Ingersoll was written to Ann Jenette after Rev. Leonard's death.

Corinth, July 19, 1862

Mrs. Leonard Whitney - My dear Madam -

Your letter did not reach me 'till yesterday - I immediately made out the proper certificate and as I think properly attended, though I am very little acquainted with the regulations upon the subject. I hope, however, that it may prove sufficient.

I was very glad to receive your letter and glad to learn that I was remembered by your husband to whom I was greatly attached.

Mr. Whitney won the respect and esteem of the whole command by uniform kindness to all and was considered by every man in the regt. as a noble, generous, gentleman.

During the time he was with us he was almost constantly by the sick and wounded and was as kind to them as though they had been his own children. At the Battle of Shiloh, he gave his blankets to the wounded, then slept upon the ground uncovered with the chilly rain pouring upon him the whole dreary night. And at that time, as I believe, laid the foundation for the disease that terminated his life.

Permit me to say that I sympathize with you deeply in your irreparable loss. Generous men are not indigenous to this world, they are exotics from the skies. There is no such thing as being consoled for their loss. Their memory is worthy of and demands the bitterest of tears. And yet, believing as you do in the immortality of the soul, the dark cloud of grief now enveloping your heart, if not dissipated, will at least be adorned and glorified by the sweet bow of Hope. I shall ever be pleased to be of assistance to you in any manner possible and I hope you will feel no delicacy in commanding me. If the certificate here with sent should prove incorrect, inform me, and I shall make it right.

I do not know where Mr. Whitney's photograph was taken. He was dissatisfied with the artist where mine was taken and went to other rooms. My impression is that the rooms are on Forth St. about a block above the Planters House, and on the same side of the street. If in St. Louis I could easily find the place and when there I will do so, unless you succeed before.

Whether your Husband left any property here belonging to you, I do not know. I will ascertain and inform you. I know he had property in his possession, but I think that it belonged to the Govt.

I am my dear madam, Your friend,

Robert G. Ingersoll

The following letter was written by Sam F. Miller to Maj. General Curtis, asking his help in securing a Lieutenancy in order for Harwood to help his family. The back is signed by S. R. Curtis - H. Z. Curtis (who

I believe was his son and later killed) and Cyrus Bussy and Maj. Gen. Halleck.

Keokuk, Aug. 28, 1862

Maj. General S. R. Curtis

Dear Sir -

Mr. Reverend Leonard Whitney of this place died in the month of April last of a fever contracted in the Military Service at Corinth.

He was a chaplain to Col. Ingersoll's 11th Ill. Cavalry - He contracted his disease by sharing his blanket on a wet night with a wounded soldier. Of all who have given their lives to their country in this struggle I very much doubt if a nobler, cleaner intellect has perished than that of Leonard Whitney. I am sure no better man or purer patriot has died in the cause He has left a wife and four children in the extremist poverty. He has a son, a noble fellow and fine soldier, in your command, in Capt. Anderson's Co. of Bussys Cavalry and friends of the family think that a true representation of these facts, by you at this War Dept. with a little personal urgency would secure the young man a Lieutenancy in the regular army and enable him to assist to support his Mother and family.

Rest assured that if you can do this it will be an Act which you may recall to mind with satisfaction when you come to settle your accounts either with your conscience or with your final Judge -

I am dear sir, Your friend,

Very truly, Sam F. Miller

P.S. His name is Harwood Whitney

Harwood did not get the appointment. On the back page of the original letters with the signatures of S.R. Curtis, H.Z. Curtis, Maj. Gen. Halleck, and Cyrus Busy, are the following notes:

Keokuk

Sept 16/62 - Respy. referred to Col. Bussy Cmdg. 3rd Iowa Cavalry for report to the character and standing of Private Whitney, Co C.

By order, H. Z. Curtis

Respy referred to the Gov. of Iowa, By order,

Maj. Gen Halleck

Hd Qrs 1st Brigade, 1st Division W.S.W.

Helena, Ark, Sep 25th/62

Major - Private Harwood Whitney is a young man of excellent morals and assuming manners, he is a good soldier and would make a good Lieutenant. There are no vacancies in my Command to which he could be assigned his promotion to a Lieutenancy in the Regular Army & would be approved by his officers who have been associated with him for more than a year. I have no better Soldier in my Command.

Very Respectfully, Cyrus Bussy

Colonel 3rd Iowa Cav Comdg.

The following letter is to Ann Jenette from Cyrus Bussy:

Head Quarters 3rd Brigade, Helena, Ark.

Dec. 1st 1862

Mrs. L. Whitney

I received your letter this morning and have complied with your request. I sent the coat this evening by Mrs. Wittenmeyer who will leave it with Harwood at St. Louis.

Will always be pleased to serve you and hope to hear from you when ever I can aid you. My wife sends her kind regards.

Very Respectfully, Your obt. Servant

Cyrus Bussy

Ann Jennette continued trying to get a pension. It appears there was some problem about Rev. Leonard going home, as in the following letter written by Col. Ingersoll, where he says he sent him home because he thought he would die and wanted him with his loved ones.

LaGrange, Ten.

June 22nd, 1863

Dear Madam,

Your letter of the 3rd reached me only a day or two ago. My Regt. is at Salisbury, eight miles from this place. I intend going there tomorrow and will then get the surgeon and give certificate such as you ask for. I gave Mr. Whitney leave to go home. I thought that he would die if he stayed and felt anxious if he was going to die, that he might be surrounded by those he loved.

I violated orders if anybody. I do not think it necessary that any certificate with regard to his absence be given.

The lawyers making applications need not tell everything they know. The main facts, that he was in the service - contracted a disease of which he died - and that he was paid to a certain date, and that he owed the U. S. nothing on any acct, whatever - I believe I sent you the Quartermasters certificate as to the indebtedness. However, it will do no hurt to have the medical certificate and I will send it if possible. Let the lawyers make the application first - saying nothing about absence and then if the papers are returned - it is time enough to enter with the details.

You speak about your son, I am about leaving my regt. and the service - under a late order whenever a regt. becomes reduced below half the original number, that the Colonel shall be mustered out of the service. My Regt. is in that condition. At first I had about eleven hundred and forty men - now about four hundred and fifty in the Regt. - that we are entitled to - so that a good many will have to be mustered out of the service. Could I give your son a position I would instantly, but it is absolutely impossible. If at any time here after I am in a position to aid him, I shall do cheerfully.

In a few days I expect to be out of war, and at home in peace, and the thought gives me great pleasure. I have seen enough of death and horror. I would not go through it all again to be a Napoleon.

I sympathize with you deeply in your great loss and think of you very often indeed. I thought a great deal of Mr. Whitney, a man of great sense, and great heart. The society of Heaven itself will be better for his genial presence. I have a good likeness of him, after having a copy taken, I will send the original to you - This shall be done immediately upon my arrival home. With a thousand wishes for your happiness.

I remain, Truly your friend

Robt. G. Ingersoll

I thank you from my inmost heart for your kind wishes for myself and dear wife –

Still attempting to secure a pension from the Army, another letter from Col. Ingersoll reads:

Peoria, Dec. 9, 1863

Mrs. Whitney -

Dear Madam,

I rec'd your letter this evening, the name of the surgeon of the 11th Ill. Cav. is Robert F. Stratton and he was surgeon at the time your husband left. L. H. Kerr is the Lt. Col. commanding the regiment. I will write to Stratton the surgeon and also the Lt. Col. and request them to attend to your matter.

I am sorry that you are having so much trouble. Anything I can do will be cheerfully done. You have our best wishes for success.

You need not be afraid of troubling me. I am more than willing to be troubled to help the wife and family of so excellent a man as your husband.

Yours truly,

Robert Ingersoll

And a letter also from Robert F. Stratton, Surgeon of the 11th Ill. Cav.

HeadQrs. 11th Ill. Cav. Near Vicksburg Miss.

Dec. 22, 1863

Mrs. Leonard Whitney

Your letter of Dec. 8th was duly received. I enclose my own certificate and also one from the Adjutant. I trust they will meet the requirements of the case. I hope you will succeed in obtaining a pension as you so well deserve.

I valued Mr. Whitney highly as a friend and companion and deeply deplore his loss. He left many warm friends in the Regt. Please remember we are willing and anxious to do anything in our power to help you.

Very truly yours,

Robert F. Stratton

Surgeon 11th Ill. Cav.

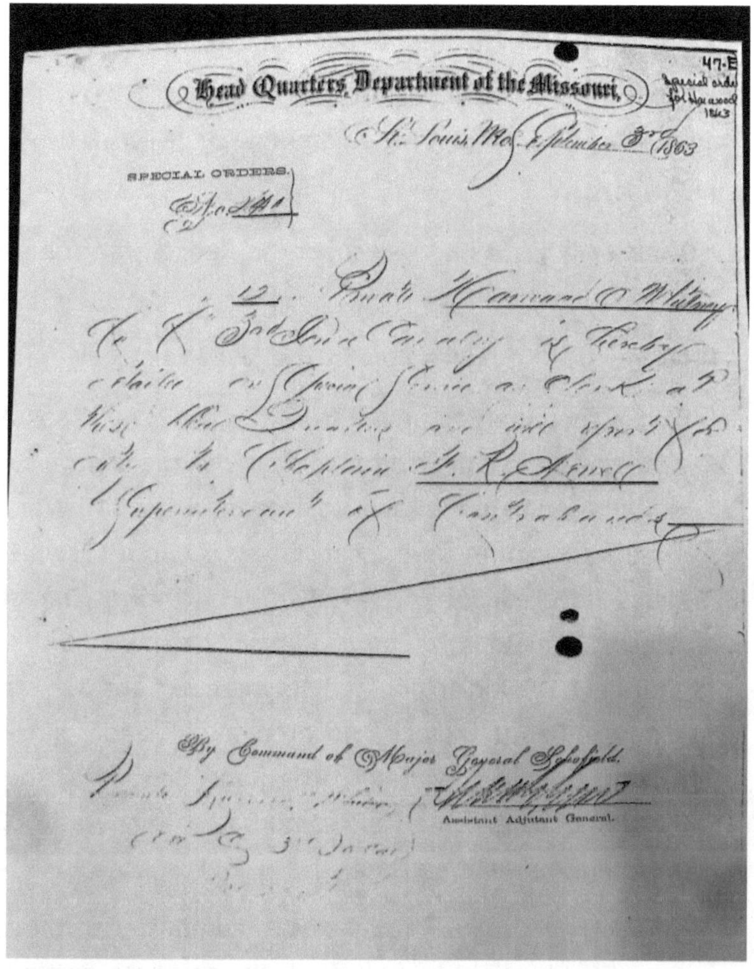

Head Quarters, Department of the Missouri,

St. Louis, Mo. September 3rd 1863

SPECIAL ORDERS.

No. [illegible]

12. Private Harwood [illegible] Co. K 3rd Iowa Cavalry is hereby detailed on Special Service as Clerk at these Head Quarters and will report for duty to Chaplain F. R. Newell Superintendent of Contrabands.

By Command of Major General Schofield.

Assistant Adjutant General.

In the meantime - Harwood, who had been in St. Louis, I surmise, since December 1862 (see the letter from Cyrus Bussy, December, 1862) received Special Orders from Headquarters of Dept. of the Missouri on Sept. 3, 1863 as clerk to a Headquarters and was to report for duty to Chaplin F. R. Newell, Superintendent of Contrabands, by command of Maj. General Schofield.

On February 2, 1864, in Keokuk, Harwood's 18-year-old brother, (Leonard's second son), Charles Edmund Whitney died. I do not know what of, or if there is any other information about him. I will try to look up old newspapers to see if there is any information. He died 2 years after his father.

On Sept. 1, 1864, Harwood was discharged from the Army after serving 3 years.

In 1989 the Daily Gate City newspaper in Keokuk ran the following article:

**Keokuk's Role in The Civil War**

> While seemingly removed from the Civil War, Keokuk did in fact play a most important role. It was the central swearing-in point for all of the Iowa volunteers in the Civil War. At one time four camps were located here: "Camp Ellsworth," 200 acres located in the area of Hawthorn, Decatur and Messenger Road; "Camp Rankin," named for Keokuk's Colonel J. W. Rankin, located between 11$^{th}$ and 12$^{th}$ streets on Grand; "Camp Halleck," located at 5$^{th}$ and Johnson; and "Camp Lincoln," located in the Rand Park area, site of the Battle Reenactment. This camp had as many as 1,000 men camped there at one time.
>
> Another of Keokuk's roles was to administer to the sick and wounded brought by boat from the southern battlegrounds. Seven Civil War hospitals were located in Keokuk with the largest, The Estes House, having 652 beds. The location of the Estes House was at 5$^{th}$ and Main Streets, now the site of Estes Park. Keokuk's National Cemetery is a direct result of the Civil War soldiers who died enroute to Keokuk or after arriving at

one of the hospitals. Both Confederate and Union soldiers are buried in this National Cemetery, one of the original twelve established by Congress July 17, 1862. It is Iowa's only National Cemetery and the first established West of the Mississippi. Keokuk provided many Civil War heroes; too many for space to allow elaboration. Among them were:

> *Major General Samuel Curtis*, victorious Commander at the Battle of Pea Ridge. Curtis served as Mayor of Keokuk and Iowa Congressman.
>
> *Colonel B. Torrence*, local educator, who served with the 1st Iowa Infantry and the 13th Iowa Cavalry.
>
> *Colonel John C Parriot*, who fought with the Iowa 8th, 12th, 14th, and Illinois 58th, and later served as Postmaster of Keokuk.
>
> *William Worth Belknap*, brevet Major General, who fought in many major battles during the Civil War, including Shiloh, Corinth, and the Vicksburg and Atlanta Campaigns. He later served as Secretary of War in President U. S. Grant's Cabinet.
>
> *John Wesley Nobel*, Colonel of the 3rd Iowa Cavalry, who was later appointed as Secretary of Interior in President Harrison's cabinet.
>
> *Hugh T. Rice*, Colonel of the 15th Iowa Infantry and later Brigadier General, who fought in many battles, including Shiloh.
>
> *Colonel John T. Rankin*, a lawyer who served as Judge of the First Judicial District and also as a State Senator.
>
> *Joseph P. Hughes*, who was appointed Surgeon General for Iowa and organized and personally took charge of the Army's hospitals in Keokuk.

> *Annie Whittenmyer*, who visited the Iowa regiments in the fields, inaugurated special diet kitchens which became a permanent part of the military system, established the first Soldier's Orphans' Homes in America and was allowed to pass through all lines at all times. Grant said of Wittenmyer, "No soldier on the firing line gave more heroic service than she rendered." She is further credited with compiling the first Army cookbook and was instrumental in getting a bill passed granting pensions to Army Nurses.

While removed from Pea Ridge, Arkansas, where one of its most famous sons secured Missouri for the Union, Keokuk was vitally involved in the Civil war.

KEOKUK CITY RIFLES - Keokuk's homeguard, a three-pronged city militia consisting of the Keokuk City Rifles, Keokuk City Rangers, and Keokuk City Artillery, was organized on the 24$^{th}$ day of April, 1861, by a number of prominent citizens. Their services tendered the mayor in protecting the city. This organization served well and ably, for there was a true, ever-present threat from secessionists and their sympathizers as near as Alexanderia and Athens, Missouri.

In 1869 Harwood was employed as an Agent for the T.P.&W. Railroad Depot in Warsaw, Ill. There is a newspaper article published Feb. 12th, 1915, about Harwood saving a 16-year-old boy, Morris Jacobs, when his horse and wagon went into the river:

Relates Incident About H. O. Whitney, a Keokuk Man Whose Death Occurred a Few Months Ago, Proved a Hero for Saving Young Lad's Life.

The Warsaw Bulletin recalls an incident in which the late Harwood O. Whitney of this city proved considerable of a hero. The incident took place in July, 1869, and the following is the story of the affair from the old Bulletin:

Wednesday afternoon, July 21, Morris Jacobs, the 16-year-old son of J. C. Jacobs, drove the Jacobs & McMahan delivery to the river to water the horse, taking with him his 8-year-old cousin. Driving into the water, his animal, which was young, was scared by a team backing against the delivery, and plunged deeper into the water. Young Jacobs could not control it and soon the rig and boys were a considerable distance from shore, the delivery upsetting. Morris, who is a fair swimmer and could have saved himself, was endeavoring to save his cousin and it looked as if both would drown when H. O. Whitney, the T.P. & W. agent, who saw the peril of the boys from the depot window, rushed down to the river, plunged in and brought the little fellow to shore, although almost exhausted himself, due to the weight of his clothing. Morris was able to save himself. The wagon was recovered by Wm. Leyhe and Albert Cherry. The horse was drowned.

It must have been during this time around 1869 that Harwood met and fell in love with Helen Jemina Hay, the youngest daughter of Charles Hay and the sister of John M. Hay. They were married on July 14, 1870 and lived in Warsaw, Ill. I have little information about this period although a trip to the Warsaw Library and researching the old newspapers may provide more.

There is one letter written by Helen Hay Whitney to her mother-in-law, Ann Jenette. I don't know what year, but Helen died in 1873.

> Warsaw, Illinois
>
> September 17th
>
> My Dear Mother,
>
> I thank you heartily for your beautiful present. I appreciate it very highly and like all good mothers, I fear you have deprived yourself of a pleasure to give your child one.
>
> I know you like the book and every time I take it up, it will remind me of you. Tell Carlton he must think of his sister Helen every day, that she loves little boys and she wants him to print her a letter and she will answer it in the same way. If he sends a few lines that will do to commence with. She will wait just two weeks for him to do it, no matter if he makes mistakes she will think it is nice for he is the only little brother she has in the world!
>
> If you are too busy to show Carlton ask Leonard to help him and encourage him to try if he does not feel disposed to.
>
> Harwood is at the office or he would send his love. Again let me thank you.
>
> Your affectionate daughter,
>
> Helen

Carlton was 10 years old and evidently still having some problems. In Rev. Leonard's letters during the Civil War, he was constantly encouraging them to "study and go to school" and to obey their mother. Carlton had more problems later on. Leonard Denison was 20 years old at this time.

In a letter written April 25, 1873 (2 months before she died) to Helen from her sister-in-law in Springfield, Ill. the sister-in-law mentions Helen's "good news" and adds: "... now do be careful of yourself and let no accident occur this time..." - evidently Helen has lost a previous child. She also mentions, "Charles' time is almost wholly occupied ... since he has become Mayor of the City, evenings as well as days so that I see very little of him." It appears Helen was called "Ellie," as this letter is addressed to her:

> Springfield
>
> April 25, 1873
>
> Dear Ellie - Your kind letter containing the announcement should not have been allowed to remain so long unanswered but if you could only look in upon this busy household day after day, you would excuse my apparent neglect.
>
> I am so glad to hear such good news from you - now do be careful of yourself and let no accident occur this time.
>
> Johnnie and Arthur have gone to a circus with Mike and I have sent the children to the kitchen in order to secure a few moments quiet for writing.
>
> I have just finished a letter to Annie Johnson in answer to an invitation for me to visit her. I think of going down and taking Arthur and Willie next week to spend a week or ten days. My

old nurse Maggie, who you will remember went with me to Warsaw, came to see me yesterday. She has just returned from Sterling - I am going to take her with me to St. Louis and leave my own nurse with the children.

Anna and her husband are going to keep house for me, and I think I will have a pleasant time and a good rest from the care of housekeeping.

I had a nice long call from Aunt Ella and Deniza the other day. I was glad to hear that Uncle Joe is improving. I was afraid he would never recover. The children were delighted with Uncle Whitney's letter and Johnnie says, "Mama I like to hear that letter over and over, but I wish he had told him the man caught the young wolves." Johnnie is reading in the 3rd Reader that Grandma Hay gave him and last Friday repeated "woodman spare that tree." I never saw a child learn faster. He is crazy to see Warsaw and Grandma Hay.

Charlie's (Charles Edw. Hay) time is almost wholly occupied now-a-days since he became Mayor of the City, evenings as well as days so that I see very little of him.

Little Annie is as cunning and smart as ever - she astonishes us sometimes by her wise sayings. I tell you she makes the boys ...?... Anna Henderson is very happily married. She is devoted to her husband and he to her. Jeanne is still single. I cannot say when she will change her state - I was glad to hear from Aunts that you are all well. Aunt Elma walked all the way out here and when she arrived, she looked so pale and tired that I got her a glass of beer and some brown bread and she felt well right before she left. She has been so delicate all

> winter. All the love that they brought to us all from you all is reciprocated. You may be sure we will look for Mother Hay in the fall with Mary Wolfolk and she must not disappoint us. I suppose you have seen Carrie Leinr and that she has told you of her visit with us. Here come the children and I must bid you a hasty goodbye – May

Helen Hay Whitney died a month and a half later, on June 19, 1873, evidently from complications of her pregnancy.

Charles Edward Hay was a lawyer and later Mayor of Springfield, Ill. I think both he and his brother, John, worked with their Uncle in his law office in Springfield, Ill. where John met Abraham Lincoln and became his private secretary around 1861.

The following information on Dr. Charles Hay is from the Biological Review of Hancock County, Warsaw Library:

> … As the years passed there were added to the family of Dr. and Mrs. Hay, six children, of whom the eldest, Edward Leonard died in infancy. Leonard Augustus Hay, the second son, retired army officer, died in Warsaw, November 12, 1904. Mary Pierce is the widow of Major Austin Coleman Woolfolk, A. O. M., United States Army and afterward a circuit judge in Minnesota. John M. Hay rose to national prominence, his last public work being as secretary of state under President Roosevelt. Charles Edward, captain of the Third Cavalry United States Army, and afterward twice elected mayor of Springfield, Illinois, is the only surviving son. Helen became the wife of Harwood Otis Whitney and died in 1873. The death of his daughter came to Dr. and Mrs. Hay as

> their greatest bereavement. Her bright sunny temper, her witty and original conversation, her devotion to those she loved and her absolute unselfishness, qualities which she seemed to derive with her name from her mother, made her the idol of her home.

We also have two letters from Helen's mother's relatives, (she was Helen Leonard), from Detroit, Michigan, written to Harwood at the time of Helen's death. These were from Mrs. Bernard (Nellie Tucker Leonard) and Bernard A. Leonard, and the other from Ellen B. True, a friend in Detroit, Michigan.

A month later Charles Edward Hay wrote the following letter to Harwood:

> Mayor's office
>
> Springfield, Ill.
>
> Aug. 27, 1873
>
> Dear Whitney, - I have been quite busy and so the time has passed away that I had promised myself to visit Warsaw again. The calculation now is that about the 15th of Sept. Johnny and John and myself will come in "grand time" for a visit of a few days.
>
> John's matrimonial prospects seem to be on the increase. Christmas seems to be his objective point. It will be very odd to think of him as a double man. I hope it will result in the best for all. After the 1st of the month I hope everything will run a little smoother as the weather will begin to grow cooler and a fat fellow like I am can navigate to a better advantage.

> The Journal will keep you generally pretty well posted as to the news.
>
> Good bye - C.E.H.

John M. Hay married Clara Stone in Cleveland, Ohio on February 4, 1874. An article about John Hay from the Cleveland newspaper of that time gives some background on John:

> John Milton Hay was born in Salem, Ill. He graduated from Brown University in 1858 and soon after entered the law office of Milton Hay, his uncle, a former partner of Abrahan Lincoln in the law business. Thus, early in his life John Hay came in touch with the man who was destined to be a tremendous figure in the history of this country. In 1861 young Hay was admitted to the bar; he took an active part in the campaign preceding Lincoln's first election and in 1861 went with Lincoln to Washington as one of Lincoln's private secretaries. He served in the field for a time during the Civil War and was brevetted a lieutenant colonel. After the war he commenced a diplomatic career in Paris, Vienna and Madrid. In 1870 he resigned and came back to America where he became a member of the editorial staff of the New York Tribune. It was In the period of his work on the Tribune that Hay produced his homely "Pike County Ballads", and these were first published in the Tribune.
>
> After five years of service with the Tribune, Hay came to Cleveland and married Miss Clara Stone, a daughter of Amasa Stone, the man whose generosity was later to bring Western Reserve University to Cleveland from Hudson. Samuel

Mather, philanthropist and civic leader also married a daughter of Amasa Stone.

The Stone-Hay wedding on Feb. 4, 1874, was a brilliant society event. The ceremony was in the Stone home at 113 Euclid Ave. Hay was always the devoted suitor and husband. Before his marriage he wrote a letter to Whitelaw Reid, then the editor of the New York Tribune, in which he said: "The fact of being in love and seeing a good woman in love also, is a wonderfully awakening thing. I would not have died before this happened for a great deal of coin,"

That Hay approached the wedding ceremony with some trepidation is shown in a letter he wrote a friend. "I am going to be married," he said in the letter. "If you want to see the last of me, be at Mr. Stone's, 113 Euclid Ave, Cleveland, on the eve of Feb. 4 and I will show you a lovely woman dressed in a white dress and a man in a black coat."

The Hays maintained a home in Cleveland at 514 Euclid Ave. It was built for them by the bride's father. That John Hay always remained the true lover is shown in one of his later tributes to his wife, thus:

One dear presence, lovelier

Than all the miracles of art,

With the gentle power to move and stir

The deepest pulses of my heart.

After the marriage Colonel and Mrs. Hay lived in New York for about one year and then returned to Cleveland. He opened an office on the Public Square. It was in this period of a 10-

year residence in Cleveland that he became most active in the city's civic and communal life. Among his interests was the public library and he served on its board. It was also in this period that much of the active work on the monumental 10-volume biography of Abraham Lincoln was done. T.G. Nicolay, the co-author of the biography, was a frequent visitor to the city in those days. It was then, too, that Hay wrote his novel, "The Breadwinner," which appeared anonymously in 1889. Many of the scenes of the story are laid in Cleveland.

The Hays gave up their Cleveland home in 1897 when the colonel accepted the post of Ambassador to England. He was in London only a year when President McKinley called him back to become Secretary of State. His work as head of the State Department is notable. It was the days of the Boxer rebellion in China, and it was in that troublous time that Hay devised the "open door" policy, which, though not a formal treaty, soon was accepted by every great power. Other great trips toward the promotion of world peace followed. Then came the news of the assassination of President McKinley.

Sick at heart and ill physically, John Hay returned to give up his post when Theodore Roosevelt was inaugurated, but Roosevelt insisted that there must be no change in the State Department and Hay kept his post. On July 1, 1905, John Hay died and the whole nation paid tribute when the funeral was held in Cleveland. Two weeks before his death he wrote these words in his diary: "I have had many blessings, domestic happiness being the greatest of all."

1870
Helen Hay
sister of
John Hay
married
H.O. Whitney
1870
Died 1873
(pregnancy
complication
John
Hay
John Hay

A letter from E.M. Putnam to John Hay when he was *Charge d' Affairs* in Paris, Vienna & Madrid until 1870 reads:

> Office of Putnam's Magazine
>
> Association Building
>
> Fourth Avenue & 23rd Street
>
> New York
>
> June 30, 1870
>
> Col. John Hay, (Madrid)
>
> Dear Sir -- We have sent to Charles E. Hay Esq, Springfield, Ill. a check for $55 – as our usual return for your excellent paper "Down the Danube." We are ambitious to send larger increment to our valued contributors - but the ambition and crowding of magazines leaves us no profit even at these rates.
>
> We feel honored by having your article and hope you will favor us with more. We are trying to keep up our magazine wholly original and American and to make it credible as our contributors will enable us to make it.
>
> With high respect dear sir,
>
> Faithfully yours, E. Putnam

Harwood must have moved back to Keokuk with his mother sometime after Helen's death although I don't know when. However, the next letter is from John Hay written to Harwood in Keokuk. I believe he had been made 1st Assistant Secretary of State for Rutherford B. Hays, 1879-1881.

Department of State, Washington

December 1, 1879

Dear Mr. Whitney,

Thanks for your kind letter. I do not feel as if I ought to be congratulated. I did not want this place - did not want to leave home and my work there but after I had declined once, the thing was put to me the second time in such a way that it would have seemed like shirking to decline again. So here I am, working like a convict, spending two or three times my pay, and wishing myself at home. But I thank you all the same for your letter and if you run across Wm. Clark, give him my compliments and thanks for the handsome paragraph you sent me.

Very Sincerely, John Hay

Mrs. Stone told me of your kind attention and her pleasant visit to Warsaw.

(Clara Hay's mother is Mrs. Stone.)

I think it was around this time that John Hay bought the lovely big house in Warsaw for his parents and widowed sister, Mrs. Mary Pierce Hay Woolfolk, who came to take care of them in 1880. Dr. Hay died on Sept. 18, 1884, and his wife died in 1893. Leonard Augustus Hay, a son and brother to John, retired to Warsaw in June 1891, and I believe he lived there too. Mary Woolfolk died in 1914 and Mr. & Mrs. Will Hay and John Hay (Charles Edward's sons) came to live there in 1917.

My great aunt Lillian Ehinger Felt (later Whitney) was a friend of Mrs. Woolfolk's and my mother and her cousin Prue. I remember taking the streetcar to visit "Aunt Mary" and the carpet with red roses in it that had been in the house since the Civil War. My great aunt Lillian inherited Mary Woolfolk's dog, "Rags", when Mary died and also an oil painting that had been bought in Paris by Leonard Augustus Hay in 1870 for his parents. It has been in our family since 1915.

In the meantime, Ann Jenette Whitney had finally received a pension on July 16, 1873, 11 years after her husband's death, of $20 per month and $2 for each child under the age of 16 starting July 1866

( No. 14. )

Ann Jenette Pension 1873

**Department of the Interior,**
PENSION OFFICE,

Washington, D. C., July 16th, 1873.

Madame

You are hereby notified that your claim for pension, as widow of Leonard Whitney Certificate No. 21.273, has been allowed at $20. per month, commencing June 12th, 1862, and $2 additional for each child while living and under the age of sixteen years, commencing July 25th 1866.

payable at the Pension Agency in Fairfield Iowa

Your pension certificate has been issued and sent to the Pension Agent at the same place, who will forward to you, upon receipt thereof, and quarterly thereafter, proper vouchers for payment thereupon. The note indorsed upon said vouchers will explain when and how they shall be executed by you, and how the payment thereupon will be made.

The fee to be paid your attorney for the prosecution of your claim is $———, and no more, and the same will be deducted from first payment by Pension Agent.

Respectfully,

J. H. Baker
Commissioner.

To Ann J. Whitney
Keokuk
Iowa.

Another letter is from Robert Ingersoll to Ann Jenette on April 17, 1877, who apparently went through Keokuk but didn't have time to stop to call on her.

Peoria, April 27, 1877

Mrs. Whitney –

My dear Madam:

I arrived at Keokuk at 7:30 on the evening of the 25th and left next morning at 5:40. As you see that it was impossible for me to call. I greatly regret this as it would have given me great pleasure to have seen you. The next time I am in Keokuk I will do myself the honor to call.

Thanking you for the ...?.. I remain.

R.. G. Ingersoll

There is another letter from John Hay to Harwood but no year in the date on it. It is from White Sulphur Springs, Va. Harwood had mentioned going to Spain, so I feel it may have been after Helen died and John came home from Europe and before 1880. As far as I know Harwood never went to Spain – and I do not know what he was going for, possibly looking for some type of job.

White Sulphur Springs, Virginia

July 21st

My dear Boy,

I believe I have always congratulated you upon your successes when I have been fortunate enough to know of them. If you are going to Spain "here's my hand". I hope you'll have a splendid time! I know they won't make you walk Spanish - I don't know what that means but I suppose it's something very bad. I hope you will be as the happiest person in the world and contented as

Your Sincere Friend,

J.H.

P.S. I intended sending the enclosed to you before - but have always forgotten it - does that word have two t's in it or not, I wonder!

Sometime during this period, Harwood's brother, Leonard Denison, left Keokuk and was married. He must have lived in Council Bluffs, Iowa. I know very little about him - he would have been 30 years old in 1880. He died in Council Bluffs on July 18, 1889, at the age of 39. We have a receipt that Harwood paid $50 on account for his funeral and paid taxes on his lot in Council Bluffs in 1889. There are two letters from a young boy named Bonaparte Whitney from Council Bluffs in 1906 and 1907 - he would have to be at least 16 if he were born before Leonard died. I have no other information or knowledge of him. When Harwood died in 1914 the deed to Leonard D. Whitney's wife's property in Council Bluffs was listed in the list for Probate. If he survived, he would be the only relative left of his family. I'm sure there would have been some record of Harwood sending him money or something in all the papers I have but there is nothing. Copies of the two rather sad letters follow:

Council Bluffs, March 14, 1906

Dear Uncle,

I received your box and was pleased with the clothes. Mother was very glad to hear from you, her sight and health has not improved any. Hoping this will find you well.

Your nephew,

Boneparte Whitney

Council Bluffs

Dec. 28, 1907

Dear Uncle,

We received your letter and mother was pleased that you remembered her. She is feeling well but cannot see. Father's old buggy horse died last Spring. Hoping you are all well.

Your nephew,

Boneparte Whitney

In September 1882 Harwood applied for a pension, a result of being bothered by hemorrhoids and piles acquired during the forced march from Rolla to Pea Ridge. There are nine affidavits, and just rewritten copies so I will not include them all but will quote from one:

> I was well acquainted with said Harwood, late Pvt. of Co. C 3rd Regt Iowa Cav Vols and have personal knowledge of the fact from being present with the Regt that in the month of Feb. 1862 in the field at Lebanon, Mo. from previous exposure on a forced march from Rolla, Mo. towards Pea Ridge, Ark. said Harwood O. Whitney was attacked with Hemorrhoids or piles and was left sick and under treatment

from Surgeon McGra..?.. Of said regiment at Lebanon, Mo. in Feb 1862.

I don't believe he got the pension as there is no other mention of it but under a new Act in 1912 for Veterans over 60 years he received a pension.

In 1883 Harwood bought the Patents for Dry Press Brick Machine (Patd, 1878) from Lewis B. Kennedy, as his agent and attorney for the right to sell his Patents in certain states.

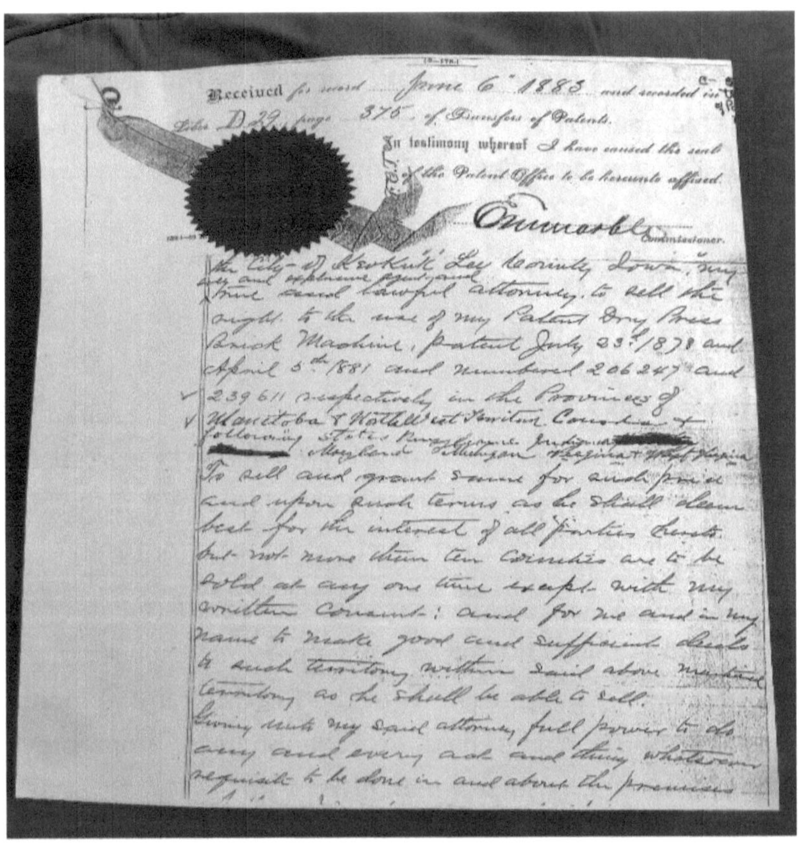

Received for record June 6th 1883 and recorded in Liber D 29, page 375 of Transfers of Patents.

In testimony whereof I have caused the seal of the Patent Office to be hereunto affixed.

[illegible] Commissioner.

the City of Keokuk Lee County Iowa, my [illegible] agent and true and lawful attorney, to sell the right to the use of my Patent Dry Press Brick Machine, Patent July 23rd 1878 and April 5th 1881 and Numbered 206247 and 239611 respectively in the Provinces of Manitoba & North West Territory Canada & following States [illegible] Maryland Michigan Virginia & West Virginia To sell and grant same for such price and upon such terms as he shall deem best for the interest of all parties hereto but not more than ten Counties are to be sold at any one time except with my written Consent; and for me and in my name to make good and sufficient deeds to such territory within said above mentioned territory as he shall be able to sell.

Giving unto my said attorney full power to do any and every act and thing whatsoever requisite to be done in and about the premises

On March 6, 1884 there is an agreement between Adrus, Leoffler & Co., Founders and Machinists, making H. O. Whitney general agent for the sale of his patent Brick Press Machines, clay crushers, & improvements, from which Harwood received 50% of the profit.

53-B
Andrus Leoffler
Letterhead
1884

Office of Andrus, Loeffler & Co.
FOUNDERS AND MACHINISTS,
MANUFACTURERS OF BRICK MACHINERY,

Nos. 213 to 220 South Fourth Street.

Keokuk, Iowa, Mch 6th 1884

Agreement between William Andrus party of the first part & H. O. Whitney party of the second part both of Keokuk Lee County Iowa

The said William Andrus hereby appoints the said H. O. Whitney General Agent for the United States for the sale of his patent Brick Press Machines Clay Crushers & improvements for which he agrees to allow said H. O. Whitney Fifty 50 per Cent of the profits above actual Cost of Manufacture of said Machines.

Said H. O. Whitney to have power of Attorney to transact all business as to sale of Machines & Territory using his discretion as to prices which must be above the Cost of Manufacture

There are many more receipts of payments for machines - he evidently paid for half of the machines at $1,000 before he sold it. There are also transfers of different patents from A. D. Thomas for improvements and various Letterheads of Andrus, Globe Iron Works (who made the machines). I don't know if any of these papers have historical value or not so I will not put them in this story (however they are available).

In 1887 Harwood was named Agent for Star Union Freight Line which was another job as he was still agent for the Brick Presses.

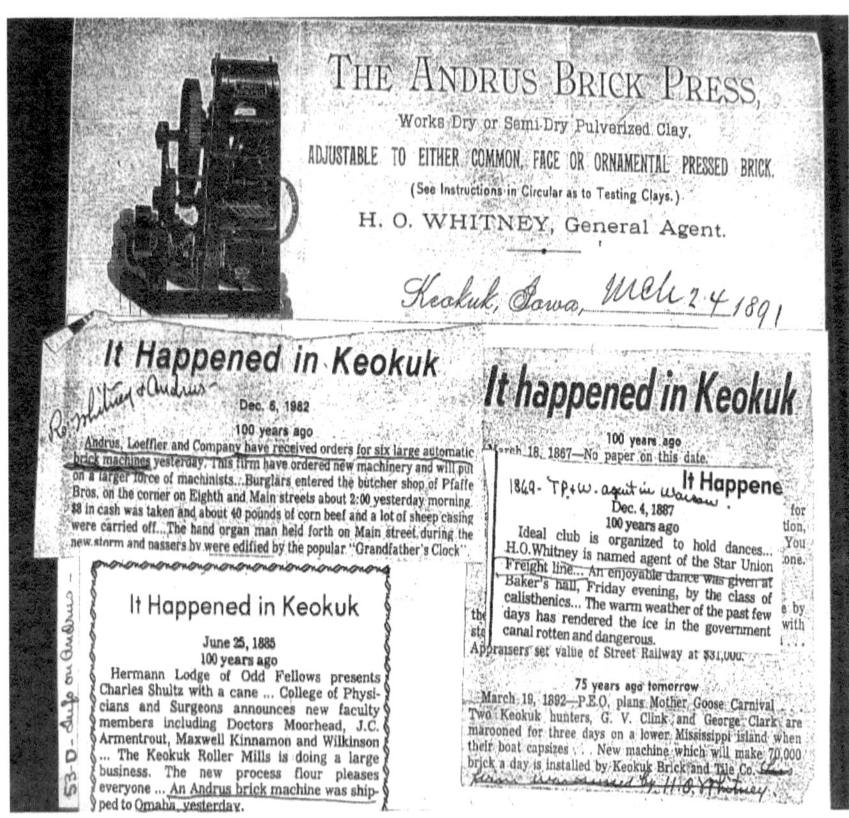

THE ANDRUS BRICK PRESS,

Works Dry or Semi-Dry Pulverized Clay,

ADJUSTABLE TO EITHER COMMON, FACE OR ORNAMENTAL PRESSED BRICK.

(See Instructions in Circular as to Testing Clays.)

H. O. WHITNEY, General Agent.

Keokuk, Iowa, Mch 24 1891

It Happened in Keokuk

Dec. 6, 1982

100 years ago

Andrus, Loeffler and Company have received orders for six large automatic brick machines yesterday. This firm have ordered new machinery and will put on a larger force of machinists...Burglars entered the butcher shop of Pfaffe Bros. on the corner on Eighth and Main streets about 2:00 yesterday morning. $8 in cash was taken and about 40 pounds of corn beef and a lot of sheep casing were carried off...The hand organ man held forth on Main street during the new storm and passers by were edified by the popular "Grandfather's Clock".

It Happened in Keokuk

June 25, 1885

100 years ago

Hermann Lodge of Odd Fellows presents Charles Shultz with a cane ... College of Physicians and Surgeons announces new faculty members including Doctors Moorhead, J.C. Armentrout, Maxwell Kinnamon and Wilkinson ... The Keokuk Roller Mills is doing a large business. The new process flour pleases everyone ... An Andrus brick machine was shipped to Omaha yesterday.

It happened in Keokuk

100 years ago

March 18, 1867—No paper on this date.

It Happene

Dec. 4, 1887

100 years ago

Ideal club is organized to hold dances... H.O.Whitney is named agent of the Star Union Freight line... An enjoyable dance was given at Baker's hall, Friday evening, by the class of calisthenics... The warm weather of the past few days has rendered the ice in the government canal rotten and dangerous.

Appraisers set value of Street Railway at $31,000.

75 years ago tomorrow

March 19, 1892—P.E.O. plans Mother Goose Carnival . . . Two Keokuk hunters, G. V. Clink and George Clark are marooned for three days on a lower Mississippi island when their boat capsizes . . . New machine which will make 70,000 brick a day is installed by Keokuk Brick and Tile Co.

In 1888 the article came out in the Iowa Historical Record written by O. Clute about Rev. Leonard's life. Harwood must have sent a copy to Sam Miller who was then a Justice on the Supreme Court in Washington, D.C. The copy of the letter from Justice Miller is very hard to read.

> Supreme Court of the United States
>
> Washington
>
> May 4, 1888
>
> My Dear Mr. Whitney -
>
> I rec'd the copies of the Iowa Historical Record sent by you and have read Mr. Clute's article about your father with much interest.
>
> In saying what I did I spoke from the fullness of my heart and gave utterance to sentiments held by all who knew him and were capable of understanding him.
>
> Mr. Perry also enjoyed it very much and as I am sure must all of the old members of the ..?.. ..?.. sat under your father's preaching.
>
> I hope your Mother and all the other members of the family are in good health and flourishing.
>
> I am your friend, Sam F Miller

I do not have much information on Harwood from 1890 until 1902. I think he was a director of the State Central Bank but I do not know when he received that position.

In 1902 he must have been trying for some political appointment as there is a letter attesting to his responsibility and honesty and character signed by notable people of the town - some of the signatures are beautiful!

54-C

petition for political appt. signed by leading men

Keokuk, Iowa, Jany. 28th, 1902.

The undersigned have known Mr. H. O. Whitney as a business man of Keokuk, who is popular with all classes, for many years.

He is a veteran of the Civil War, having served three years in the Third Regiment of Iowa Cavalry, and was honorably discharged.

He has filled several positions of trust and responsibility requiring the best of business sagacity, the record of which as to honesty and ability are all highly to his credit.

He has been a life-long Republican, and has actively sustained the party upon all occasions.

We take pleasure in recommending him as an honest, capable and efficient business man, in whatever he undertakes.

James C. Davis (Lawyer)

(President State Central Savings Bank)

Geo. D. Rand

Mr. Whitney is one of our very best citizens and no man in the community stands higher - John N. Irwin (Ex. Minister to Portugal)

Wells M. Irwin (Irwin Phillips Wholesale Grocers)

Saml E. Carey. I endorse what Mr Irwin says to the fullest extent

Howard Tucker (President Iowa Insurance Co)

(Wholesale Grocer)

(Cashier Commercial Bank)

(Wholesale Grocer)

54-D

A. H. Evans (Ex Grand Commander G.A.R. State of Iowa)

I take great pleasure in certifying that I have known Mr Whiting for over twenty years and I know him to be all that is claimed for him above

H. B. Blood

A. W. Trimble (Genl atty C.B. & Q. Ry. Co.)

E. B. [illegible] Minister Westminster Pres. Church

Felix T. Hughes (Judge Superior Court)

Palmer Trimble (atty C.B. & Q. Ry Co)

Geo. E. Rix (Cashier State Central Savings Bank)

David J. Ayres (Ex. Mayor & Ex. Postmaster)

J. H. Cole (Supt. Mississippi Bridge)

Edmund Jaeger (President Commercial Bank)

W. P. Darwin - Wholesale Carpet Co.

[illegible] (Cashier Keokuk National Bank)

J. M. Bisbee Assistant Postmaster

Henry R. Miller (brother of Admiral Miller)

B. O. Tuber (Tuber Lumber Co)

A. C. Goodrich Genl. Manager Keokuk & Western Ry Co

I. F. Kiedaisch (Wholesale Drugs)

Howard L. Connable (Wholesale Clothing)

Joseph Bruce (POST MASTER)

[illegible] Mattlese Huiskamp Shoe Manfg Co.

Luke Huiskamp " " "

F. B. [illegible] (Keokuk National Bank)

A. Hollingsworth (Lawyer)

W. J. Roberts (Lawyer)

[illegible]

[illegible] 1/10 of Burlington [illegible]

John Hay again enters the picture in 1901. John Hay's only son is killed in a fall from a window. Harwood is sent a printed card of "thanks" edged in black:

> *Mr. and Mrs. Hay, finding it impossible to acknowledge separately the many messages and letters of condolence which they have receive since the death of their son, beg to be allowed to express in this manner their deep and grateful appreciation of the kindness of their friends in this time of their sorrow.*
>
> *July 2, 1901*
>
> *Washington D.C.*

On February 6th, 1902, Harwood attended the wedding in Washington of John Hay's daughter Helen (named for her Aunt Helen) to Payne Whitney. John Hay was still Secretary of State. The following is a typewritten copy of the letter from Harwood to a cousin written in 1908 telling of the wedding, his trip, and some background information on the family.

> 525 N Eighth St., Keokuk, Iowa
>
> April 23, 1908
>
> Mrs. Emily F. Collins
>
> 60 Newbury Ave.
>
> Atlantic, Mass.
>
> My dear Cousin:
>
> Your very welcome and interesting letter of March 10th was duly received. While I fully intended to make a prompt reply,

events in the nature of illness and death of my wife's father and mother, brought about postponement until now; and even now I may be unable to reply accurately to all your questions.

I have a book of about 690 pages, Whitney Genealogy, published by Fredrick Clifton Pierce of Chicago, which says that John Whitney came from London, England to Watertown, Mass. in 1635. According to this book I am a descendant of John and Eleanor Whitney and belong to the Massachusetts Whitneys, as did also Hon. W. C. Whitney of New York, who appears in this book with a distinguished record. I was not personally acquainted with W. C. Whitney but was probably remotely related.

I will explain that W.C. Whitney's eldest son is named Harry Payne Whitney while his youngest son is named Payne Whitney. The youngest son, Payne, is the husband of Helen Hay Whitney.

Harwood Otis Whitney (myself) was born at Bennington, Vermont, April 17, 1844. I was married at Warsaw, Ill. July 14th, 1870, to Helen J. Hay, the youngest daughter of Dr. Charles Hay, and the youngest sister of Secretary of State John Hay, whose oldest daughter is named Helen after her Aunt, omitting the "J". She is now Mrs. Payne Whitney or Helen Hay Whitney.

My first wife, Helen Hay Whitney, died June 10th, 1873. I was remarried in Keokuk, Iowa, June 15th, 1904, to Mrs. Lillian E. Felt.

The marriage ceremony of Helen Hay Whitney to Mr. Payne Whitney occurred Feb. 6th, 1902. I received an invitation to the wedding and wrote Secretary Hay that I accepted the invitation, but with my old bachelor habits, I preferred to be entertained at a hotel. He immediately wrote me that he had reserved rooms at The Hotel Gordon, which was within one block of his home. Upon my arrival at Washington, late at night, I was delighted with the elegant suite of rooms that had been reserved for me at this fine hotel. Supposing that I would be allowed to pay my own bill, I had everything charged to my room. After the wedding I concluded to pay my bill and take cheaper rooms and remain in Washington a few days longer and did not need such an expensive suite of rooms. He said, “I would advise you to remain where you are, sir.” Then I wrote a note to Secretary Hay and asked him to instruct the hotel to allow me to pay my bill. He replied, “I am very sorry that you have decided not to accept my hospitality as other of my friends have who have come to the wedding.” He enclosed his card, which read simply “The Secretary of State" and wrote across it, “You will allow Mr. Whitney to pay his own hotel bill, as he declined my hospitality” and further invited me to attend a cabinet meeting with him the next morning and be introduced to the President.

I pushed the card down in my side pocket and said no more to the hotel officials. I could not afford to put myself on record as declining his hospitality. He knew I would not present his card to the hotel, when he wrote it.

The Secretary's family is a delightful one. Mrs. Hay is a charming woman with great force of character. Helen Hay Whitney is beautiful and brilliant in literary affairs. She has written several volumes of poetry and has published some beautiful books for children. Her book published last year (1907) is an illustrated one called "The Bed-time Book." The wedding was a brilliant one, and the presents princely, but the newspapers have described the affair so often better than I could, that I refrain from the attempt. They are now living in the palatial residence on Fifth Ave., New York, presented to them by their uncle, Oliver Payne, who is a bachelor and multimillionaire, and who resides in New York City.

All this account of the great wealth of the participants of this wedding has been published and the facts are of more interest to those who expect to participate than to myself, but in order to answer your questions I have mentioned them and enclose some newspaper clippings which may interest you.

It is extraordinary that at 94 years of age, you could write such an interesting letter, and I extend to you my congratulations and thanks.

There is a firm, Joell Munsell's Sons, Albany, N.Y. who deal in American Genealogies, or family histories, etc., and have them for sale. If you would send for their catalog, it might be of interest to you.

The record of our family is as follows:

<u>Rev. Leonard Whitney.</u>

Born at Williston, Vermont, Oct 23, 1812

Died at Keokuk, Iowa, June 12, 1862 (age 50 years)

Harwood Otis Whitney.

Born at Bennington, Vt. April 17, 1844

Charles Edmund Whitney.

Born at Canandaigua, N.Y. Oct. 5, 1846

Died at Keokuk, Iowa Feb. 2, 1864 (age 18)

Leonard Denison Whitney.

Born at Canandaigua, N.Y. June 20, 1850

Died at Council Bluffs, Iowa, July 18, 1889 (age 39)

Nettie Whitney. (Infant)

Born at Keokuk, Iowa, Feb 7, 1858

Died Oct. 15th, 1858 (age 9 months)

Carlton Perry Whitney.

Born at Keokuk, Iowa, Sept. 8th, 1860

Married to Miss Carie Belle Masson at Keosauqua, Iowa, Dec. 13, 1894

One child, Marguerite Masson Whitney, born at Keosauqua, Iowa, March 24, 1896

Mrs. Ann Jennette Whitney. Wife of Leonard Whitney.

Born at Bennington, Vt. Jan. 12th, 1825

Died at Keokuk, Iowa, March 8th, 1904 (age 79)

On July 28, 1902, Harwood received a letter from John Hay:

> Newbury, N.H.
>
> July 28, 1902
>
> Dear Whitney:
>
> Many thanks for the clipping.
>
> I am here for a rest, of which I was in grievous need.
>
> Helen and her husband have just arrived here after a very pleasant trip in Europe, spent mostly in the Valley of the Loire among the historic chateaux of France.
>
> Alice and your Wadsworth have concluded their plans to be married here in September - a very quiet wedding. I am a little disappointed as I wanted an exact duplicate of Helen's wedding - but the other arrangement better suited the young people's plan.
>
> All wish to be kindly remembered,
>
> Very Sincerely,
>
> John Hay

On March 8, 1904, Harwood's Mother, Ann Jenette, died. She had been an invalid for years, in a wheelchair and always needing the care of a girl. Through the years, Harwood's brother, Carlton, grew up without a father. One brother died at 18, another at 39. After the death of his first wife, Helen, Harwood went back to live with his mother and Carlton. He spent many years taking care of them. Carlton had many emotional problems, mainly in 1886 and 1887. Ann Jenette would not allow him to go away for treatment. I will not go into details at this time. Carlton must have improved as he ultimately married Carrie Belle Masson of Keosauqua, Iowa, in 1894. He ran a Grain and Feed business there with Harwood's occasional help. They had one daughter, Marguerite Masson Whitney in 1896. Marguerite married James H. Addison in 1921, but he died in 1925; they had no children. Carlton died in 1929 and his wife went to live with her daughter in Omaha.

On June 15, 1904, two months after his mother died, Harwood married Lillian Ehinger Felt. Harwood was 60 years of age and Lillian was 48. They moved into the Whitney home on 8th and Franklin. Lillian Ehinger had been married to George K. Felt of Montrose in 1882. He and his father were engaged in the lumber business in Montrose and Bedford, Iowa. He died of lung trouble in 1886, a few hours after they had returned from a trip by train and wagon to a ranch near Albuquerque, N.M. where they had gone in hopes of a cure. As a widow she went to live with her parents, Dr. George E. Ehinger and Cornelia Palmer Ehinger, at their home at 524 Concert.

In 1904 when Lillian married Harwood, her parents went to live with their son and his wife and daughter, Dr. Clyde and Ella Long Ehinger in Westchester, Pa. Aunt Lilly had lived most of her life taking care of her parents. She was very social, and their home was continually filled with friends and relatives for meals and visits. She was very active in the Unitarian Church, having been treasurer for years. She gave to Harwood the social "niceties" he had been unable to enjoy for many years.

A clipping from the paper at that time states:

> Among the many beautiful presents received by Mr. & Mrs. Harwood O. Whitney on the occasion of their wedding

> Wednesday evening, is a handsome davenport, greatly appreciated by the groom as coming from the officers and directors of the State Central Savings Bank of which institution he is a director.

John Hay died July 1, 1905. In August 1905 Harwood received the following letter from Mrs. Clara Hay:

> Newburg, N.H.
>
> August 5th, 1905
>
> Dear Mr. Whitney,
>
> I have not written to you about the legacy my husband left to you as I have not yet been able to arrange about it. One of my sons-in-law who is also an executor being in Europe and nothing can be done until his return.
>
> My husband always had a high regard for you and in memory of his sister Helen he wishes to make a substantial demonstration of it.
>
> I cannot yet realize what has happened, it seems only that he is away on a journey and that he will return someday as he has done so often before.
>
> I am overwhelmed by the tributes of love and respect which came to me from all quarters of the globe, and I am hoping that he knows what all the world thought of him. I assure you that I appreciate all your kind words of sympathy -
>
> Gratefully and sincerely yours,
>
> Clara S. Hay

On September 13, 1905 the following letter to Harwood informed him that John Hay had left him $2,000. The letter is signed by Payne Whitney and J Wadsworth:

> Payne Whitney
>
> 51 Wall Street
>
> New York
>
> September 13, 1905
>
> Harwood Otis Whitney, Esq.,
>
> Keokuk, Iowa.
>
> Dear Sir: - Pursuant to the will of the late John Hay, we herewith hand you New York draft for two thousand (2,000) dollars payable to your order. Kindly sign the enclosed receipts and return to Payne Whitney, 51 Wall Street. New York City.
>
> Please cash or deposit the draft at your earliest convenience and oblige.
>
> Yours very truly,
>
> Payne Whitney
>
> J. Wadsworth, Jr.
>
> Executors, Estate of John Hay

Payne Whitney and Helen Hay Whitney were the parents of John Hay "Jock" Whitney, who was Ambassador to England under President Eisenhower, etc.

James Wadsworth and Alice Hay Wadsworth were the parents of Evelyn who married Senator Steward Symington, and grandparents of Rep. James Symington.

In 1906 Harwood tried one more time for a political position. He evidently wrote to Clara Hay to ask her help in acquiring some sort of appointment by the President[1]. I do not have any idea what it was. Mrs. Hay answered on Feb. 5, 1906:

> 800 16th St.
>
> Washington D.C.
>
> Feb. 5th
>
> Dear Mr. Whitney - I have communicated with the President, and he says he will appoint you if he possibly can - he will have to gain the assent of the two Senators, but he hopes to be able to do so.
>
> Sincerely yours, -
>
> Clara S. Hay

This was followed two days later with the following letter:

> 800 16th Street
>
> Washington D.C.
>
> Feb. 8th, 1906

---

[1] (Author's note: this was President Roosevelt)

Dear Mr. Whitney - I am very sorry to have to tell you that I have just received a letter from the President. He says - "In this case, tho it is the kind of thing I have refused to do in any other instance I at once set about getting the consent of the Iowa delegation - But I found it an absolute impossibility. Senator Allison took a much ..?.. position than he usually does, and the rest of the delegation would not consider the matter. It appears that they have been definitely and for some time committed to another man and that they all feel that they could not in honor go back upon him - and that to do what I desire would cause great political trouble and some political scandal.

So, you see it is not possible and I can not tell you how sorry I am that I have not been able to help you in this matter.

I feel under great obligations to the President for trying to do this and I know you also appreciate his efforts in your behalf.

I wish it could have been otherwise, but politics seem to be always mixed up with any government appointment and it is impossible to separate them.

Sincerely yours,

Clara S. Hay

The last letter I have is a copy of a letter written by Harwood to Clara Hay. He obviously realized then, what an imposition he had asked.

Keokuk, Ia.

Feb. 13, 1906

Dear Mrs. Hay,

I sincerely regret that I allowed my selfishness to put you to such trouble.

I did not realize the obstacles to be removed before the President could with propriety make the appointment.

That the President should have so interested himself at your request is a great proof of his friendship for you and although unmerited by me, I am just as grateful and appreciate it as highly as I would if I had received the appointment.

I only wish it were within my power to reciprocate. All I can say is that I am very grateful both to you and our great President.

Yours Sincerely,

Harwood O. Whitney

Harwood and Aunt Lilly had eight more years together. She fixed up the Whitney home, adding a lovely porch and also adding some of the things from her parents' home after they died in Westchester, Pa. in 1908 (within a month of each other). I'm sure the house was always open to friends and relatives. The Ehinger cousins came and went constantly, and all looked to Aunt Lilly as the "Grand Dame" of the family. But the Ehinger family is yet another story!

Harwood died May 27, 1914 leaving no children and no other known relatives (that I know of) in Vermont, either Harwoods or Whitneys.

I later came across a cousin, Flora Harwood Talham - 1917 – Bennington, but have not followed up on that lead.

In 1925 Dr. Clyde and Ella Ehinger, Aunt Lily's brother, came back to Keokuk at Aunt Lily's insistence, from the forest cabin they had retired to in Washington State. Together they bought the old Marshall house at 8th and Grand (700 Grand Ave) in Keokuk, remodeled it and moved in. There was lots of room for Grandfather's books.

The Marshall house was built in 1853, during the time Rev. Leonard was preaching in Keokuk, and at that time it was located at the northeast limits of the city of Keokuk. Aunt Lily died in 1930. Dr. Clyde Ehringer, my Grandfather, died in 1935 and Grandmother Ella Ehinger died in 1936. My mother, Lillian Ehringer Koppenhafer, inherited this home and lived in it until her death. This is another very interesting story, for another time.

And so ends the saga. I have tried not to add too much more than documented material that we have. I have always thought it would make an interesting "Historical Novel" for someone with the expertise and imagination and insight into personalities, who could see into the lives and the world of Rev. Leonard. He was so intelligent, forceful, strong, searching for answers that were not in the usual or approved pathways of thinking or preaching - daring to take a rough road in order to find what he believed. It was a time of a new freedom in thinking and religion. Yet he was a devoted father and loving, tender husband and found himself at a loss to cope with the horror and death of war - the senselessness of it all. I feel it helped destroy him.

Harwood, having had the advantage of growing up with a strong father, suffered the economic deprivation that his father could not overcome and, I feel, spent his life trying to find social and economic prestige. It is said he was quite a "ladies' man" during his 30 years as a bachelor. Finally, he found a compatible companion and enjoyed a comfortable home in his final years.

The three other brothers were raised by a young Mother who, I feel, was high strung, prone to illnesses and complaints and possibly spoiling her boys - a woman not meant to live the hard domineering, lonely life she was handed. Carlton had a multitude of problems and the other two I don't know much about. I often wonder if it was all physical that they died so young?

And now I have done my job. I have organized and documented it all, and maybe my daughters will write the novel!

Lois Koppenhafer Lefler

=====

From "Yesterdays: Reminiscences of Long Ago", Virginia Wilcox Ivins, (1915) p.99:

*At the corner of Eighth and Franklin Street is a frame cottage that was once the home of Reverend Leonard Whitney, a Unitarian Minister here, a most scholarly man. As simple as a child in his ways and possessed of a sweet benevolence that was beautifully exemplified in the devotion of his life to others. He entered the army at the beginning of the Civil War and was untiring in his ministrations to the sick and wounded. In one of the memorable battles, he took off both of his coats to wrap about some of them during a heavy rain and as a consequence took cold and died from the effects of it. He was mourned by a great circle of friends - not only those of his own church, but of many other faiths, who though they might differ with him on many tenets of faith, were as one in their love and respect for him. His son, Harwood Whitney, has occupied the old home until quite recently, when he too died (1914) leaving a wife, but no children.*

# Appendix A

## Ontario Messenger – Extra

## A Sermon

## By L. Whitney,

***Pastor of the Free Church of***

***Canandaigua, N.Y.***

***Parallel between the***

***Traitor Judas Iscariot, and***

***The Authors and Supporters of***

***The Fugitive Slave Bill***

***"Verily I say unto you inasmuch as ye have done it unto any of the least of these my brethren, ye have done it unto me." Matt.25$^{th}$: 40.***

Most men in a Christian land are more ready to admit the doctrine of a judgment than to consider for what they are to be judged – more ready to confess themselves sinners in general terms than to consider what sin is. Their attention has been so much occupied with the doctrines of "total depravity" and the "imputed sin" of their father Adam, that they seem to have forgotten their own. If it is not so, why is it, that as well in the church as out of the church, those very sins abound, that as sure as the words of Christ are true, shall be a millstone about the neck in that day when all men shall be judged according to their works? Our text seems well intended to bring men to their senses on this subject.

And what are those great sins, put by our Savior as the representatives of all others on this solemn occasion? And what are those great duties of the gospel of the Christian life, of such transcendent importance as to stand alone at the "judgment seat of Christ?" Are they what men in general – what the church even, puts foremost and uppermost as the test of Christian character? Of acceptance with God? If our Lord has truly described this scene, are men's great sins reckoned there, their supposed errors in doctrine? Their honest doubts of a "Trinity", "total depravity" by Adam's fall, (a fact which Christ, in all his teaching forgot to mention), a "vicarious atonement," and such like? Are they neglect of the forms of religion? – of baptism, the supper, the meetings of the church, stated preaching, and the "regular means of grace?" No such thing. However important these things may be to some minds as means, they are neither the substance nor the end of true religion. I know not that Christ ever condemned a single sinner for such sins. Certain it is he has not dignified them with a place at his judgment seat.

And what are the great duties he has exalted there? The duty of possessing an "evangelical faith" – of experiencing a "change of nature" – of confessing him as the anxious seat – of uniting with the church, and of a "good and regular standing" there? Not one word of it. However well all this may be, it is not religion, or so much as a sign of religion, as to be brought into account at that day when "every man shall be rewarded according to his works."

But there are sins and there are duties which shall be remembered at the bar of God, at the judgment of Christ. They are of the substance of human character. They try the heart and reins of the children of men. They are indicated by that infallible standard of our Savior, "ye shall know them by their fruits – by their works shall ye know them." And what are these great sins and great duties that determine the moral character of men? The passage of scripture standing in connection with our text, can leave us in no doubt what they are. They are sins against our fellow men, and duties to our fellow men. They are expressed in language so common and simple that a child can understand them; and with an obligation so apparent that every human heart must respond to them. They commend themselves to every man's conscience. Hear them. Learn of Christ what makes a righteous man, and what makes a sinner. "Then shall the king say unto them on his right hand, come ye blessed of my Father, inherit the kingdom prepared for you from the foundation of the world. For I was an hungered and ye gave me meat; I was thirsty and ye gave me drink; I was a stranger and ye took me in; naked and ye clothed me; I was sick and ye visited me; I was in prison and ye came unto me. Then shall the righteous answer him, saying, "Lord, when saw we thee hungered and fed thee? Or thirsty and gave thee drink? When saw we thee a stranger and took thee in? Or naked and clothed thee? Or when saw we thee sick or in prison and came unto thee? And the king shall answer and say unto them, verily I say unto you, inasmuch as ye have done it unto one of the least of these my brethren, ye have done it unto me."

Then shall he say also unto them on the left hand, "depart from me ye cursed into everlasting fire reared of the devil and his angels. For I was hungered and ye gave me no meat; I was thirsty and you gave me no drink; I was a stranger and ye took me not in; naked and ye clothed me not; sick and in prison and ye visited me not."

Then shall they also answer him, saying, "Lord when saw we thee as hungered or thirsty or a stranger or naked or sick and in prison and did not minister unto thee?"

Then shall he answer them saying, "verily I say unto you, inasmuch as ye did it not to any one of the least of these, ye did it not to me."

These words, like much of the teaching of our Savior, involve a great general principle. They are not to be limited to these specific duties to our fellow men, or the neglect of them. They cover the whole field of humanity. And as our Lord puts himself, in his own person as the representative of all men, even "the least" so the duties he enjoins are general, obliging every man not only to give bread to the hungry and drink to the thirsty, to shelter the stranger and visit the sick and the prisoner, but to do all the good he can to all men, as he has opportunity. In short, it is a most solemn sanction of that law of love to our neighbor which worketh no ill to him, which is the fulfilling of the whole law and which is so forcibly expressed in the golden rule of our Savior. – "All things whatsoever ye would that men should do unto you, do ye even so unto them."

This passage of scripture includes all these great principles of human duty. It carries them all up to the judgment seat of Christ. It reminds us of their most common and most touching and pressing particulars. It extends them to the whole human family, and only the more, the more miserable and needy and distressed and wronged they are. And it enforces all these duties, and protects all these needy ones, by all the solemnities of the judgmental, and by all the sacredness of the person of our Lord Jesus Christ, by the body and blood of the son of God. We may here pause (not to defend these plain inferences for they lie upon the face of the text), but to ask, why is it so? Why is love not to our neighbor – why are these good works to our fellow creatures so exalted? Why is a life of divine humanity thus singled out and made the great test of religion, of Christianity, of salvation? Why is not even the first commandment mentioned in connection with the judgment? Why did not Christ say, "Come ye blessed of my Father, for ye have loved them. Come ye blessed for ye have proved your love to God by saying in many a long prayer, Lord, Lord, Lord, Lord" – ye have compassed sea and land to make proselytes – ye have built him many and costly houses of worship and gone there three times every Sabbath day to keep it holy and do your duty – ye have kept all his ordinances and propitiated his favor by looking and feeling solemn in every attitude of devotion?

Why, I say, are not these common and imposing tokens set up to distinguish between the church and the world, the righteous and the wicked here, so much a mentioned or thought of at the judgment?

For the very good reason, we may presume, that they are not sure tests of human character. Bad men may do all these things as well as good men. They may do all these things and neglect the "weightier matters of the law, judgment and mercy." They may do them all and retain all their pride and selfishness and cast and oppression and inhumanity and be entirely destitute of the spirit or life of Christ. The old Pharisees will be remembered as conspicuous examples of this kind of piety. Their love to God, if measured by their worship and prayers and sacrifices and solemn meetings was absolutely unbounded. But when weighed in the balance of Christianity – a religion of "good will to men," they were found wanting. They were unjust, proud, aristocratic respecters of persons, sectarian, bigoted, they 'devoured widows' houses, hunted Jesus as a Fugitive, and he plainly told them, that even the publicans and harlots entered the kingdom of God before them. Religion in this way was always cheap. Giving costly sacrifices to God for the unrestrained privilege of oppressing and trampling upon his children, is a vicarious atonement that the worse men have always believed in.

If this, God's Earth, can only be turned into a free hunting ground of the poor and defenseless, the rich and powerful have always been willing to pay Him a handsome *percent* in prayers and offerings for the privilege.

Such a religion is cheap in another sense. Men are *afraid* to rob God. They dare not directly contend with the Almighty. Hence the worse men strive in some way to propitiate His favor. They profess to know and to love Him, though in works they deny him.

Not so with their fellow men. The poor and weak and ignorant can be trodden under foot with impunity. Here in the direction of their greatest temptation, they fancy a class of rights entirely unprotected. They say to themselves in their folly, "might makes right and there is no higher law." We can take advantage of men's necessities, of their ignorance or weakness or vices – we can sell the righteous for silver and the poor for a pair of shoes, and the Lord will not see it. Or if he does, we will pay him with our devotions and costly offerings.

Thus, those whose foolish heart is darkened with selfishness and lust are tempted to reason. And though the Lord looks down from Heaven and laughs at their folly, they at last come to reconcile to themselves, love to God whom they have not seen with hatred of their brother whom they have seen. And who does not see in this the sad necessity of making practical love to our fellow men, our regard for their equal rights, our relief of their sufferings and necessities, the only standard of pure and undefiled religion?

Who does not see the wisdom and beauty and glory of our text, in throwing over poor starving, crushed, bruised, bleeding humanity, the most solemn sanctions of the Divine Law, and even the sacred shield of Christ's dear body? God's throne is forever secure. No wave of evil can ever dash against it – no wrong can ever rob him of his essential blessedness. And though men do not "love God with all their heart," they can inflict no evil upon the Almighty. They only injure themselves. Not so with the second commandment. "He that hateth his brother is a murderer." And from that day when the first murderer tried to shield himself from guilt by the impious question, "am I my brother's keeper?" to the present hour, the violation of this same law of love to our neighbor has been the great source of all the evils and miseries that have cursed the human family. At this moment, all that we deplore as vice and crime, all the selfishness and oppression, the division and discord, the wrath and strife, the wars and fighting and blood with which earth is filled, have their origin in man's want of love and respect for his fellow man. Let all men at once know what it is to love their neighbor as themselves – to regard the rights and interests and feelings and affections and relations of every other human being as dear and sacred as their own and selfishness and crime, wrong and violence, intemperance, slavery and war, and every such thing, would flee away. Men look and long and wait for such a time, but they mistake the means of its accomplishment. They expect "peace on earth and good will towards men," while they live in habitual violation of the only law which makes such a state possible. "Behold the kingdom of God is within you." "Thou shalt love thy neighbor as thyself." "Bear ye one another's burdens and so fulfill the law of Christ." That this good time coming may arrive, that the whole creation which groaneth and travaileth in pain together until now may be delivered from its long night of bondage and the kingdom of God come, and his will be done on earth as it is done in Heaven, this "higher law" must be enthroned in every human heart and be translated into a practical reality. It is only a heavenly life of brotherhood and love that can ever bring heaven down to earth.

How needful it was then, that this law should be expressed in every variety of form, particular applications and violations so extensively amplified in the scriptures and its solen sanctions so doubly guarded. And so, in fact we find it. While only about one-third of the preceptive portion of the scriptures is devoted to the duties we owe directly to God, about two-thirds are occupied with the duties we owe to our fellow men. The Bible is full of the duties we owe our neighbor and of warnings against oppression, every invasion of the rights, even of the least of our brethren.

But among them all, there is perhaps none which invests *human nature* with such dignity and sacredness as our text – "inasmuch as ye have done it unto one of the least of these my brethren ye have done it unto me."

Does any little soul, whose manhood and sympathies have been dwarfed by the spirit and can't of sect, tell me that Christ here means only a brother in the church? Let him prove to me, that only church members hunger and thirst and are naked, and strangers, and prisoners; or if they do that, we are bound to relieve such only, and I may listen to him. But when he has done this a still heavier task is before him. He must further prove that he who was sent because "God so loved the world," to be the "Savior of the world," and who "by the grace of God tasted death for every man" only came to such or cares for such, or loves such – that he did not come to preach the gospel to all the poor, to proclaim liberty to the captives, the opening of the prison doors to them that are bound. That he did not come to heal all their diseases, to undo the heavy burdens, to draw all men unto him, not to condemn, but to save the world. For until all this and much more is provided, I must still think the mission of Christ to the world was not to infuse a narrow and selfish, but a disinterested and universal love, not to relieve the sorrows and protect the rights of the few, but to exalt and sanctify human nature, to invest it with the sacredness of his own divine humanity.

And our text on the free and to the true spirit of the passage does all this – does it from the lips of the Lord of glory – does it from the judgement seat of Christ. And woe to the man – and woe to the ruler, and woe to the nation that heeds not the warning. Let them know henceforth and forever, that human nature is a solemn, sacred treasure, near to the heart of God and his well-beloved son. Let them know that the poorest man, the most ignorant, degraded, despised, hated, scorned, wronged, oppressed man, that the weakest and the "least" man, gives in evidence at the bar of God. Yea, let him know that Christ himself, by his own words, is insulted and wronged, and despised, and rejected in the person of the "least human being" whose rights are trodden down, and whose claims are rejected.

In the spirit and in the very words of this text, to despise any human being is to despise Christ. To insult any human being is to insult Christ. To wrong any human being is to wrong Christ. To neglect the wants and sorrows and sufferings of any human being is to neglect Christ. While to love and do good to any human being is to love and do good to Christ. Are we ready to exclaim, "this is a hard saying, who can bear it?"

We must bear it or deny Jesus in the house of his friend. For man is his friend, and those poor and despised ones, the very ones he peculiarly protects – the very ones to try our faith in the gospel and our love to Christ. How solemn is the thought that in the "least" human being or race of human beings, despised, wronged, oppressed, outraged, "the son of God is crucified afresh and put to an open shame." And yet how cheering that the least aid and comfort shown them, though it be but a shelter for the night to hide the outcast, or a cup of cold water to cheer him on his journey, shall not lose its reward, for it is done unto Christ.

I propose to apply this teaching of our Savior to the Fugitive Slave Law – a law that has become so infamously notorious that it can need no explanation. And I feel the more called upon to do so since Dr. Ford, and Dr. Spencer, and Dr. Cox, and Dr. Sharpe, and Dr. Spring, and Dr. Hawks, and I don't know how many Drs., who have delivered very able discourses upon this lower law, seem by a simultaneous lapse of memory, to have overlooked this important passage.

Moses they know, and Paul they know, but Christ in his most solemn and important instruction upon this subject, they seem for the time, to have jointly and severally forgotten. Whether it was "the fear of man which bringeth a snare," or "a gift that perverteth judgment," "the dissevered fragments of a once glorious Union" – or that they did not find this passage to jingle well with buying and selling and hunting and enslaving their fellow men, I leave others to judge. Sufficient it is for me that I find this passage and others like unto it in the New Testament, not the Old, in the words of Christ, not Moses, and I find in them a "Higher Law" – a warning to all tyrants and a sacred protection to the person and rights of every human being which the "Chief Priests and Rulers" can never annul or evade. "There they stand and there they will stand forever," – warning them as they value their own rights, to regard the equal rights of every other man. Warning all men from the solemn scenes of the judgment, that our Lord Jesus Christ in his own person is insulted and denied, whenever the rights of his "least" human brothers are betrayed.

And in how clear a light does this set the whole subject of "Human Slavery," in all its nature and relations and laws, and "solemn compacts?" It has, you know, long been a vexed question with certain statesmen and divines, whether Slavery is a sin *per se*, a wrong in itself. Let our text decide the question. Would it be a sin *per se* to enslave Jesus Christ if he were now upon the earth? He is upon the earth if his words are true. Any wrong or any kindness done to the "least" human brother is done unto him. So, He says. If it would not be a sin *per se* to enslave Jesus Christ – to buy and sell Him – to doom him to unpaid toil in the cotton field – to whip and chain Him – to hunt Him down with dogs and guns – i.e. bow his mind to ignorance and his "back to the smiters" – to make him a beast of burden without hope and without God in the world – then it is plainly not a sin *per se* to enslave the "least" of his brethren. The principle is the same. Christ has made it the same by his own words and acts. He has identified his humanity with universal humanity; even the weakest and "least" form of it. If there is any difference in the application of the principle, it is against those who enslave the "least of his brethren." If the teaching of Christ has made the two cases parallel, all must pronounce the latter the meanest and most cowardly act. When upon earth, Jesus had repeatedly shown his miraculous power, and when he was arrested as a Fugitive, he could have called Twelve Legions of Angels to rescue him. But his "least brethren" have no such power or aid. In this world and especially in the Christian land, they have no helper, and their betrayal is but the easy and cowardly triumph of might over right. So especially is it under the Fugitive Slave Law.

The betrayal of the straggling Fugitive who has come up from the prison house of bondage by the combined strength of 20,000,000 freemen is a crime that for baseness has no parallel, either in sacred or profane history. And if we consent to do it under any law, to do it in any how, our history will be more profane than any that has borne the name. The original larceny upon the African coast, the "taking and converting," which another law of Congress in the better days of the Republic pronounced *Piracy,* is the sweetest virtue compared with this. That is at the worst, an individual concern carried on in solitude in the face of much danger by a few free-booters bred to the trade, and who claim no higher law than force, and ask the protection of no other. But this is claimed to be a cool, deliberate, solemn compact, entered into by 20,000,000 of Christian people 'for value received' to hunt down a few of the weakest and least of Christ's brethren, beneath his own Altars – to re-enslave those who have waded through seas of suffering to regain their "inalienable rights" – to chain and send back to a second death, those who have come up through great tribulation from a land of Bibles and churches and Christian Liberty!

Has this crime any parallel? Do your minds revert to Judas Iscariot who for 30 pieces of silver betrayed his Lord and Master? Though this *silver* (which was the price of blood) may have suggested the name of the party that emulates his virtue, I had rather meet his crime at the Judgment seat of Christ than the more enlightened and combined and concentrated baseness of guilt of the betrayer of the Fugitive Slave in the year of Christ 1851. Extravagant as such a declaration may seem to some, I hope to make it good by an appeal to our own sense of justice, the teaching of Jesus, and a fair comparison of their crimes.

I know men have been accustomed to look upon the treachery of Judas as without parallel. This betrayer of innocent blood for money has long been looked upon as without one redeeming quality – as little less than the incarnate devil, that entered into him with the sop. But we apprehend it is the character of Jesus, more than that of Judas or his crime, that has thus separated him from his brother traitors. The nature of the crime is the same in all cases where human nature is betrayed. Christ has made it the same by his own words, and it commends itself to our sense of right.

Then, whether the betrayal of the "least of his brethren" of the poorest and most ignorant Fugitive Slave equals the crime of Judas Iscariot, must depend upon other circumstances of guilt than the character of Jesus. Let all these circumstances be carefully considered.

That the Moral Character of the Fugitive falls below Him who was *without sin* matters not. Let him who is without sin cast the first stone. It was not sinless, but sinful human nature that Christ came to protect and save. All of his human brethren are sinners but that does not make the betrayal of the "least" of them less a crime in his sight. He makes no difference between selling the righteous for silver or the poor sinner for a pair of shoes. In both cases *Christ* is *sold*.

And as to his *personal dignity* and miraculous power, that certainly lends a heroism to the crime of Judas that his modern imitators cannot boast. Their treachery against human nature and human rights is a perfectly safe business. They frame iniquity by law and can call out the Army and Navy to hunt down and deliver up the "least" and the weakest and most defenseless of men. In this view, then, the crime of Judas was moral heroism, moral sublimity, compared with that of the authors and supporters of the Fugitive Slave Law.

But it may be said Judas betrayed his friend and benefactor and this aggravated his guilt. And what is the American slave but the friend and benefactor of those who betray him and trample him into the dust? If he is a stranger, let them be careful to entertain strangers for thereby some have entertained Angels unawares – "thou shalt not oppress the stranger." If he is an enemy, why not let him go? Why pursue him and take him back to their embrace? But is he not the best *friend and benefactor* of those who thus wantonly betray him?

If Jesus could say "mine own familial friend, in whom I trusted, which did eat of my bread, hath lifted up his heel against me" – "he that dippeth with me in the dish shall betray me," with what literal truth can the American slave appropriate the same language? The wretches who betray his rights and hunt him as a partridge upon the mountains, and those whose fields are tilled, whose children are nursed, whose backs are warmed, and whose stomachs are fed from the fruits of his own toil and sweat and blood. His labor creates the great staples that feed and clothe the nation. – And if we are not all the friends of the slave it is our fault, not his. And those who betray him, like Judas Iscariot, are guilty of betraying their best friend.

Is it farther said that Judas delivered up Jesus to be put to death, to be crucified, and that therefore his crime was greater than that of those who only deliver up the "least" of his brethren to slavery?

I ask you to pause and consider. Did Judas *know* or even expect Christ would be put to death? It is not in proof. The evidence is all the other way. Our Lord had not yet had his trial. And Judas must have known that no crime could be proved against the 'just one', as well as we know that none can be alleged against the innocent Fugitive. He must have anticipated an honorable acquittal at the trial, especially as there is no evidence that the commissioner, then as now, was bribed with a double fee to condemn Jesus. Judas merely served for his fee as a Marshall before the trial to get Jesus before a commissioner. That he did not anticipate the sad result of his treachery is quite evident from the brief record the Evangelist has given us of his end. Then Judas which had betrayed him, when he saw that he was condemned, repented himself, and brought again the thirty pieces of silver to the Chief Priests and Elders, saying, I have sinned in that I have betrayed the innocent blood. And he cast down the pieces of silver in the Temple and departed and went and hanged himself.

But suppose Judas did know that his friend would be put to death. Would you think better of him if he had only betrayed his Lord and Master to a "bondage worse than death?" Would you think better of this traitor if he had only helped put the irons onto the limbs of Jesus and delivered him up as a "chattel personal" or sold him as a beast in the market? I know not how this may strike others, but for one, I think the baseness of such an act would have added infamy to this son of perdition, in all coming time. But those who in our time betray Christ in the person of the poor Fugitive cannot plead ignorance of the result of their crime. *They know* what American slavery is. They know that to deliver any man up to slavery is to reduce him, soul and body, as near the condition of a brute as possible. They know that the very nature and safety of the whole infernal system demand it. They know that however well fed and clothed and cared for the slave may be as a piece of property, that it is the whole design and tendency of slavery to crush and mar that human body which Christ has made as sacred as his own, and to put out in the human soul all the light and progress and hope which he came to purify and exalt and bless in every human being.

I see then in the crime of Judas nothing to raise him higher in infamy and guilt, and much to make him fall short of his humble followers of our own time.

And now, if on examination, we find nothing in the motives and influences which govern the latter in betraying the Fugitive more worthy than those which induced the model traitor to betray Jesus, he must at last lose his well-earned notoriety. Surely, he must cease to be the "observed of all observers," in infamy, in a country where *treason to human nature is the only passport to office and honor and* "sits in Moses' seat."

Let us compare the motives of the ancient and the modern Judas. I am well satisfied the parallel extends much farther than we have supposed. If it were only for base gain, for the thirty pieces of silver that Judas betrayed his Master, it would appear that he yielded to a comparatively small temptation. That is only about fifteen dollars our money, while the "least of his brethren" will readily sell for some hundreds in our Christian market. It is true our "commissioners" here at the North only get ten dollars as a direct fee for their treachery, but then it is claimed that all our commerce and cotton and factories are directly interested in doing this "disagreeable duty."

Then if we put the case upon the sole ground of "value received" I think our statesmen and divines have demonstrated that in some shape our modern Judas gets more for his services than Judas of old. If he does a baser deed, he don't do it so cheap. To be sure we ought not to pride ourselves too much on this trifling difference. There is a difference in the value of money now, and then. And we can have no assurance that he who would betray human rights for money at all – who would betray the "least" brother of Christ for dollars and cents, would not sell Christ *himself* at the market price, however low that price might be.

But what evidence, let me ask, is there that money was the only motive that made Judas a traitor, when the probability is all the other way? Why divest him of those patriotic motives and that deference to the Rulers and the Law, which we award to all good citizens now? I am well satisfied great injustice has been done him in this regard. Judas Iscariot was a man as well as a traitor, and it is not unreasonable to suppose that he loved his country and her laws, that he was a Union-loving Law-abiding citizen of Judea. Does that betrayer of the Fugitive Slave plead in defense of the wrong done him his love of the Union which he thinks can only be cemented by his sweat and tears and blood? Let him with more reason extend a like charity to his brother traitor. For be it known to all men that the very Fugitive Law under which Jesus of Nazareth was betrayed and captured seems to have had its origin in the same patriotism – in this same fear for the safety of the Jewish Union. This is not fancy, but sober fact. Remarkable as is the coincidence, the pen of inspiration has preserved to us this strange prototype of our own times. You may find it in the 11th chapter of the Gospel of John. "Then gathered the Chief Priests and Pharisees a council, and said, what do we? for this man doeth many miracles. If we let him thus alone all men will believe on him, and the *Romans will come and take away both our place and nation.* And one of them named Caiaphas, being the High Priest that same year, said unto them, ye know nothing at all, nor consider that it is expedient for us that one man should die for the people, and that the whole nation parish not. And this he spake not of himself: but being high Priest that year he prophesied that Jesus should die for the nation. "Then from that day forth they took council together for to put him to death." So, it seems the doctrine of expediency and compromise with wrong is not a modern doctrine. And ours are not the first or the only times when chief statesmen and Chief Priests have thought the betrayal of innocent blood the only way to preserve the national existence and save the Union. But then, as now, there were believers in a higher law than expediency or compromise. And though this was the sad necessity, the patriotic motive which impelled the unionists of that day to put Jesus to death, that higher law informs us that "by wicked hands he was crucified and slain," and those who caused his death are called "murderers." Still, it is no more than charitable to suppose that such a man as Judas would largely partake of this kind of patriotism. He seems to have been constitutionally fitted for compromise and concession. The very man for the crisis. The very man to deny his former principles and conquer his prejudices to save the union. How uncharitable then to suppose Judas was not influenced by the patriotism of the times, especially as it fell upon him, from the high places of office and power – of cabinets and councils, and the union meetings of the Chief Priests and Pharisees?

And besides, he doubtless held in great reverence the rulers and the laws of the land. For though he was a thief, when he was treasurer and "kept the bag" I do insist this shall not impeach his general standing for law and order. If it did, what shall we say of those staunch friends of the Union and the Treasury who follow in the footsteps of their illustrious predecessor now? And Judas had the "commandment," the lower law on his side coming from the proper authorities – endorsed by the Chief Priests. At the council of Caiaphas, to take Jesus and save the nation, a fugitive bill had been passed in these words – "Now both the Chief Priests and the Pharisees had given a commandment that if any man knew where he (Jesus) were, he should shew it that they might take him."

Perhaps Judas thought there was no higher law, till it struck him amid the awful and terrific scenes of the crucifixion. The Chief Priests who had always opposed and persecuted Jesus, had doubtless preached "law and order" sermons, the duty of passive submission to the powers that be, and the Roman authorities stood ready to back their commandment and execute the law. Still, it must have been a very disagreeable duty to betray and capture this one Fugitive. It was so, else it was a very low time at Jerusalem in patriotism – in love of law and order, and union, and sacred compacts. Many of the numerous friends and disciples of Jesus must have known where he had fled, for Jesus walked no more openly among the Jews after the passage of his "fugitive law" but went thence into a country near to the wilderness. But only one could be found in all Judea who loved the Union well enough to obey this law.

And to him it was evidently a disagreeable duty. "Any man can do an agreeable duty," but even the son of perdition did not find it agreeable to betray this innocent man. It may be that the ghost of a higher law which his Master had taught him, haunted his imagination, or that fragments of the old law and the Prophets still lingered in his memory – "hide the outcast – betray not him that wandereth – deliver those drawn unto death." And when Judas at last conquered his prejudices enough to betray him into the hands of his enemies, the deed was done more in sorrow than in anger. For he thought he had obeyed the law, and perhaps saved the Union of his nation, he had lost himself. And "what is a man profited, though he gain the whole world, and lose his own soul?"

But to the everlasting credit of this traitor, it is recorded that when he came to witness the sad result of his treason, he would not keep the price of blood and life itself was no longer endurable. As a repentant sinner he lays down his office, his wicked fee and his life together in obedience to the higher law which he had broken, and which was now uttering its fearful retributions in his conscience.

And here finally, is an important particular in which the parallel between Judas and his brethren utterly fails. Judas did repent himself of his treason, made all the restitution in his power, and confessed that he had "betrayed the innocent blood." But these authors and supporters of the Fugitive Slave Bill still persist in their iniquity to grow bold in sin and their feet make haste to shed blood. "Because sentence against an evil work is not executed speedily, their hearts seem fully set in them to do evil." Not like their brother traitor are they moved to sorrow and repentance at the sad result of their doings.

Though half naked and starving men and women and children, amid the snows of winter, are fleeing for their lives and seeking shelter from their bloody edict in a strange land – though others are hunted and shot down as a partridge upon the mountains, parents torn from the embrace of their families never more to return, and freemen dragged from their own hearth stones and carried off to a hopeless bondage, and though a Shadrach is delivered from their fiery furnace "by a strong hand and an outstretched arm," their hearts are unmoved and they will acknowledge no higher law. Nay, in them seems fulfilled the scripture, "evil men and seducers wax worse and worse, deceiving and being deceived."

They not only propose to cement this Union with the betrayal of innocent blood, of thousands of Christ's own brethren, but to make this whole people guilty of the treason. They would make the sin of Judas Iscariot honorable and baptize it in the name of *patriotism* and *religion.* To this end at this hour, all the power of the government, the public sentiment and the religion of this land are invoked. Treason to humanity and therefore to Christ, is the only passport to office. Obedience to God and his higher law, is treason against the government. "Soundness" in patriotism and religion are tried by their affinity to Judas, not to Christ. And the only "sound" gospel is the gospel according to him who sold his Lord for money and to save the Union.

Do you call this an exaggeration? I ask if it is anything but the sorrowful truth reduced to plain language? Are not the direct support of human slavery and the execution of this infamous law, sought to be made the controlling public sentiment political and religious, of this whole land? What though we may seek to cover up the odious thing with soft words – by talking of our "peculiar institution," our devotion to the Union, our love of law and order and the constitution.

The Lord looks down from heaven and laughs at our hypocrisy, and the Lord Jesus Christ thunders from his judgment seat –

"inasmuch as ye do it unto one of the least of these my brethren ye do it unto me."

In the face of these facts shall we condemn Judas and let these traitors go? If it was wrong in him to betray one innocent man to save a nation from perishing, how can it be right to sacrifice thousands and millions, even to save the Union?

And if the law did not screen Judas from guilt in betraying the innocent, how shall it shield those who are guilty of the wholesale betrayal of those whom Christ has made his own representatives? And if the reward of Judas, his obedience to the law of the land and his love of the Union of his nation did not save him from being called a "Devil" and the son of perdition, what name shall we give that combined consolidated depravity which seeks to make this arch traitor a model of *patriotism and religion,* and his deed of darkness the everyday duty of all good citizens and the church of the living God? And if, for this one act of treason to human nature, with his repentance and restitution and confession, such was the sad end of Judas Iscariot, what shall the end be of these who seek to make his crime *perpetual* by the sanctions of law and religion, and who by every act of teachery and injustice and wrong and outrage done to the "least" of his brethren, crucify the Lord afresh and put him to an open shame?

Let him who receives the wrong as done to himself answer.

Then shall he say also to them on the left hand, depart from me ye cursed into everlasting fire, prepared for the devil and his angels. For I was an hungered and ye gave me no meat; I was thirsty and ye gave me no drink; I was a stranger and ye took me not in; naked and ye clothed me not; sick and in prison and ye visited me not.

Then shall they also answer him, saying Lord, when saw we thee an hungered, or a thirst, or a stranger, or naked, or sick, or in prison, and did not minister unto thee?

Then shall he answer them, saying, verily I say unto you inasmuch as ye did it not to one of the least of these, ye did it not to me."

And these shall go away into everlasting punishment.

# Appendix B

## American Heritage Magazine

## February 1960 Volume 11, Issue 2

## Grant At Shiloh

Bruce Catton

*Surprised and almost overwhelmed, He stubbornly refused to admit defeat. His cool conduct saved his army and his job.*

For a time early in the spring of 1862, it seemed that Union armies were about to destroy the Confederacy in the west. A hitherto inconspicuous officer named U. S. Grant had, in close succession captured the two major Rebel strongholds in Tennessee, Forts Henry and Donelson; an aggressive follow-up might have overwhelmed the badly disorganized Confederates. But the Union high command hesitated, and a fine opportunity was wasted. Grant was ordered south toward the important railhead at Corinth, Mississippi, on an expedition that was little more than a reconnaissance action; then he was briefly held back by an unfounded charge of insubordination. Meanwhile the Confederate commander, Albert Sidney Johnston, gathered his scattered forces and prepared for a sudden and devastating counterthrust at Grant's unsuspecting army, which was bivouacked along the banks of the Tennessee River at Pittsburg Landing. In the battle that was to take place around a rural meetinghouse nearby called "Shiloh Church," the Union advantage in the west was nearly lost – and with it, the promising future of U. S. Grant. The story of this crucial moment in his life is taken from Grant Moves South, a continuation by Mr. Catton of the late Lloyd Lewis' projected multivolume biography, which began with Captain Sam Grant. It will be published this month by Little, Brown. The photography at left, taken by Brady about a year after Shiloh, is one of a set of wet plates found in an upstate New York barn in 1949.

When March began, the Confederacy was facing less than destruction of its power in the west. It reacted with great vigor – Richmond could see, as clearly as anyone else, that the loss of the Mississippi must ultimately be fatal – and reinforcements were summoned, even at the cost of stripping the seacoast of defenders who were badly needed where they were. Five thousand troops were sent to Corinth, on the north border of the state, from New Orleans, and Braxton Bragg was rushed up with 10,000 more from the Gulf Coast; but it took time to move these troops, just as it took time for P. G. T. Beauregard and Leonidas Polk to come down from Columbus in Kentucky, and for Albert Sidney Johnston and W. V. Hardee to move down from Murfreesboro in Tennessee, and by any logical appraisal of the situation, the Confederacy did not have time enough. But in the end, it was given forty-nine days – seven weeks from the fall of Fort Donelson to the opening day of Shiloh – and this was just time enough.

By the end of March, Johnston had between forty and forty-five thousand men at Corinth, with able lieutenants to lead them. Twenty-five miles away, across the Tennessee line, with Grant, with a slightly smaller army; coming down from Nashville was Don Carlos Buell, with an army about the size of Grant's. Johnston's only chance was to beat Grant before Buell arrived, and when April began, he undertook to do this. His army had been hastily put together, most of his soldiers had never been under fire before and were imperfectly trained, and staff organization was so poor that, when the advance began, the different divisions got into one another's way, straggled all over the landscape, and made such bad progress that Beauregard, in despair, wanted to cancel the whole operation, on logical ground that such a stumbling, disorganized offensive could not possibly succeed. But he drove his men on toward Pittsburg Landing.

So as the Confederate army, which had been considered too weak and dispirited to do anything better than await destruction, was about to launch a sudden, shattering offensive; and in the ironic chance of war the offensive was to strike the one Union Army commander in Tennessee who, in the campaign now approaching its surprising climax, had been trying without success to bring on a fight. Striking him, it would find him unready – as if the hoped-for battle were inconceivable unless it were imposed by him on his opponent. Grant had learned much in war's brutal school, but his military education was still incomplete. Now he was about to learn a great deal more – at prodigious cost to himself and to some thousands of young men who, without quite realizing it, had joined the Union Army in order to pay for his education.

Grant was developing as a military realist. The war had taught him a few good lessons: that when untrained armies face each other, neither general gains by deferring a fight until the training of his own men is perfected; that in any hard battle there comes a time when both armies are ready to quit, and that the one which can nerve itself for one more attack at such a time is very likely to win; that troop morale is better in an active campaign than in training camp; that war means fighting so that feints and demonstrations accomplish little, and the real object of a campaign is not to make the enemy retreat but to destroy him root and branch.

These were good things to learn, and in learning them Grant had done little more than sharpen his naturally aggressive instincts. But he had the defects of his qualities, and experience had not yet applied a corrective. He underestimated both the fighting heart and the initiative of his enemy, believing that a Confederate army in his front was likely to be very passive, and in his devotion to the offensive he was likely to overlook defense. Apparently, he was only slightly impressed by the possibility that the enemy might strike first.

A newspaper correspondent assayed the headquarters feeling correctly when, at the end of March, he wrote that there would be a big fight just as soon as Buell's army arrived: "Within two weeks, measures will have been accomplished that will render retreat by the Rebel army at Corinth impossible." Writing to his wife, Grant said that "a big fight may be looked for some place before a great while," and added that he believed his would be the last big battle in the west.

Like a great many of his soldiers, Grant had been unwell. Whether, as the men believed, the water supply around Shiloh was contaminated, or whether the standard diet of fried pork and hardtack was having its natural effect, there was a great deal of camp diarrhea, which Grant in a letter referred to as "Dioreah" and which the rank and file commonly mentioned derisively as "the Tennessee quickstep." Grant recovered from this malady, but shortly thereafter he received a painful injury to his leg. On the evening of April 4, Confederate cavalry jumped a picket post on the Corinth Road a few miles from the landing, and Grant rode out to see about it. Returning with W. H. L. Wallace and Colonel James B. McPherson, he found the night so impenetrably dark (a heavy rain was coming down) that there was nothing a rider could do but trust to his horse to stay on the road. Grant's horse lost his footing and fell in the mud, pinning Grant's leg under him and wrenching his ankle severely. Grant's boot had to be cut off, and for the next day or so he needed crutches when he walked.

Grant believed that as soon as Buell's men arrived, the advance could begin. His own army contained six divisions, the newest of which had been made up from six green regiments that had just reached camp; its command went to Brigadier General Benjamin M. Prentiss. Five divisions, with a total of possibly 37,000 men, were camped on high ground between the creeks near Pittsburg Landing. The sixth, Lew Wallace's division of 7,500, was stationed on the western bank of the Tennessee at Crump's Landing, half a dozen miles downstream. There had been increasing contacts with aggressive Confederate patrols in the last few days, and these roused a suspicion that some sort of attack on Wallace's men might be brewing. Brigadier General William Tecumseh Sherman had been alerted to be ready to send help, if necessary, but the general assumption was that the Rebels meant no particular harm along the main Federal front. One Federal explained, long afterward, that "the almost absolute necessity that no battle should be fought before the arrival of Buell's army seemed to forbid scouting or anything that might appear aggressive," and Sherman said much the same thing when an officer on outpost duty told him he had seen Rebel infantry not far beyond the Union lines. "I have got positive orders," Sherman told him, "To do nothing that will have a tendency to bring on a general engagement until Buell arrives." To Colonel J. J. Appler of the 53rd Ohio, Sherman was more snappish. Appler formed his regiment in line and sent word to Sherman that the enemy was in sight; for his pains he got the reply, "Take your damn regiment back to Ohio. There is no enemy nearer than Corinth."

Sherman did not notify headquarters that there was plenty of contact with Rebels on his front, and on the afternoon of April 5 Grant went to the front to see for himself. Everything seemed to be fairly quiet – undeniably there was a good deal of Confederate activity not far off, but it seemed to be mostly reconnaissance parties – and Grant accepted Sherman's appraisal. When he returned to his headquarters at Savannah, Tennessee, Grant wired to Major General Henry W. Halleck who commanded the union armies in the west: I HAVE SCARCELY THE FAINTEST IDEA OF AN ATTACK (GENERAL ONE) BEING MADE UPON US BUT WILL BE PREPARED SHOULD SUCH A THING TAKE PLACE. After the battle had taken place, Grant admitted that his outposts had been skirmishing freely with Confederate patrols for two days: "I did not believe, however, that they intended to make a determined attack but were simply making reconnaissance in force."

The head of Buell's column reached Savannah around noon on April 5. Colonel Jason Ammen, an old acquaintance of Grant, commanded a brigade in the leading division, which was under General William Nelson; and at some time during the afternoon Grant and Nelson stopped at Ammen's tent to discuss plans. Ammen said his men were not tired and could easily march down to Pittsburg Landing that afternoon, if need be. Grant told him to take it easy, and in his diary, Ammen recorded Grant's words this way: "You cannot march through the swamps; make the troops comfortable; I will send boats for you Monday or Tuesday, or sometime early in the week. There will be no fight at Pittsburg Landing; we will have to go to Corinth, where the Rebels are fortified. If they come to attack us, we can whip them, as I have more than twice as many troops as I had at Fort Donelson." Then Grant rode off, saying he had an engagement that evening.

The Union army's position at Pittsburg Landing seemed strong, even though the five divisions were arrayed rather loosely. The ground was high, the deep creeks protected both flanks, and if the Confederates did attack, they would have to come in head-on, in a straight frontal assault. Proper field entrenchments would have made the position invulnerable, but no trenches had been dug – partly because professional soldiers just then believed that an army which dug itself in would lose its aggressive touch. Buell and the head of his column were supposed to reach Savannah on Sunday, April 6. Once they arrived things could begin to happen.

The soldiers waited in the Tennessee springtime and admired the budding leaves and the peach-tree blossoms, and bathed in the little streams that ran down to the Tennessee. An Iowa soldier, looking at the innumerable tents scattered through "The delightful Tennessee forest," felt that this vast camp had the appearance of a "gigantic picnic." There was a noisy, holiday air over the place. Untrained soldiers kept discharging their muskets in the woods, moved by nothing more than a simple desire to see if things would go off after a rain, and regimental bands were playing; on the river, a steam calliope on one of the transports brayed out patriotic tunes. That evening, quite unnoticed, Johnston arrayed his men in order of battle, remarking grimly: "I intend to hammer 'em. I think we will hammer them beyond doubt." His army was so near that his pickets stood at ease in the dark and enjoyed the music of the Union bands.

Grant's aide-de-camp, John Rawlins, was awakened early on Sunday morning, April 6. The mail steamer from Cairo reached Savannah at three o'clock disembarking a passenger who came up the hill from the landing to headquarters – Captain W. S. Hillyer, a member of Grant's staff who had just returned from a trip down-river. Hillyer's arrival aroused Rawlins, who found himself unable thereafter to go back to sleep. He got up and dressed with the first light of dawn and went down to Grant's office to look at the mail.

While Rawlins sorted the mail, Grant himself came into the headquarters office. Headquarters today was to be moved from Savannah to Pittsburg Landing, and order had been issued the evening before to prepare an early breakfast and to have the horses saddled and ready to be put aboard Grant's steamer, Tigress, which lay at the landing with steam up.

Grant went through his mail in the office and chatted casually with an Illinois officer who had just returned from leave, and at six o'clock, or a little later, breakfast was announced. Grant and his officers had just begun the meal when the quiet of the spring morning was unexpectedly broken by the sound of dull concussions from far upstream – cannon firing, somewhere in the vicinity of Pittsburg landing.

Grant sat motionless for a moment, an untasted cup of coffee in his hand. A private soldier detailed for headquarters duty came in from outside to confirm what everyone had sensed: judging by the sound, this was a real fight and not just a skirmish. Grant set his cup down, stood up, and said: "Gentlemen, the ball is in motion. Let's be off." Within fifteen minutes, the General, staff, clerks, orderlies, and horses were aboard the Tigress, and the steamer was moving upstream. Before the boat left, Grant wrote two hasty notes. One, to General Nelson, said simply "An attack having been made on our forces, you will move your entire command to the river opposite Pittsburgh. You can obtain a guide easily in the village." The other, addressed to Buell, was slightly more detailed. It read: *Heavy firing is heard up the river, indicating plainly that an attack has been made upon our most advanced positions. I have been looking for this but did not believe the attack could be made before Monday or Tuesday. This necessitates my joining the forces up the river instead of meeting you today, as I had contemplated. I have directed General Nelson to move up the river with his division. He can march to opposite Pittsburg.*

The note is interesting for its bearing on the puzzling question: Precisely what had Grant been expecting in the way of enemy action? This morning, he was writing, "I have been looking for this"; the afternoon before he had assured Halleck that he anticipated nothing like a general attack to his position. Apparently, he did feel that Lew Wallace's force might be attacked, and he may have taken this morning's gunfire for confirmation of that suspicion. He had warned both Sherman and W. H. L. Wallace that an attack at Crump's Landing seemed quite likely and that both men should be prepared to reinforce that spot at a moment's notice. Saturday night he had Colonel McPherson – who had become one of is most trusted staff members – stay with W. H. L. Wallace at Pittsburg Landing, the significance of this being that this division was the reserve, held ready to reinforce any trouble spot in case of need. Both Sherman and Prentiss, who had the forward line, sent patrols very early Sunday morning to see what might lie in front of them. McPherson wrote that "it was well known that the enemy was approaching our lines," and on Sunday Grant had notified Halleck that the Confederates in and around Corinth were present in great strength. He believed that

Johnston had 80,000 men with him, and he suspected that some of these were arrayed along the line of the Mobile and Ohio Railroad, which ran from Corinth up to the recently evacuated Confederate stronghold at Columbus – ideally situated, if his suspicions were correct, to strike the Union flank at Crump's Landing. Clearly enough, Grant had believed that some sort of fight might soon be thrust upon him; the one thing he had not anticipated was what was actually happening – a massive drive on his front by the entire Confederate army.

The Tigress went up the river. The sound of cannon and musket fire was coming in more and more clearly, and somewhere between 7 and 7:30 a.m. the steamer closed in by the bank at Crump's Landing, next to Lew Wallace's headquarters boat. Wallace was on deck waiting, and Grant leaned over the railing of his own boat and called out his orders: Wallace was to hold his division ready to march on receipt of orders, and he was also to send patrols out to the west to see whether the Confederates were moving toward him as well as toward the troops around Shiloh Church. Wallace agreed. He was an ambitious man, deeply wanting to win fame as a soldier. What would happen in the next twenty-four hours would put military fame out of his reach, although fame at last would be his: Ben Hur would come out of the brain that could not quite create victory in battle. To the end of his days, he would try to explain the baffling things that went wrong on this sixth of April. So far, none of them had gone wrong, and Wallace faced the day with confidence. The Tigress swung away from the bank and went upstream, and at eight o'clock or a little later nosed into the bank at Pittsburgh Landing. Grant got on his horse and went ashore, to ride straight into the middle of the great Battle of Shiloh.

At the moment of going shore, it was evident that an enormous fight was going on and that it was not going well for the Union army. Off to the southwest – not two miles away, and obviously drawing closer – there was a tremendous noise of battle, continuous racket of rifle fire, heavy thud of artillery, the sound of thousands of men shouting. Smoke was drifting up from the woods, and a dismaying crowd of stragglers, weaponless and winded, was knotting up on the hillside that went from the river to the high ground; panicky men, disorganized and unmanned, who had been shoved unready into their first battle and who had gone for the rear in wild desperation, officers of rank among them. There were hordes of stragglers in the rear of every army in every battle in the Civil War, but Shiloh was the one battle that put them on display; a man running from the battle area here was in effect a man running down a funnel, for even the dullest fugitive could see that the only road to safety was the road to the steamboat landing, and men who in any other fight would be drifting across square miles of open country were packed in a solid mass, cowering under the lee of the bluff above the river. They were beginning to assemble now, with the day hardly more than begun, and they would continue to assemble all day long, pathetic evidence that troops with inadequate training and no battle experience whatever had been called on to stand up to one of the worst combats of the entire war.

There was a great deal for the commanding general to do, and Grant promptly set about it. The volume of firing warned that the men up front would need ammunition, and Grant put his staff to work to organize an ammunition train so that there might be a steady supply of cartridges. The job was intricate: The Union Army's weapons had not yet been standardized, and in Sherman's division alone cartridges of six different calibers had to be supplied. Another staff officer was sent downstream on the Tigress, with orders for Lew Wallace to bring up his division as fast as possible. Something had to be done about the stragglers, and Grant seized two Iowa regiments which, having disembarked a few minutes earlier, were lined up on the bluff awaiting orders; as soon as they had been given ammunition, they were to form across the roads a little way from the landing and halt all fugitives, holding themselves ready at the same time to obey further orders. The colonel of one of the regiments, James T. Reid of the 15$^{th}$ Iowa, looked blank when Grant gave him these instructions, and Grand had to identify himself with the remark: "I am General Grant." Then, having sent most of his staff off on various tasks, Grant set out for the front to see for himself what was happening.

What was happening was both simple and complex, confusing in its innumerable details but appallingly clear in its general drift. This was not one battle but a vast number of intense and bewildering small battles, each one overlapping with its neighbors and yet strangely isolated, the only true pattern coming from the inexorable application of overwhelming force on a loose battle line which had come into being without any central direction but solely in response to immense pressure. Of the five Federal divisional commanders involved, only one had been a professional soldier. The two divisions which had been hit first and hardest and which, on Grant's arrival, had been fighting the longest, contained few regiments that had ever fought before. Reinforcements had gone forward, not in response to any general plan, but simply because officers at the front were calling desperately for help. Fugitives from the combat area were coming to the rear almost as fast as the new troops were going forward; as the two tides flowed past and through each other, Grant lost forever the belief that he had held thus far – that the ordinary soldiers of the Confederacy were halfheartedly serving a cause that never fired their inmost loyalties. The one unmistakable fact now was that these ordinary soldiers of the confederacy – no better trained and no more experienced than Grant's own men – were fighting with sustained fury and were giving his army the worst of it. His immediate and most pressing task was to stave off unredeemed disaster.

Grant went first to W. H. L. Wallace, commanding what was supposed to be the reserve division, and got from him a sketchy picture of what had happened so far.

At dawn, the Union army had been grouped loosely in preparation for a march on Corinth. Up in front, nearest the Confederates, were the divisions of Sherman and Prentiss, with McClernand's and Stephen A. Hurlbut's divisions lined up back of them and Wallace's division in the rear. At three in the morning, Prentiss – no professional, but a stout fighter with combat experience in the Mexican War – had sent three companies from the 25$^{th}$ Missouri out on a long reconnaissance. These soldiers groping past the Federal picket line, and drifting to the right, in front of Sherman's division, had bumped into Confederate skirmishers at five o'clock, or thereabouts. They had attacked at once, and before long Prentiss had sent other Missourians forward to support them. Meanwhile, Sherman's 77th Ohio had also gone forward on the prowl, and it too had kicked up a fight with unidentified Rebels in the murky woodlands. (One of the many oddities about this battle was that it began with Federals attacking Confederates). The advance elements had fought hard for a short time, and then the Confederate offensive had begun to roll, and ever since then the men in Blue had tried desperately to hold on to what they had.

Sherman was on the right. Prentiss was to his left, not in immediate contact, and isolated on Prentiss' left was a lone brigade from Sherman's division, three midwestern regiments under Colonel David Stuart. Albert Sidney Johnston was attacking with his entire army, less than three brigades held back as reserve, an army amassed in three consecutive battle lines, each line following closely behind the one ahead: a defective tactical arrangement because it meant that Confederate troops would be hopelessly scrambled once the fighting became intimate, but a powerhouse nonetheless because it put more than 30,000 men in a broad mass to attack, little more than a third of their number.

Sherman's men got it first. Unluckiest of all the new regiments, on a day when everybody's luck was bad, was the 53rd Ohio. It got into line, fired two volleys, then heard its colonel howl: "Fall back and save yourselves!" The colonel ran for the rear and cowered behind a log, white-faced; two companies of the 5th stayed and fought, and the rest lit out for the steamboat landing. By the end of the day, scattered portions of this regiment were fighting in three separate Union regiments. The 71st Ohio also lost its colonel, who spurred his horse for the rear the moment the fighting began. In the confusion that followed, the 71st was hit hard by an Alabama regiment and fled in a wild, disorganized stampede. The 6th Iowa, doing its best in its first fight, found that its colonel was drunk. He tried to put the regiment through pointless, impossible maneuvers in the face of a Confederate attack, and was placed under arrest by the brigade commander.

(Growing sober a bit later, he took a musket and fought in the ranks of some other regiment as a private soldier.) Sherman's division was driven back and so was Prentiss', and when McClernand and Hurlbut got their men in beside them, the Confederate attack seemed to increase in intensity. One of McClernand's brigadiers said later that his troops lost more men in their first five minutes of action than in all the rest of the day. Now Wallace's troops were going into action, and by ten in the morning practically all of Grant's army was strung out on a loose, uneven front, fighting desperately.

Grant went on to see the other divisional commanders. Iowa soldiers in Hurlbut's division saw him riding up, attended by two or three staff officers. He was wearing a sword today, and a buff sash; one officer said Grant's face "wore an anxious look, yet bore no evidence of excitement or trepidation," and he trotted forward with a leisurely air. Another soldier said Grant was smoking a cigar, seemingly as cool as if he were making a routine inspection, and he believed that the sight reassured the men, who felt that the worst must be over. Grant visited Sherman briefly. Sherman's horse had been shot, he had a minor wound in one hand, he was covered with dust, and his tie had worked around to the side so that it stuck out under one ear; but this man, who had been so nervous in the early days at Kentucky that he lost his command and was called insane, was cool and at his ease in the heat of actual battle; and when Grant asked how things were going Sherman said the situation was not too bad, except that he did need more ammunition. Grant told him that arrangements for ammunition had already been made and cantered off to see Prentiss. When he wrote his memoirs, long afterward, Grant remarked that on this first day at Shiloh, "I never deemed it important to stay long with Sherman." The intimacy that would bind these two men together for all the rest of the war was born this day at Shiloh.

Prentiss had been driven back into an eroded lane that ran parallel with the Confederate front, with a stretch of woodland behind it and a nondescript field overgrown with brambles out in front, and here his raw troops were making a determined stand. W. H. L. Wallace and most of his division joined them here, now or a little later, and the resistance these soldiers put up was so effective that the Confederates were held at bay for five or six hours; they referred to this section ever after, as the hornets' nest. Grant told Prentiss to hold his ground at all hazards – an order which Prentiss would obey with dogged fidelity – and cantered off. As Grant and his escort rode past the 5th Ohio battery, the captain of the battery saw his own father riding along as a member of Grant's cavalry escort.

Grant and his staff drew up in an open space, while Grant studied the situation. The fire was heavy and Captain Hillyer, who never pretended to be the stoical military type, confessed that he and most of the others were in an agony of apprehension. Grant seemed almost to enjoy it, as a man might enjoy being out in the rain on a hot day. One staff officer nudged Hillyer and begged: "Go tell the Old Man to leave here, for God's sake!" Hillyer shook his head: "Tell him yourself. He'll think me afraid, and so I am, but he shan't think so." At last someone mustered the nerve to ride up and tell Grant, "General, we must leave this place. It isn't necessary to stay here. If we do, we shall all be dead in five minutes." Grant looked about him, muttered, "I guess that's so," and led the cavalcade away.

Now and then there would be a brief lull somewhere along the front, but these breathing spells never lasted long nor spread all along the line. Morning wore away, and afternoon came, and the fight went on unabated. The tough knot of resistance at the hornets' nest remained, despite repeated Confederate attacks, but elsewhere the Union lines were crowded back steadily; by the day's end, McClernand noted that his division had occupied eight separate battle lines between dawn and dusk. Beaten men kept drifting to the rear, and when they met fresh troops coming up, they would cry that their regiments had been destroyed and that this was the Bull Run story all over again. One regiment that was moving toward the firing line passed the 4151st Illinois, which had been badly shot up, and the Illinois colonel called out to the new troops: "Fill your canteens. Some of you will be in hell before night and you'll need water." A battery in Sherman's division had to limber up and retreat in a hurry, and one gun, swinging around, locked itself around a green tree, the trunk jammed in hard between wheel and gun barrel. All the gunners fled on foot except for the drivers who rode the six horses attached to the gun; these, lying flat on the animals' necks, too frightened even to look around, flogged their steeds unmercifully, and the poor beasts bucked and pawed the ground and did their unavailing best to gallop; and the other soldiers, themselves beset by panic and fear, looked on and howled with sudden laughter at the sight. Cannoneers from some other battery at last came over and got the gun clear. As men from the 4151st Illinois fled up a narrow ravine the advancing Confederates overtook them, lined both sides of the ravine, and shot as fast as they could load and fire. A survivor of this unhappy regiment wrote that the Confederates were right on top of them – "It was like shooting into a flock of sheep" – and a Mississippi major who had taken part in the assault reflected afterward, "I never saw such cruel work during the war."

In the violence of battle, bizarre things happened. Many men ran from Prentiss' line in the hornets' nest; some of them regaining a little nerve, crept back to the fight, and the boldest took a place behind a stout tree on the firing line. Others followed him, and in no time a grotesque tail of thirty or forty men, each clutching the waist of the man in front of him, swayed out behind that tree, while a distracted company officer, unable to control either himself or his men, paced insanely back and forth from end to end of this line. In W. H. L. Wallace's division, six men were lined up in a single file behind one six-inch sapling, each one firing past the ones in front of him, the blast from their muskets scorching and almost deafening the man at the head of the line. A sixty-year-old private in the 8$^{th}$ Illinois refused to retreat when his regiment went to the rear, falling in with another unit and fighting there, doing the same when this regiment fell back; that evening, rejoining his comrades, he displayed notes signed by several captains and one colonel, certifying that he had been fighting and not straggling. Amid heavy fighting, an Iowa private told that his brother had been killed, asked: "Where is he?" A comrade pointed to the body, which lay not far away. The Iowan, who had been in the act of loading, walked over, musket muzzle in one hand, ramrod in the other. He bent, saw that his brother was dead, then put the butt of the musket beside the dead man's head, finished loading, and fired. He stayed there as long as his regiment held its position, loading and firing beside his brother's body. One soldier saw a comrade hit by a bullet that did not even break his sin, fall to the ground and writhe in wild agony, grasping at leaves and sticks with frantic hands; and he realized that a thing he had been told by a veteran was true – that a spent bullet could cause more immediate pain than a serious wound.

It went on for hour after hour, and the Union army was driven back closer and closer to the high ground above the steamboat landing – all except the hard core in the hornet's nest, which seemed immovable. Grant visited Prentiss here, late in the afternoon, when the hornet's nest was a blunt salient jutting far out in front of the rest of the line; again he told Prentiss to hold his ground, and rode off to patch up the sagging remainder of the battle line as best he could. He saw Colonel A. L. Chetlain, dismounted and pale from a recent illness, with his badly battered 11th Illinois, coming back out of action; placed the regiment in support of a battery; told Chetlain to go back to the landing and lie down - "You ought not to have come out today"; and then dropped a word of encouragement. "I think they have done all they are going to do," he said. "We have fresh troops coming, and tomorrow we'll finish them." Yet the fresh troops did not arrive, neither Lew Wallace's division – both Rawlins and McPherson had been sent to hurry it along – nor Buell's men from Savannah, and they were needed desperately.

Grant was placing many troops personally that afternoon. It may be that his biggest single contribution to what was finally classed as a victory was the encouragement he gave to badly beaten troops, simply by his presence and his obstinate refusal to act as if things were going badly. The 15th Illinois, driven from its position, badly mauled when a Union battery took it under fire, minus its field officers and able to muster no more than a hundred men, was led by Grant to a new fighting position. The 8th Ohio, driven from the area around the hornets' nest, met Grant and was sent back into the fight; driven back again, the regiment encountered Grant once more and was directed to another place in the firing line. The 11th Iowa, broken and in retreat, managed to re-form; as it did so, Grant rode up and ordered it to counterattack. Later, retiring once more, it again met Grant, and was again ordered forward. He found time to chat with Major William W. Belknap of this regiment; he asked for his name and recalled that the Major's father had been "Colonel Belknap of the old army," and added that they had served together as officers in the recent Mexican War.

Briefly, in midafternoon, Grant saw Buell, who had come down from Savannah on a steamboat. The two men talked, and accounts of their conversation conflict, which makes little difference – there was not much for them to say since the general situation spoke eloquently for itself. Grant wanted Buell's troops at the earliest possible moment, and Buell would get them to the scene as quickly as he could. Rawlins later insisted that Buell asked Grant what preparations he had made for retreat and said that Grant replied that he still thought he was going to win. Grant added, according to another account, that, if necessary, they would make a bridge of boats to the far side of the river and protect it with artillery. The bank above the landing was jammed with stragglers when Buell arrived – 5,000 of them at least and possibly more – and Grant believed that the spectacle made Buell feel that the situation was much worse than it really was. Buell for his part, wrote that Grant seemed dull, and he insisted that "there was none of that masterly confidence which had since been assumed with reference to the occasion." The two men came ashore, mounted, and then went their separate ways. Buell believed that the number of stragglers may have been as high at 15,000 and said that at the top of the bluff all was confusion.

The confusion was genuine enough. Most of the men who huddled in the lee of the bank seemed totally demoralized. Wild rumors were in circulation; the whole army had surrendered, a Rebel officer had been seen patrolling a lot of dismounted Federal cavalry, fugitives were going to build rafts and float down the river all the way to Paducah and safety. Here and there officers made earnest but completely fruitless efforts to rally the men. A member of Grant's staff, returning to the landing, saw a mounted officer riding back and forth; the men heard him unmoved, and one was heard to remark casually, "That man talks well, doesn't he?"

Late in the afternoon there came a lull, right on the heels of disaster. The men in the hornets' nest were still fighting, but by now they were isolated. They had killed General Johnston himself when that energetic leader exposed himself too bravely in their front, but they had lost contact with the troops to their right and left and now they were all but surrounded. W. H. L. Wallace undertook to pull his men out and was mortally wounded; most of his soldiers got away and went off toward the landing badly disorganized. At one open place, a demoralized crowd heading for the rear was overtaken by a single gun galloping toward the landing; they assumed it was one of their own pieces joining the retreat. Suddenly the gun wheeled, the gun crew dismounted and unlimbered it and began to fire rapidly into the backs of the fugitives; this was part of a Confederate battery, spearheading a new attack. One Federal in the crowd said that the Confederates coolly went on loading and firing while fugitives continued to scamper past. There were enough Union soldiers present, he said, to pick up the gun, carriage, caisson and horses and hurl them into the Tennessee but no one made any effort to capture the gun or silence the gunners.

The hornets' nest finally caved in. Prentiss had done precisely what he had been told to do – hold on at all hazards – and so had his men, but now the end came. After Wallace's men left, the little division was surrounded. A long line of confederate guns plastered the front at close range, and infantry swept past the flanks and got into the rear. Survivors dimly recalled a scene of complete confusion. A Texas colonel recalled that when Prentiss' lines finally cracked, a federal officer galloped forward to meet the Confederate line of battle crying: "Boys, for God's sake, stop firing, you are killing your friends!" He and his horse were shot dead, and the line came sweeping on. Another federal officer was killed as he rode toward the rear in, of all things, a buggy; then while the Southerners regrouped for a new assault, there was a general cry of "White flag!" and "Cease firing!" and the uproar of battle died. Prentiss had surrendered with approximately 2,200 men. With the surrender, a half hour of comparative silence came down on the field.

The Federals did not realize it, but conditions in the Confederate army – it was Beauregard's army now that Johnston was dead – were just about as disorganized as in their own. During much of the battle effective control of the Confederate attack had been exercised by a group of staff officers from the three Confederate corps, the Corp commanders having been thrown out of effective touch with most of their troops. At the time Johnston lost his life, Beauregard had Hardee and a handful of staff officers rounding up stragglers to form improvised battalions to renew the attack on the Federal right – just as Grant, at about the same moment, had men creating similar formations out of disorganized men in his own rear. After Prentiss' surrender, crowds of Confederates wandered through the hornets' nest, gaping at the prisoners, picking up souvenirs, and acting as if the battle had ended. At this stage, it is probable that neither army had more than half of its men on the firing line.

The lull came just in time. Grant had his chief of staff, Colonel Joseph D. Webster, assembling all the siege guns and field artillery he could find in a compact line a quarter of a mile inland from the landing, overlooking a ravine formed by a backwater that came in from the Tennessee; and Webster was working hard at his job – he had fifty guns or more, arranged in a great shallow crescent, and if Beauregard's troops were going to reach the river they would have to overrun this powerful battery. Off in the woods, Confederate artillery was still firing, and shells were striking around the landing – so many that the ammunition-supply steamer, Rocket, cast off its lines and steamed downriver to get out of range. Webster's guns began firing in reply, and the gunboats, Tyler and Lexington, moved in near the mouth of the backwater and opened fire with their heavy navel guns; the whole, said a staff officer, making "a noise not exceeded by anything I ever heard afterward." A staff officer at Grant's side was killed by one of the Confederate missiles.

A newspaper correspondent saw Grant sitting on his horse in the midst of all of this, apparently unruffled. News of Prentiss' surrender had spread and most of the men around the landing were very gloomy, and someone found the nerve to ask Grant if he did not think the situation extremely dark. "Oh no," said Grant. "They can't break our lines tonight – it is too late. Tomorrow, we shall attack them with fresh troops and drive them, of course." The correspondent describing this incident said long afterward that "from that moment I never doubted Grant would be recognized not only as a great soldier but a great man."

And now with the fragmented Union army backed up almost to the river's edge, the long-awaited help arrived. Nelson's division appeared on the far side of Tennessee and steamboats began to bring the men to the landing. They came ashore proudly, with bands paying, through the depressing backwash of stragglers, teamsters, dismounted cavalry, and men whose fighting instincts had evaporated. Some of these seemed to be quite unmoved by the arrival of the fresh troops. Leading his brigade ashore colonel Ammen had to crowd through a huge mass of listless soldiers; an earnest chaplain was exhorting these men, "in whang-doodle style," repeating in frantic voice: "Rally, men, rally and we may yet be saved! Oh rally, for God and your country's sake, rally..." No one was paying the least attention, and Ammen broke in: "Shut up, you Goddamned old fool, or I'll break your head. Get out of the way." Some of the rear guard took new heart when they saw Nelsons men marching in. One of Grant's soldiers wrote that he could never forget the new hope that came to him when he heard Nelson's band playing "Hail Columbia." And he said the men all around him cheered "till the whole woods on either bank fairly shook for joy."

The moment of crisis was over. Nelson's men were assigned to support Webster's huge battery, General Hurlbut was put to work organizing temporary units of stragglers; the still unbroken parts of Grants army were drawn up to the right and the artillery opened a stupendous cannonade. The Confederate attack, as a matter of fact, was about over for the day; a brigade or two had got into the ravine in front of the heavy guns and was trying in vain to renew the fight, but Beauregard could see that for the time being his army was utterly fought out, and he was ordering a halt and a general regrouping in preparation for another fight in the morning.

Once Websters bombardment got into full voice it was stupendous. The 81st Ohio was in position a little in front, and men said the thunderous discharges behind them knocked their hats off. One soldier wrote that the concussion almost broke his neck and inflicted the sharpest pains he felt in all the war: "Guns pounded away all night long. The sensation at every shot was that of being lifted two feet and slammed down with a healthy whack." Two weeks later, he said, his ears still "played me all sorts of pranks and tricks," and the ordinary creaking and clicking of wagon wheels sounded like volleys of musketry. In the 6th Iowa, also drawn up close to the guns, the violent concussion drew blood from men's noses and ears and gave permanent injury to some soldiers' hearing. Out in the river, the Lexington and the Tyler continued to slam in their eight-inch shells, firing down the length of the supposed location of the confederate battle line. Since this line was withdrawn, they did little actual damage, but they were ordered to keep on firing at intervals throughout the night so as to keep the exhausted Southerners from sleeping. After dark a heavy rain began to fall, with intermittent thunder and lightning, the rolling crash of thunder mingling with explosions from the guns, red flames from the massed batteries streaking out in the wet darkness: one federal veteran probably spoke for everyone in both armies when he wrote of it as a "weird, wearisome and wrathful night."

The danger had passed, but not everyone was ready to recognize the fact. A surgeon in the 55th Illinois, which had been drawn up in support of the line of guns, found Grant nearby and ventured to remark: "General, things are going decidedly against us today." Grant told him: "Not at all, sir. We are whipping them there now." The doctor, with some reason, felt that not another man in the army would have said that just then. In the midst of the rain a staff officer found Grant and others grouped around a smoldering fire of straw. McPherson rode up, after inspecting the lines, and Grant greeted him with a cheerful, "Well Mac, how is it?" McPherson was not encouraging; at least a third of the army was out of action, he said, and all the rest were disheartened. Grant said nothing, and McPherson sought to prompt him by asking: "General Grant, under this condition of affairs, what do you proposed to do sir? Shall I make preparations for retreat?" Grant snapped back: "Retreat? No. I propose to attack at daylight and whip them."

Nelson's division was over the river now, and more of Buell's troops were coming up on the other side, waiting to be ferried across; and finally, the lost division of Lew Wallace came marching up to take position on the right. Wallace had had a miserable day. Some of Grant's impatient staff officers felt that he had been inert and slothful, but apparently the man had simply been misled by a complete misunderstanding about the roads he was supposed to take. He had marched his division off on a wrong road under this misunderstanding, had been forced to make a laborious countermarch, and was now reaching the scene many hours too late, his great day of opportunity gone forever – if his division could have come in early in the afternoon, on the Confederate flank it would almost certainly brought about a smashing Union victory. Not until near the end of his own life would Grant come to see that Wallace had been much more sinned against than sinning that Sunday at Shiloh.

It was a horrible night for everyone – a night of black darkness, insistent rain, jarring noise, and acute physical discomfort. Thousands upon thousands of men had been wounded and the ones who had not been hurt were completely exhausted and had no chance to get a decent rest. Grant tried to make a go of it lying under a tree on the bluff near the landing but the pain in his injured ankle kept him awake, and along toward midnight he hobbled off to the log house that was supposed to be his headquarters. It had been put into service as a hospital and was full of moaning, wounded men with many more laying outside awaiting attention. After one look at all of this Grant went back into the rain. Years later, recalling all of it, he wrote: "The sight was more unendurable than encountering the enemy's fire, and I returned to my tree in the rain."

Late that night though, Sherman came to see him. Sherman had found himself in the heat of the enemy's fire that day, but now he was licked. As far as he could see, the important next step was "to put the river between us and the enemy and recuperate," and he hunted up Grant to see when and how the retreat could be arranged. He came upon Grant at last, at midnight or later, standing under the tree in the heavy rain, hat slouched down over his face, coat-collar up around his ears, a dimly glowing lantern in his hand, cigar clenched between his teeth. Sherman looked at him, then "moved" as he put it later, "by some wise and sudden instinct" not to talk about retreat, he said: "Well, Grant, we've had the devil's own day, haven't we?" Grant said, "Yes," and his cigar glowed in the darkness as he gave a quick hard puff at it. "Yes, Lick 'em tomorrow, though."

So ended Sunday, April 6, at Pittsburg Landing.

Two exhausted armies pulled themselves out of the mud at dawn on Monday, April 7, stumbled into line, and made ready to go on with the battle. There really was no need for any more fighting because the ultimate decision had already been reached. Johnston and Beauregard had one slim chance to cancel all that the Federals had won at Fort Henry and Fort Donelson, one desperate hope to restore the balance that had been upset during the winter, and they had come within a hand's grasp of seizing it. But when the night and the storm came down on April 6, with Webster's great row of guns pounding the thickets and ravines, with Buell's soldiers shouldering their way through the fugitives on the riverbank, and with Lew Wallace's men marching across the Owl Creek bridge, the business was settled. There might be more killing, with much bloodshed and agony to be drawn from young men not yet hurt, but for the Confederates the moment when the main current of the war could be reversed had passed.

The opposing armies had paid a dreadful price for what had been done on the first day. General Johnston was dead. W. H. L. Wallace was dying, Prentiss was a prisoner, and fully 17,000 of other ranks had been killed, wounded, or captured. There had been immense losses from straggling and probably no more than half of the men who had taken up their muskets Sunday morning were in line ready to fight on Monday. The concentrated fury of the fighting had been appalling and it left its mark for all the rest of the war. The southern novelist George W. Cable was to write sadly that New Orleans "had never really been glad again after the awful day of Shiloh" and a Union veteran said that the most any Union soldier could say of any later fight was: "I was worse scared than I was at Shiloh."

The Federal army had all of the advantage that day. Beauregard was able to muster no more than 20,000 infantry, and every man had fought hard the day before; nor had any man had a decent sleep on Sunday night. Grant's veterans were no better off, but reinforcements were on hand. On his left, Grant had Buell's men. Nelson's division, and that of Brigadier General Alexander McCook, and two brigades from the division of Brigadier General Thomas L.

Crittenden. These soldiers were bone-tired from a forced march. McCook's division had hiked thirty miles on Sunday and had been ferried across the river at midnight, had stood in the mud in pelting rain most of the rest of the night, so miserably uncomfortable that one veteran remembered that night as the worst of his entire three years' service. But they had not fought, their organization was complete, and they considered themselves the saviors of Grant's army and accordingly were somewhat cocky. On the right of Buell's troops were three battered divisions from Grant's army – Hurlbut's, McClernand's and Sherman's – and on the left flank was Lew Wallace's unfought division. Grant's orders were to attack at dawn, and as the gray light streaked the sodden fields and thickets, the big line began to roll forward.

Grant rode over to see Wallace just before the attack began. He looked fresh and unworried, and when he said, "Good morning," he did not sound like a man who had been within inches of a disastrous defeat twelve hours earlier. Looking back long afterward, Wallace put into words a thought that struck many men, at various times – "If we had studied to be undramatic, we could not have succeeded better."

Overpowered they might be, but Confederates were very stubborn about giving up the ground they had won. In the main it was like Sunday's battle, a soldiers' fight, a tangled series of desperate small combats all going on at once. As Lew Wallace said before the battle ended, "The two armies as a general thing degenerated into mere fighting swarms;" tactical formations and maneuvers were forgotten and in advance or retreat only one rule prevailed – "to watch the flag and stay with it." The confederates slowly gave ground but until the middle of the day things were fairly even. Then the Federal advantage in numbers began to tell; by two in the afternoon the Confederate front was ready to cave in, and when one of Beauregard's staff came to the general in the rear of Shiloh Church and suggested that it was time to retreat, Beauregard said that he had the same idea. "I intend to withdraw in a few moments." Rear guard lines were set up, the Confederates began to pull away, and Grant, seeing the change, picked up two regiments, formed them in line of battle, and led them forward for one final blow. Reaching a proper vantage point, he ordered the men to charge, and it seemed to him that this broke the last enemy resistance.

But the Confederates were leaving anyway, and after the most perfunctory of pursuits the Federals let them go with blessings on them. No one in Grant's army wanted to keep in touch with these foes any longer than the law required. Buell was not the man to crowd anybody, and Beauregard got his shattered army off on the muddy roads toward Corinth.

From this distance it seems clear that the great missed opportunity at Shiloh was the failure to press the retiring Confederates pitilessly during the twenty-four hours following Beauregard's withdrawal. The Union army was worn out and its command arrangements were very imperfect: but the Confederates' plight was desperate. They were, in short, ready to be had, and a driving chase down the muddy roads to Corinth might have knocked them out of the war for good. Braxton Bragg, who was one of the most dour pessimists in either army but who nevertheless had a clear military eye, wrote to Beauregard on the morning after the battle: "If we are pursued by a vigorous force we will lose all in our rear. The whole road presents the scene of a rout, and no mortal power could restrain it."

One solid blow on April 8 could have shattered the Confederate army beyond repair, but the Federal army was not up to it. The Federals followed their foes just long enough to make sure that they had actually left the premises and then stopped, and although Grant exhorted both Sherman and McClernand to jam the Rebel rear guard with cavalry and infantry in hot pursuit, nothing much came of it. The Unionists went into the camps they had occupied before the battle began and Confederates loitered just out of gunshot range, and the terrible Battle of Shiloh was over. Between them, Grant and Buell had lost more than 13,000 men, Beauregard had lost more than 10,000 and the greatest battle ever fought on the North American continent up to that date had come to an end.

It had been a very near thing indeed, and the most that could be said for the Northerners was that they had beaten off an unexpected attack, and yet one of the decisive struggles of the Civil War had been won. The end of the war was a long way off in April of 1862, yet when the exhausted Confederates drifted southwest from Pittsburg Landing a faint foreknowledge of what the end would be went down the road with them. The Northern victory had been purely negative, but it was of far-reaching consequence. For this was one battle which the Confederacy had to win in order to survive, and the Confederacy had not quite been able to win it. In the long run many things killed the dream of Southern independence: one of them compacted in the wilderness above the Tennessee river was made up of the desperate fighting of many Middle Western soldiers, the power of the row of guns on the bluff in the twilight ... and with these, the unbreakable stubbornness of Ulysses S. Grant.

Leonard Whitney.

# APPENDIX C

## Iowa Historical Record

## Vol. IV. April, 1888 No. 2

## Leonard Whitney

IOWA HISTORICAL RECORD

VOL. IV. APRIL, 1888. NO. 2.

LEONARD WHITNEY.

IN the fall of 1874 I became minister of the Unitarian church in Keokuk. No sooner had I entered upon my work than I began to meet daily with evidences of the strong influence over the congregation and the people of the city which had been wielded, during his life, by the Rev. Leonard Whitney, organizer and first minister of the church. During my four years as pastor there I heard from strong men and women of all classes words of loyal friendship and high appreciation of him. And now as I go from time to time to visit friends in Keokuk, or to preach to the congregation Mr. Whitney organized, I see and hear the testimony that though dead he yet speaketh. I would gladly have left the preparation of this paper to one of the friends who knew him in life. But many of these have passed on, and those remaining hesitate to undertake the work. Happily some who knew him best have given most able help in this tribute to a noble man. And many others, whose names can not even be mentioned here, have recounted to me their memories of their friend and minister.

From the homes of New England have gone forth a multitude of men and women who have shaped the thought and

In the fall of 1874, I became minister of the Unitarian church in Keokuk. No sooner had I entered upon my work than I began to meet daily with evidence of the strong influence over the congregation and the people of the city which had been wielded, during his life, by Rev. Leonard Whitney, organizer and first minister of the church. During my four years as pastor there I heard from strong men and women of all class's words of loyal friendship and high appreciation of him. And now as I go from time to time to visit friends in Keokuk, or to preach to the congregation Mr. Whitney organized, I see and hear the testimony that though dead he yet speaketh. I would gladly have left the preparation of this paper to one of the friends who knew him in life. But many of these have passed on, and those remaining hesitate to undertake the work. Happily, some who knew him best have given most able help in this tribute to a noble man. And many others, whose names can not even be mentioned here, have recounted to me their memories of their friend and minister.

From the homes of the New England have gone forth a multitude of men and women who have shaped the thought and activities of all the mighty West. In one of these homes in Conway, Mass., Otis Whitney was born in 1781. In 1803 he married Sarah Edmunds, daughter of Joseph and Rosamond Barton Edmunds. Joseph had been a privateers-man during the Revolutionary War, and his many stories of adventure had a strong fascination for the boys and young men of his acquaintance. The father of Joseph Edmunds had been a Quaker preacher and had transmitted to his son a noble strain of independence. Rosamond Barton, wife of Joseph Edmunds, was one of the Rhode Island Bartons, and was related to the Bartons of Revolutionary fame, hence in the veins of Sarah Edmunds, wife of Otis Whitney, there pulsated a pure and strong love of justice and liberty for every human being, and that religion of the Spirit that rises above the narrow technicalities of creeds. And, personally, she was a woman of strong mental and moral qualities.

Otis Whitney was a descendant of a sturdy family that, before his day and since, has produced many able farmers, mechanics and merchants, many brilliant clergymen, lawyers, and statesmen. Otis was a man of clear head and practical turn. His efficiency provided his family with the comforts usually found in a well-to-do New England home. He was a farmer, and his children were born and grew up amid the freedom, the independence, the intelligence and industry that then characterized the rural population of New England. Both he and his wife were members of the Baptist church, in which faith they lived honorable lives and met peaceful deaths.

Among the children born to Otis and his wife came Leonard, on October 23, 1811. With such parentage he received vigor of body and mind. In such a home his native qualities developed healthfully.

He grew to an active boy and became leader of all sports and mischief in the neighborhood. He was strong, quick, impulsive, wayward, and generous. He was by no means distressingly good in the Sunday-school-library-book style. His parents and his teachers found him difficult to manage. But he was the friend of the weak. He responded readily to what was generous, just and kind. The district school and the academy gave him his early education which his father urged the restless boy to continue by going to college. But he had dreams of adventures amid strange scenes, fostered perhaps by the sea tales of his grandfather, Joseph Edmunds, the old privateers-man. When sixteen years old he went to Boston and shipped for a voyage. But before the vessel sailed, he had seen enough of the charms of the sea life to change his mind. He succeeded in getting free from the engagement and never again had a return of the longing for the sea.

The experiences of his Boston trip, acting on a mind singularly receptive, turned his attention to the sober purposes of life. He worked with interest on his father's farm. He attended school at Hinesburg, Vt., and made good progress in his studies. He chose the profession of law as his work for life, and for several years gave himself to its study. In August 1835, he was admitted to practice at the Chittenden County Court, Burlington, Vt., by the unanimous consent of the bar. He spent several years in the practice of law at Ann Arbor, Mich, and at Auburn, N.Y. There is no record accessible to me as to his success at the bar. Probably it was not promising. I suspect he was not by nature fitted in mind and morals to succeed in any but the higher fields of law practice and circumstances never allowed him to enter those fields. Work, study, and anxiety brought him poor health and he went to Saratoga Springs to rest. While there he visited not infrequently at the home of an old friend who had settled nearby as the pastor of the Baptist Church in Union Village, the Rev. William Arthur, father of the late President Chester A. Arthur. His old friend had a strong influence over the young lawyer. During the summer he united with Mr. Arthur's church, decided to give up law, and to become a Baptist minister. That fall he began his ministerial work as pastor of the Baptist church at Bennington, in his native state.

He met the lady to whom, the next year, he married, Ann Jeanette Harwood, only daughter of Asahel Harwood of Bennington. He preached with ability and sincerity and his work was acceptable among his people. Leaving Bennington, he preached at Penton, Vt., at Reading, Pa., and the Navy Yard Baptist church at Washington, D. C. and then with the church at Canandaigua, N. Y. All the while his religion was growing too large for his creed. His humanity was too deep and loving to allow him to excuse crimes because they were popular and national. He preached justice and liberty for all, even if their skins were black. His moral perception was so strong and so sensitive that he was roused mightily by the Fugitive Slave Law [passed in 1850] and poured his impassioned feelings into his sermons. Those sermons were not without wide influence. A friend who had heard one of them wrote to him as follows:

*Washington, 11 Jan. 1851. Friend Whitney – I want you to send me a copy, prepared for publication, of the sermon preached by you in which you say: "They had fugitive law in old times. The authorities commanded that if any knew where Jesus was, they should deliver him up." Undoubtedly many knew where he was and doubtless too the chief priests preached, as the Doctors of Divinity do now, that it was their duty to obey the civil authorities and deliver him up. But in all Judea, there was found but one Silver Grey.*

*One of the merchant princes of New York and a man high in influence as well as information says he will print it in fine form for gratuitous distribution if I will procure the copy. Grave Senators scream and yell almost with joy when the argument is thus told to them. They say that the minute it gets out it will go through all the papers, that it is just one of those things that must carry, that as soon as it is named, the wonder is that somebody had not thought of it before. Such was the effect when I told it at a dinner party of Senators, members of congress, etc. So, make it elevated, concise, sufficiently moderate, but yieldingly conclusive and severe, and send it along. It will come into good hands.*

*Very truly yours, M. O. Wilder*

His religious opinions had been gradually changing for some years. Probably the Anti-Slavery agitation had much to do in helping this change. He soon found himself out of sympathy with the beliefs of a part of his Canandaigua flock, and with difference of opinion there came among some of his people bitterness of feeling. His conscience urged him on. He could not stifle his thoughts. He could not put a padlock on his lips. His hearers who disagreed with him were, doubtless, just as earnest and faithful. They believed the Baptist system, and it was their right to expect their minister to teach that system. A conflict came. A church meeting was called, and Mr. Whitney was excluded from the church for heresy. But many of his congregation were with him. These others who became interested organized the "Free Church of Canandaigua," rented a hall and invited Mr. Whitney to be their minister. He accepted and for five years preached to them the word of the Spirit as his eager ear caught its enchanting message. All the time his thought was enlarging. He became acquainted with Dr. Hosmer, minister of the Unitarian

Church in Buffalo, and with the noble Samuel J. May of Syracuse, both of whom he exchanged pulpits and found himself in essential sympathy with both.

He went west as a religious pioneer. He was called to a church in Peoria and to a new movement in Keokuk. His ambition was never great. Keokuk was the smaller place with the smaller salary. He accepted its call and became its minister in October 1853. He had been only a short time in Keokuk when he had an invitation to the pastorate of the Unitarian Church in Rochester, N. Y. which he declined. His society in Keokuk erected a building which was dedicated in 1856 and Mr. Whitney entered upon his years of valuable service His geniality as a man, his generosity as a friend, his eloquence as a preacher, his power as a thinker, and the genuine religiousness of his nature called into his church a company of men and women of remarkable ability, some of whom have since reached a wider than national fame and influence. Hon. Samuel F. Miller, now senior justice on the United States Supreme Bench, was then a young lawyer in Keokuk. He became one of Mr. Whitney's most faithful friends. Hon. Geo. W. McCrary, a rising young man from Van Buren County, Iowa, went to Keokuk to study law. He and his amiable wife also found in the Unitarian Church a congenial religious home. Mr. Briggs, editor of the Gate City, then as now one of the most influential papers in Iowa, became an attendant on Mr. Whitney's preaching and one of his warmest admirers. Dr. Freeman Knowles, who had brought from his birthplace in Maine, a keen New England mind, and his wife, whose religious nature and mental power fitted her for the noblest society, and their daughter, Emma, were drawn to his preaching. Able businessmen were there not a few. George Williams, C. H. Perry, E. H. Harrison, Wm. Leighton, and their wives, were all fed mentally and spiritually by the power of their preacher.

J. M. Hiatt, S. W. Tucker, R. B. Ogden and their wives found in him a leader who they could gladly follow. Most of these early friends have crossed the river or have moved to other fields of business. But all of whom I have met are heartily loyal to this spiritual leader of their early or mature manhood and womanhood, and all are enthusiastic in their appreciation of his genius.

Still the strong man and the able leader found his labors hindered because some of those who loved him as a man and who were in sympathy with his religious philosophy could not agree with him in all respects in the practical application of that philosophy. Slavery was the all-absorbing topic in society and in politics. Mr. Whitney's soul was on fire with the love of liberty. His direct mind and sensitive moral nature went, sure as the needle to the pole, straight to the immediate freedom of the slave. Not all his people were able to think with him. He could not rest except in sermon and in prayer, his love of justice and freedom found frequent and burning expressions. Not all his people could see that duty demanded this constant and ardent utterance. Just then the Rebellion, terrible in its suffering and bloodshed, but glorious in the reward of justice and liberty it won, was urged on by the sadly mistaken South. Mr. Whitney's heart and mind could then rest only in active service. He had spoken for liberty and now wanted to work for liberty. He sought and obtained the appointment of chaplain to the Eleventh Illinois Cavalry, of which R. G. Ingersoll was Colonel. He gave up his parish and joined his regiment with enthusiasm.

For this work he was peculiarly fitted. He was genial in spirit; he met all men in a happy way. He had an appreciation of man; he could detect the divine human through the lowliest and most sinful guise. He was unselfish; he gave gladly his last crust to the suffering. He was entirely without sanctimonious pretense; he went among the men as a brother, a friend, a sympathetic helper. The officers and the men were drawn to him at once. The relations between him and them were cordial and brotherly. He was their minister in the true sense – their helper, their leader in the best things. Of the appreciation in which he was held in the regiment the following letter from his honored colonel gives generous testimony:

*New York. January 6th, 1888. Rev. O. Clute. My Dear Sir: - It gives me great pleasure to write a few words in reference to the Rev. Leonard Whitney. He was one of the best, one of the purest, one of the noblest men I ever knew. He was in the highest sense a deeply religious man – that is to say, he lived in accordance with his ideal. There was about him neither can't nor hypocrisy. He did not pretend to be better than others – he wished only to make others better.*

*While I knew him his entire time was occupied in doing good to others. He was a perpetual consolation to the sick and wounded – an example for all. He won the respect of every man who knew him, and his influence was only good.*

*He was a thorough believer in the religion of good works, and he lived in exact accordance with his belief.*

*He as truly gave his life for his country as though he had died on the field of battle.*

*Yours truly, - R. G. Ingersoll*

Not long after his regiment took the field it was engaged in one of the fiercest battles of the war – Pittsburg Landing. The story of that fight I need not write. It is known to all. But all do not know the self-sacrificing service that the chaplain gave to the sick, the wounded, the suffering, and the dying. His was the large nature that rose nobly to the large occasion. Those who saw him on the field, amid the ghastly suffering, have tears in their voices as they tell today the story. It is related of him that seeing a wounded soldier unable to leave the field he leaped from his horse, put the poor fellow in the saddle, and directed him to the nearest hospital-boat. To another he gave his blankets; to others he gave his clothes, tearing up his shirts and handkerchiefs to make bandages for the wounded. Many a maimed soldier remembers with grateful heart and tearful eyes his heroic acts of love and mercy on that bloody field. In a letter to his wife, written after the battle, when faint, weary, sick and talking of coming home, he said: "I have no horse, saddle, bridle, quilt, blanket or encumbrance of any sort or kind. I gave them all up to the wounded on the battlefield and have not seen them since; they helped those in sad need, and they are welcome to them."

The exposure to pitiless rain, to the chilling night air, to sleeping on the wet ground, to insidious malaria, bought on a fever. He was sent on a hospital boat to St. Louis in charge of the Sisters of Mercy who gave to him and to all in their care, the most faithful attention. He went from St. Louis to his home and friends in Keokuk. The disease made rapid advances. His family and his many devoted friends gave him every care. But care could not avail; love could not beat back the march of that enemy that at some time overtakes us all. On June 12, 1862, his struggle ended, his soul went home.

In estimating the work and character of Mr. Whitney it is fortunate that we have the help of some of the able men who were influenced by his ability, and warmly drawn to him in personal friendship. One of these, widely and highly honored, writes:

*Washington D.C. December 21, 1887. Rev. Oscar Clute – My Dear Friend – Your letter of the 15th inst. was received by me about the 20th, when I was so busy in disposing of the business of the court, preparatory to the recess of the Christmas Holidays, that I had no time to make any response, so that it has been delayed until now. I hope it is not too late, for it gives me great pleasure to speak of the Rev. Leonard Whitney, with whom my relations were of the most intimate character. Indeed, I fear that what I may say about him will be rather the result of the most affectionate remembrance of a devoted personal friend, rather than a critical historical statement.*

*I do not know precisely in what year Mr. Whitney came to Keokuk; somewhere I should think between 1852 and 1854. There was no organized congregation of Unitarians there when he came, but a number of the most intelligent citizens of the place had been Unitarians in other localities or were inclined to a more liberal form of Christian doctrine than was taught in any of the orthodox churches. A room was rented, and Mr. Whitney preached to these persons and to all others who came to hear him. This continued for several years, the place of worship changing as the exigencies of the case required.*

*Mr. Whitney was, I think, a native of Vermont, where the families of Whitneys are numerous, and I have since met more than one person bearing his full name of Leonard Whitney. He was, I should think, forty years of age when he came to Keokuk, and as I understood, had been a Baptist minister but had left the ministry of that church because he could no longer hold to is principles. This change of conviction may have led to his over-estimate of the evils incident to creeds. Certainly, he was an aggressive preacher and gave much of his time and energy in the pulpit to showing the untruthfulness of popular doctrines. And if there was in the character of his preaching anything which to me seemed objectionable it was the vigor with which he denounced what he thought to be the erroneous principles of the prevailing creeds of the Christian churches generally.*

*This developed a seeming inconsistency in his character, for his social relations not only with the members of the other churches of Keokuk, but with their clergymen, were of the most cordial character. He was respected and beloved by all of them, and in his intercourse with the world at large, with his friends and with his family, he was the kindest and tenderest friend and the most affectionate father and husband. But he seemed impelled by a solemn sense of duty which had fallen to his lot to expose those errors in the orthodox creeds which he believed led to contention and evil in the Christian churches, and in accordance with the energy of his nature and the strength of his convictions he was not choice in the selection of the words by which he denounced those errors.*

*He was a man of very vigorous thought and still more vigorous language. Some of the illustrations of his arguments have remained with me through long years and absence from the theatre of his services. Perhaps I cannot better show the man than by reproducing one of these.*

*The years of 1857 and 1858 found the people of the city of Keokuk utterly prostrated by the financial crisis which pervaded the United States, but which fell with peculiar force upon that place, because it had been a prosperous town and its citizens venturesome in their desire to make money by speculation, and particularly in real estate. The result of this crisis was to leave many people, who believed that they had accumulated fortunes, struggling with absolute poverty and in debt beyond any hope of relief. This condition of things was accompanied or followed, as is very often the case, by a great religious revival in which under the influence of religious zeal the occasion was improved to turn the attention of those who had been thus unfortunate, to a land where sorrows never come. The interest awakened was very extended and the number who joined the different churches during this revival was quite remarkable. As Mr. Whitney did not believe in this mode of adding to the church, nor in a permanent good influence on persons who professed a change of life and heart under this kind of teaching, he took occasion to preach a sermon on the subject of revivals, in which he, with his usual force, pointed out his belief that such motives as had induced the additions to the churches under the circumstances then existing were not of a character to prove lasting with the individuals nor credible to those bodies in the end. In illustration of his view of the matter, he said: "Those who have thus been seriously distressed by losses of corner lots in Keokuk have only transferred the same earthly affection to their faith in the corner lots which they desire to secure in the New Jerusalem."*

*I do not know that this illustration was original with Mr. Whitney. I am very sure I never heard it before or since, and its force as a mental photograph of what he supposed to be the moving principle in such revivals of religion can hardly be equaled.*

*It is with more pleasure, however, that I give illustrations of his warmth of heart, showing the practical benevolence of his nature. On a Sabbath in mid-winter when he was expected to preach to his congregation, not then very large, he failed to appear, so that after some singing and reading from the book of prayers the people dispersed. During the succeeding week it was ascertained that Mr. Whitney had that morning started in a snowstorm from his home, which was some distance from the place of worship. On his way he had to pass the house of a widow who was in very poor circumstances, and it occurred to him to drop into the house and enquire into her situation. He found her with a family of children, without fire, without wood to make one, and if she had anything to eat, no means of cooking it. He instantly set himself to work, went to some neighboring house and got a few sticks of wood, sawed them into the requisite lengths, split them up, started a fire in the widow's stove, and saw that she had something to eat. With his attentions to her the time passed so quickly that before he had finished, it was too late for him to preach. Of course, this became known to a few of his congregation and the next Sunday when he addressed the members who attended, in a short and modest way he stated the cause of his detention and said that he had no regrets for himself and no apology to make for his failure to attend upon the previous Sabbath.*

*The circumstances attending Mr. Whitney's death constitute a tribute to the tenderness of his heart and the nobility of his character which must endear him to the memory of his friends as long as they live to remember anything. In the early part of the late civil war, he was appointed by Col. Robert G. Ingersoll as chaplain of his regiment, the Eleventh Illinois Cavalry. I do not stop here to make any criticism upon Col. Ingersoll's religious principles, either then or now, but it seems probable the friendship between him and Mr. Whitney may have been strengthened by the fact that at that date, over thirty years ago, each of them was aware that the other was struggling for light on the great subject of religious thought. Whatever may be your opinion or mine in regard to Col. Ingersoll's present opinions on those subjects, no one can deny the integrity of his character or the purity of his purposes in the course he pursues on that subject.*

*Mr. Whitney accepted the place of chaplain, immediately joined his regiment, and within a very few days found himself at the battle of*

*Pittsburg Landing, as we all know it, or the Battle of Shiloh, as it is called by the men who fought on the other side. It will be remembered that after a hard day's fight our soldiers laid down on the ground, where the darkness had overtaken them, and that a rain fell during a large part of the night. Notwithstanding the bad weather and his fatigued condition, Mr. Whitney occupied the entire night in going around over the field, looking after the sick, the wounded, and the dying, and in doing all that he was capable of in the way of relieving their sufferings. Many of these wounded he found without covering, cold, unprotected and to one he gave his overcoat, to another his coat, to another his waistcoat, and still continued to go on through the rain and cold.*

*I do not desire to harass the feelings of your readers by descriptions of the sufferings which he attempted to relieve, nor of those which he must himself have encountered in this first essay of his duties as chaplain of his regiment, nor by recalling the unfortunate result to Mr. Whitney and to his congregation at Keokuk. The feelings of affection and distress to himself which are recalled by the incident compel me to be brief. I can only add that during that night he contracted a disease from which he died within two or three weeks, and indeed was hardly able to be brought home before that event occurred.*

*His grave lies in the most beautiful part of the cemetery of Keokuk among those of other citizens who have died and been buried there. Adjoining this is a national cemetery where the bodies of those who died in the army have been interred. On Decoration Day once a year, the people of that city, as of other sections, meet and scatter roses on the graves of their friends and heroes. For many years after his death, and as long as I was able personally to attend those decoration services, I never failed to visit the grave of my departed friend and contribute my floral testimony to his memory. It was a pleasant thing as I would sit near his last resting place and watch the people who came to see it, to note that no grave in all that city of the dead received more consideration or was visited by more sorrowing hearts than that of Leonard Whitney.*

*Mr. Whitney died in the prime of life, died regretted and mourned by the population of an entire city, died without an enemy, and his loss was an irreparable one. He left a widow and four children. Through the kindness of Col. Perry and some others, he had secured a comfortable house in a pleasant part of the city. He was indifferent to making money, perhaps too much so, and his wife and young children were left in struggling circumstances. Perhaps the pervading influence of his earnest example, of his devotion to duty, of his generous character, and of his self-denying consecration to the cause of humanity and the Christian religion, as he understood them, were worth more to those he left behind than any money could have been.*

*He was a true man, with a noble heart and a commanding intellect. He died a martyr to his sense of duty. "Of such is the kingdom of Heaven."*

*Sam F. Miller.*

Desiring a word from one or two who had known Mr. Whitney in the army that I could incorporate into this paper, I addressed a note to Col. R. G. Ingersoll. In response came the cordial letter printed a few pages in advance. Afterwards I found among Mr. Whitney's papers the following letter from Col. Ingersoll written a short time after Mr. Whitney's death.

*Corinth, July 19th 1862*

*Mrs. Leonard Whitney. –*

*My Dear Madam – Your letter did not reach me till yesterday. I immediately made out the proper certificate and as I think, properly attested, though I am very little acquainted with the regulations on the subject. I hope, however, that it may prove sufficient. I was very glad to receive your letter and glad to learn that I was remembered by your husband, to whom I was greatly attached. Mr. Whitney won the respect and esteem of the whole command by uniform kindness to all and was considered by every man in the regiment as a noble, generous gentleman.*

*During the time he was with us he was almost constantly by the sick and wounded and was as kind to them as though they had been his own children. At the battle of Shiloh, he gave his blankets to the wounded, then slept upon the ground uncovered, with the chilling rain pouring upon him the whole dreary night, and at that time, as I believe, laid the foundation for the disease that terminated his life.*

*Permit me to say that I sympathize with you deeply in your irreparable loss. Generous men are not indigenous to this world. They are exotics from the skies. There is no such thing as being consoled for their loss. Their memory is worthy of and demands the bitterest of tears. And yet, believing as you do in the immortality of the soul, the dark cloud of grief now enveloping your heart, if not dissipated, will at least be adorned and glorified by the sweet bow of Hope.*

*I shall ever be pleased to be of assistance to you in any manner possible, and I hope you will feel no delicacy in commanding me. If the certificate herewith sent should prove incorrect, inform me and it shall be made right.*

*I am, my dear madam, your friend,*

*Robert G. Ingersoll.*

Twenty-three years after Mr. Whitney's death his congregation in Keokuk, desiring to express their love for him, and to tell the children and young people of the church something of its noble founder, held a memorial service in his honor. The congregation and the Sunday School met together in the beautiful church dedicated in 1874, standing on the site of the one built soon after Mr. Whitney first came to them – a church in striking contrast with the humble hall in which his people first listened to his inspiring words.

The congregation and Sunday School joined in a devotional service and in memorial hymns. Then those who had personally known him, or who had come to honor him by learning of his work and his character, spoke about him with sincere loyalty. Rev. R. Hassall, Messrs. M. R. King, S. W. Tucker, J. M. Shaffer, R. B. Ogden, and J. M. Hiatt gave addresses and letters were read from some who were unable to be present. It would be a pleasure to quote liberally from all speakers, but I must confine myself to some brief extracts. J. M. Hiatt said:

*"Sham and can't and hypocrisy Whitney hated as fiercely as did Carlyle. But not, as with Carlyle, did his hatred run into bitterness and misanthropy. It was because he loved mankind and the truth, and reverenced the divinity incarnate, that he hated these things. They were obstacles to human progress and happiness, and opposed to divine verity, hence his unresting war upon them. While fully recognizing moral worth and intellectual culture, he could not perceive the factitious distinctions that exist among men. The cabman and the king alike had immortal souls, and to him stood upon*

*the same platform. The worldly-wise would say he betrayed great want of tact, of policy, and in his lack of discrimination. That he failed in consequence to aggrandize himself, his church, and his cause as he otherwise might have done. Policy was no part of his character. He lived too near the soul of things. What the truth could not gather, to him must remain ungathered. He would not have played upon human weakness or pandered to human vanities to have made the world's emperor.*

S. W. Tucker, whose family received Mr. Whitney as a welcome guest on his first arrival in Keokuk, said:

*The admirers and appreciators of Mr. Whitney were not confined to his society. He had frequent hearers from the other denominations. His efforts were mostly arguments. He had a natural gift in argument which may have been confirmed by his study of law. This style was attractive to inquirers outside of his immediate people.*

From one who knew him in the field comes this hearty word:

*Washington, D.C. January 4th, 1888*

*Rev. Oscar Clute –*

*My Dear Sir – I considered Mr. Whitney one of the most faithful, laborious, and devoted men in the service. Although not in his regiment yet, the Fifteenth Iowa, of which I was in 1862 a field officer, was near the Eleventh Illinois Cavalry, I had occasional opportunities for observing the conduct of Mr. Whitney. I was at once impressed by his energy and thorough devotion to the men and their interests. As nurse as well as chaplain, he met their wants. He smoothed the pillow of the sick and gave good words to the ears of the despondent and dying. In season and out of season, on that slow, tedious, muddy, toilsome, and sickening march from Shiloh to Corinth - where the wasting weakness of that camp disease which is the terror of all soldiers, reduced the men to skeletons and the ranks by numbers – Mr. Whitney cheered the faltering, nerved the weak, and was, whenever I saw him, thoroughly equal to the occasion.*

*Very truly yours,*

*Wm. W. Belknap*

Hon. George W. McCrary, who has exemplified as a member of congress, as a cabinet officer, and as United States Judge of the Eighth Judicial District, the principles which, when a student and a young lawyer, he heard in the sermons of Mr. Whitney, sends me the following communication:

*Kansas City, Mo., December 18th, 1887*

*Rev. Oscar Clute – My Dear Sir – You ask me for some personal recollections of Rev. Leonard Whitney, and it is with pleasure that I respond, prompted as I am by a great admiration for his talents and character, and a sincere regard for his memory.*

*Mr. Whitney was, I believe, the pioneer Unitarian minister of Iowa. Others had preached within the bounds of the state before him, but if I am not mistaken, he was the first minister of the Unitarian faith regularly settled over a church within the state. He was installed over the Keokuk church, I think, in 1853. When I went to that place to commence the study of the law in the fall of 1854 he was preaching to a small congregation of exceptionally strong people, in a hall near the corner of Main and Fourth streets. The Keokuk church at that time numbered among its supporters such men as Samuel F. Miller, now senior justice of the Supreme Court of the United States, Col. C. H. Perry, Dr. Freeman Knowles, Wm. Leighton, E. H. Harrison, J. M.*

*Hiatt, and others of scarcely less prominence, all of whom were much devoted to Mr. Whitney.*

*As a preacher Mr. Whitney was chiefly distinguished for the force and power of his logic. It was an education to hear him from Sunday to Sunday. His was for a long time the only Unitarian pulpit in Iowa. He stood at his post, surrounded by his little band of devoted followers, and right manfully defended the Liberal Faith. In his day controversial preaching by the liberal clergy was necessary. It is, happily, not so now. Mr. Whitney and his church were a target for many sharp shots from all the surrounding pulpits. I knew and admired the orthodox clergy of Keokuk of that day, and I do them no injustice when I say that Mr. Whitney was more than a match for them all. On one occasion I remember he had mercilessly exposed the unreasonableness of certain popular theological doctrines, and a neighboring minister had replied soundly berating him for speaking so of sacred things and insisting that the doctrines in question only seemed unreasonable because finite minds can not understand the reasoning of the infinite. In reply Mr. Whitney exclaimed with great force: "I cannot accept these things on the ground that I do not understand them, for as an honest man, I am bound to reject them because I do understand them."*

*But he did not always debate in his pulpit. In spirit he was gentle and charitable and preached much upon topics of duty and practical living. Once I remember a curious circumstance happened which will illustrate something of his deep religious faith as well as his readiness as a speaker. He was preaching in the evening and his subject was immortality. Suddenly the gas went almost out, so that for a time the church became dark. He stopped his discourse while the darkness continued, which was several moments, and when the light returned, as it did very suddenly, he said, "So, my friends, I believe it will be with us all. For a moment at the end of life's journey, darkness may come over us, but it will be but for a moment, and will be followed by the glorious light and joy of eternity."*

*As a preacher he was far above the average. His power was the result of great ability coupled with evident sincerity. He never descended to hair splitting niceties, but always grasped the vital questions touching the subject in hand. He had no patience with arguments founded on isolated passages of scripture. He adopted a very different method of argument. The attributes of God as understood by all Christians were taken as his premises, and from these he went with unerring certainty to his conclusions. God is love, therefor nothing can proceed from him that is not prompted by love. God is justice, therefore no punishment that is not just can proceed from him. God's mercy endureth forever, and therefore will always be with every child. God is wisdom, therefor his chastisements must be wise, hence cannot be aimless nor endless. These are samples of his inexorable logic. Many others might be added. His sermons cast in this mold and delivered with a fervent eloquence not often seen, produced a marked effect upon his hearers. They appealed with equal power to the head and the heart, to the intellect and affections.*

*Mr. Whitney was deeply interested in the anti-slavery cause and could not see it to be his duty to keep silent upon that subject. He was one of the few ministers in southern Iowa who preached openly and boldly against slavery from 1854 until the war. I remember well one of his sermons preached, I think in 1856, in which he arraigned the slave power as hostile to the Union and predicted that war would come if they persisted in their course, and that the result of war would be the destruction of slavery and the establishment of the Union founded upon liberty and justice, and therefore destined to be perpetual. Having preached thus for many years, he naturally felt, when the war came, that he ought to do something more than preach for the cause he loved so well. He doubted whether a Unitarian minister could get a place as chaplain, and this gave him some trouble. Hearing, however, that the famous Col. Robert G. Ingersoll had raised a regiment of the Illinois cavalry, he naturally surmised that Mr. Ingersoll would not object to him on account of his heterodoxy. He accordingly wrote Col Ingersoll a letter applying for the chaplaincy of the regiment, and saying, "If appointed I promise to take care of the sick and wounded half the time, to fight half the time, and preach the remainder." He got the place, and he had the reputation among the officers and the soldiers who knew him of being one of the best chaplains in the army.*

*At the great three days battle of Shiloh, he devoted himself day and night, and through rain and storm, to taking care of the wounded. He stripped himself of one article of clothing after another in order to cover the wounded, and thus by exposing himself contacted the sickness from which he died, having given his life for the cause as truly as did those who were killed in the battle.*

*Mr. Whitney was a man warm-hearted, generous, charitable, devoted to friends and forgiving toward enemies. I have known him to go about the city of Keokuk on many occasions soliciting aid for worthy poor people. He was a deeply religious man and he lived up to his profession. His life was one of devotion to duty, and to the right as he saw it.*

*Very sincerely yours, Geo. W. McCrary.*

Mr. Whitney still lives in a world made better by his presence. Often in Keokuk one hears men and women, now gray-haired fathers and mothers, tell of their lives being straightened and sweetened by his influence. The children of those who, sick and needy, were helped by his work and sacrifice, rise up and call him blessed. Civil liberty towards which his generous nature went out in entire devotion, now extends its welcome and its care to every human being. Spiritual liberty, in defense of which his loyal soul gladly endured opprobrium and obscurity, is making rapid progress. The love of God and the love of man which to this clear-brained and warm-hearted follower of Jesus were the essence of religion, are constantly coming to wider recognition. He lived here for truth and goodness, he worked for his fellow-men, his aspiring soul looked in joy to God. Surely, in the nearer presence of God he still lives and still works for all noble things.

O. Clute - Iowa City,

Iowa, March 11th, 1888.

# APPENDIX D

## Robert G. Ingersoll

## August 11, 1833 – July 21, 1899

## Nicknamed "The Great Agnostic"

From Wikipedia

Robert Green Ingersoll was an American lawyer, writer and orator during the Golden Age of Free Thought, who campaigned in defense of agnosticism.

Born in Dresden, New York, his father, John Ingersoll, was an abolitionist sympathizing Congregational preacher, whose radical opinions caused him and his family to relocate frequently. For a time, Rev. John Ingersoll substituted as preacher for American revivalist Charles G. Finney while Finney was on tour in Europe. Upon Finney's return, Rev. Ingersoll remained for a few months as co-pastor/associate pastor with Finney. The elder Ingersoll's later pastoral experiences influenced young Robert negatively, however, as The Elmira Telegram described in 1890:

*Though for many years the most noted of American infidels, Colonel Ingersoll, was born and reared in a devoutly Christian household. His father, John Ingersoll, was a Congregationalist minister and a man of mark in his time, a deep thinker, a logical and eloquent speaker, broad minded and generously tolerant of the views of others. The popular impression which credits Ingersoll's infidelity in the main to his father's severe orthodoxy and the austere and gloomy surroundings in which his boyhood was spent, is wholly wrong. On the contrary, the elder Ingersoll's liberal views were a source of constant trouble between him and his parishioners. They caused him to frequently change his charges, and several times made him the defendant in church trials. His ministerial career was, in fact, substantially brought to a close by a church trial which occurred while he was a pastor of the Congregational Church at Madison, Ohio, and at which his third wife appeared as the prosecutor. Upon this occasion he was charged with prevarication and unministerial conduct. The evidence adduced – the trial is one of the abiding traditions of the dull little town of Madison – was of the most trivial and ridiculous character, but the committee which heard it decided that though he had done "nothing inconsistent with his Christian character," he was "inconsistent with his ministerial character," and forbade him to preach in the future. Elder John went before the higher church authorities and was permitted to continue his clerical labors. However, he soon removed to Wisconsin, going from there to Illinois, where he died. The Madison trial occurred when young Robert was nine years old, and it was the unjust and bigoted treatment his father received which made him the enemy, first of Calvinism, and later of Christianity in its other forms.*

**Lawyer.** Later that year the family settled in Marion, Illinois, where Robert and his brother, Ebon Clarke Ingersoll, were admitted to the bar in 1854. A country historian writing 22 years later noted that local residents considered the Ingersolls as a "very intellectual family but being Abolitionists and the boys being deists, rendered obnoxious to our people in that respect."

While in Marion he learned law from Judge Willis Allen and served as deputy clerk for John M. Cunningham, Williamson County Clerk and Circuit Clerk. In 1855, after Cunningham was named registrar for the federal land office in southeastern Illinois at Shawneetown, Illinois, Ingersoll followed him to the riverfront city along the Ohio River. After a brief time there, he accepted the deputy clerk position with John E. Hall, the county clerk and circuit clerk of Gallatin County, and also a son-in-law of John Hart Crenshaw. On November 11, 1856, Ingersol caught Hall in his arms when the son of a political opponent assassinated his employer in their office.

When he relocated to Shawneetown, he continued to read law with Judge William G. Bowman who had a large library of both law and the classics. In addition to his job as a clerk, he and his brother began their law practice using the name E.C. and R.G. Ingersoll. During this time, they also had an office in Raleigh, Illinois, then the county seat of neighboring Saline County. As attorneys following the court circuit he often practiced alongside Cunningham's soon-to-be son-in-law, John A. Kogan, the state's attorney and political ally to Hall.

With his earlier mentor Cunningham having moved back to Marion after the land office's closing in 1856, and Logan's relocation to Benton, Illinois, after his marriage that autumn, Ingersoll and his brother moved to Peoria, Illinois, where they finally settled in 1857.

Ingersoll was involved with several major trials as an attorney, notably the Star Route trials, a major political scandal in which his clients were acquitted. He also defended a New Jersey man charged with blasphemy. Although he did not win the acquittal, his vigorous defense is considered to have discredited blasphemy laws and few other prosecutions followed.

For a time, Ingersoll represented con artist James Reavis, the "Baron of Arizona", pronouncing his Peralta Land Grant claim valid.

**Civil War.** With the beginning of the American Civil War, he raised the 11th Regiment Volunteer Cavalry of the Union Army and assumed command. The regiment fought in the Battle of Shiloh. Ingersoll was later captured in a skirmish with the Confederates near Lexington, Tennessee on December 18, 1862, then paroled – i.e. released on his oath that he would not fight again against the Confederate States of America until formally exchanged for a capture of Confederate soldiers or officers of like rank who were often under parole themselves, making the practice a matter of honor and formality, which could be extended to individuals or even entire regiments *en-*

*masse*. This was an old practice which was still commonly observed early in the war, until the Dix-Hill Cartel broke down under political distress. Unable to perform his duties under his officer's commission while paroled, he tendered his resignation as commanding officer on June 30, 1863.

**Entry into politics.** After the war, he served as Illinois Attorney General. He was a prominent member of the Republican Party and, though he never held elective office, he was nonetheless an active participant in politics. According to Robert Nisbet, Ingersoll was a "staunch Republican." His speech nominating James G. Blaine for the 1876 presidential election was unsuccessful as Rutherford B. Hayes received the Republican nomination, but the speech itself, known as the "Plumed Knight" speech was considered a model of political oratory. His opinions on slavery, women's suffrage, and other issues of the time would sometimes become part of the mainstream, but his atheism/agnosticism effectively prevented him from ever pursuing or holding political offices higher than that of state attorney general. Illinois Republicans tried to persuade him to campaign for governor on the condition that Ingersoll conceal his agnosticism during the campaign, which he refused to do.

**Oratory and free thought.** On October 30, 1880, Ingersoll was introduced as "The Great Agnostic" by Rev. Henry Ward Beecher, before a political speech delivered to a large audience at the Academy of Music in Brooklyn. In an unpublished 1881 lecture entitled "The Great Infidels," he attacked the doctrine of Hell: "All the meanness, all the revenge, all the selfishness, all the cruelty, all the hatred, all the infamy of which the heart of man is capable, grew, blossomed, and bore fruit in this one word – Hell." He opposed the

Chinese Exclusion Act and supported a more lenient policy toward Chinese workers coming to the United States.

**Membership of The Lambs.** Ingersoll was elected to The Lambs Theatre Club in 1889 and gave an address to their first public "gambol" at the Broadway Theatre on March 3, 1891. His address "brought many laughs."

**Death.** Ingersoll died from congestive heart failure at the age of 65. Soon after his death, his brother-in-law, Clinton P. Farrell, collected copies of Ingersoll's speeches for publication. The 12-volume "Dresden Editions" kept interest in Ingersoll's ideas alive and preserved his speeches for future generations. Ingersoll's ashes were interred in Arlington National Cemetery.

**Legacy.** Susan Jacoby credits Ingersoll for the revival of Thomas Paine's reputation in American intellectual history, which had decreased after the publication of The Age of Reason published during 1794-95. Paine postulated that men, not God, had written the Bible, and Ingersoll included this work in his lectures on freethinking. As the only freethinker of his time with a wide audience outside of the unbelieving circle, he reintroduced Paine's ideas to a new generation. In 2005, a popular edition of Ingersoll's work was published by Steerforth Press Edited by the Pulitzer Prize winning music critic, Tim Page, *What's God Got to do With It: Robert Ingersoll on Free Speech, Honest Talk on the Separation of Church and State* brought Ingersoll's thinking to a new audience.

**Friendship with Walt Whitman.** Ingersoll enjoyed a friendship with the poet Walt Whitman, who considered Ingersol the greatest orator of his time. "It should not be surprising that I am drawn to Ingersoll, for he is 'Leaves of Grass' ... he lives, embodies, the individuality I preach. I see in Bob Ingersoll the noblest specimen – American-flavored – pure out of the soil, spreading, giving, demanding light." The feeling was mutual. Upon Whitman's death in 1892, Ingersoll delivered the eulogy at the poet's funeral. The eulogy was published to great acclaim and is considered a classic

# Appendix E

# John Milton Hay

**From Wikipedia**

John Milton Hay (October 8, 1838 – July 1, 1905) was an American statesman and official whose career in government stretched over almost half a century. Beginning as a private secretary and an assistant for Abraham Lincoln, he became a diplomat. He served as United States Secretary of State under Presidents William McKinley and Theodore Roosevelt. Hay was also a biographer of Lincoln and wrote poetry and other literature throughout his life.

Born in Salem, Indiana to an anti-slavery family that moved to Warsaw, Illinois, Hay showed great potential from an early age, and his family sent him to Brown University. After graduation in 1858, Hay read law in his uncle's office in Springfield, Illinois, adjacent to that of Lincoln. Hay worked for Lincoln's successful presidential campaign and became one of his private secretaries in the White House. Throughout the American Civil War, Hay was close to Lincoln and stood by his deathbed after the President was shot. In addition to his other literary works, Hay co-authored, with John George Nicolay, a ten-volume biography of Lincoln that helped shape the assassinated president's historical image.

After Lincoln's death, Hay spent several years at diplomatic posts in Europe, then worked for the New York Tribune under Horace Greely and Whitelaw Reid. Hay remained active in politics, and from 1879 to 1881 served as Assistant Secretary of State. Afterward he returned to the private sector, remaining there until President McKinley, to whom he had been a major backer, made him the Ambassador to the United Kingdom in 1897. Hay became the Secretary of State the following year.

Hay served for nearly seven years as Secretary of State under President McKinley and, after McKinley's assassination, under Theodore Roosevelt. Hay was responsible for negotiating the Open

Door Policy, which kept China open to trade with all countries on an equal basis, with international powers. By negotiating the Hay-Pauneforte Treaty with the United Kingdom, the (ultimately unratified) Hay-Herran Treaty with Columbia, and finally the Hay-Bunau-Varilla Treaty with the newly independent Republic of Panama, Hay also cleared the way for the building of the Panama Canal.

**Early Life.** John Milton Hay was born in Salem, Indiana, on October 8, 1838. He was the third son of Dr. Charles Hay and the former Helen Leonard. Charles Hay, born in Lexington, Kentucky, hated slavery and moved to the North in the early 1830s. A doctor, he practiced in Salem. Helen's father, David Leonard, had moved his family west from Assonet, Massachusetts, in 1818, but died in route to Vincennes, Indiana, and Helen relocated to Salem in 1830 to teach school. They married there in 1831. Charles was not successful in Salem, and moved with his wife and children to Warsaw, Illinois, in 1841.

John attended the local schools, and in 1849 his uncle Milton Hay invited John to live at his home in Pittsfield, Pike County, and attend a well-regarded local school, the John D. Thompson Academy. Milton was a friend of Springfield attorney Abraham Lincoln and had read law in the firm of Stuart and Lincoln. In Pittsfield, John first met John Nicolay who at the time was a 20-year-old newspaperman. Once John Hay completed his studies there, the 13-year-old was sent to live with his grandfather in Springfield and attend school there. His parents and Uncle Milton (who financed the boy's education) sent him to Brown University in Providence, Rhode Island, alma mater of his late maternal grandfather.

**Student and Lincoln supporter.** Hay enrolled at Brown in 1855. Although he enjoyed college life, he did not find it easy: his Western clothing and accent made him stand out; he was not well prepared academically and was often sick. Hay nevertheless gained a reputation as a star student and became a part of Providence's literary circle that included Sarah Helen Whitman and Nora Perry. He wrote poetry and experimented with hashish. Hay received his Master of Arts in 1858, and was, like his grandfather before him, Class Poet. He returned to Illinois. Milton Hay had moved his practice to Springfield, and John became a clerk in his firm, where he could study law. Milton Hay's firm was one of the most prestigious in Illinois. Lincoln maintained offices next door and was a rising star in the Republican Party. Hay recalled an earlier encounter with Lincoln:

*He came into the law office where I was reading … with a copy of 'Harper's Magazine' in hand, containing Senator Douglas's famous article on Popular Sovereignty [whether residents of each territory could decide on slavery]. Lincoln seemed greatly roused by what he had read. Entering the office without a salutation, he said: "This will never do. He puts the moral element out of this question. It won't stay out."*

Hay then made speeches and wrote newspaper articles boosting Lincoln. When Nicolay, who had been Lincoln's private secretary for the campaign, found he needed help with the huge amounts of correspondence, Hay worked full time for Lincoln for six months.

After Lincoln was elected, Nicolay, who continued as Lincolns private secretary, recommended that Hay be hired to assist him at the White House. Lincoln is reported to have said, "We can't take all Illinois with us down to Washington" but then "Well, let Hay come." Kushner and Sherrill were dubious about "the story of Lincoln's offhand appointment of Hay" as fitting well into Hay's self-image of never having been an office-seeker, but poorly into the realities of Springfield polities of the 1860's. Hay must have expected some reward for handling Lincoln's correspondence for months. Hay biographer John Taliaferro suggests that Lincoln engaged Nicolay and Hay to assist him, rather than more seasoned men, both "out of loyalty and surely because of the competence and compatibility that his two young aides had demonstrated." Historian Joshua Zeitz argues that Lincoln was moved to hire Hay when Milton agreed to pay his nephew's salary for six months.

**AMERICAN CIVIL WAR. Secretary to Lincoln.** Milton Hay desired that his nephew go to Washington as a qualified attorney, and John Hay was admitted to the bar in Illinois on February 4, 1861. On February 11 he embarked with President-elect on a circuitous journey to Washington. By this time several Southern states had succeeded to form the Confederate States of America in reaction to the election of Lincoln, seen as an opponent of slavery. When Lincoln was sworn in on March 4, Hay and Nicolay moved into the White House, sharing a shabby bedroom. As there was only authority for payment of one presidential secretary (Nicolay), Hay was appointed to a post in the Interior Department at $1,600 per year, seconded to service at the White House. They were available to Lincoln 24 hours a day. As Lincoln took no vacations as president and worked seven days a week, often until 11 pm (or later during crucial battles,) the burden on his secretaries was heavy.

Hay and Nicolay divided their responsibilities, Nicolay tending to assist Lincoln in his office and in meetings, while Hay dealt with the correspondence, which was voluminous. Both men tried to shield Lincoln from office-seekers and others who wanted to meet with the

President. Unlike the dour Nicolay, Hay, with his charm, escaped much of the hard feelings from those denied Lincoln's presence. Abolitionist Thomas Wentworth Higginson described Hay as "a nice young fellow who unfortunately looks about seventeen and is oppressed with the necessity of behaving like seventy." Hay continued to write, anonymously, for newspapers, sending in columns calculated to make Lincoln appear a sorrowful man, religious and competent, giving of his life and health to preserve the Union. Similarly, Hay served as what Taliaferro deemed a White House propagandist in his columns explaining away losses such as that at First Bull Run in July 1861.

Despite the heavy workload – Hay wrote that he was busy 20 hours a day – he tried to make as normal a life as possible, eating meals with Nicolay at Willard's Hotel, going to the theater with Abraham and Mary Todd Lincoln, and reading *Les Misérables* in French. Hay, still in his early 20's, spent time both in barrooms and at cultured get-togethers in the homes of Washington's elite. The two secretaries often clashed with Mary Lincoln, who resorted to various stratagems to get the dilapidated White House restored without depleting Lincoln's salary, which had to cover entertainment and other expenses. Despite the secretaries' objections, Mrs. Lincoln was generally the victor and managed to save almost 70% of her husband's salary in his four years in office.

After the death of Lincoln's 11-year-old son Willie in February 1862 (an event not mentioned in Hay's diary or correspondence), "it was Hay who became, if not a surrogate son, then a young man who stirred a higher form of parental nurturing that Lincoln, despite his best intentions, did not successfully bestow on either of his surviving children.

Lincoln and his two secretaries. Hay is on the right.

According to Hay biographer Robert Gale, "Hay came to adore Lincoln for his goodness, patience, understanding, sense of humor, humility, magnanimity, sense of justice, healthy skepticism, resilience and power, love of the common man, and mystical patriotism." Speaker of the House, Galusha Grow, stated, "Lincoln was very much attached to him"; writer Charles G. Halpine, who knew Hay then, later recorded that "Lincoln loved him as a son."

Hay and Nicolay accompanied Lincoln to Gettysburg, Pennsylvania, for the dedication of the cemetery there, where were interred many of those who fell at the Battle of Gettysburg. Although they made much of Lincoln's brief Gettysburg Address in their 1890 multi-volume biography of Lincoln, Hay's diary states "the President, in a firm, free, way, with more grace than is his wont, said his half-dozen lines of consecration."

**Presidential Emissary.** Lincoln sent Hay away from the White House on various missions. In August 1861, Hay escorted Mary Lincoln and her children to Long Branch, New Jersey, a resort on the Jersey Shore, both as their caretaker and as a means of giving Hay a much-needed break. The following month, Lincoln sent him to Missouri to deliver a letter to Union General John C. Fremont, who had irritated the President with military blunders and by freeing local slaves without authorization, endangering Lincolns attempts to keep the border states in the Union.

In April 1863, Lincoln sent Hay to the Union-occupied South Carolina coast to report back on the ironclad vessels being used in an attempt to recapture Charleston Harbor. Hay then went on to the Florida coast. He returned to Florida in January 1864 after Lincoln had announced his Ten Percent Plan, that if ten percent of the 1860 electorate in a state took oaths of loyalty and to support emancipation, they could form a government with federal protection. Lincoln considered Florida, with its small population, a good test case, and made Hay a major, sending him to see if he could get sufficient men to take the oath. Hay spent a month in the state during February and March 1864, but Union defeats there reduced the area under federal control. Believing his mission impractical, he sailed back to Washington.

In July 1864, New York Publisher Horace Greeley sent word to Lincoln that there were Southern peace emissaries in Canada. Lincoln doubted that they actually spoke for Confederate president Jefferson Davis but had Hay journey to New York to persuade the publisher to go to Niagara Falls, Ontario, to meet with them and bring them to Washington. Greeley reported to Lincoln that the emissaries lacked accreditation by Davis but were confident they could bring both sides together. Lincoln sent Hay to Ontario with what became known as the Niagara Manifesto: that if the South laid down its arms, freed the slaves, and reentered the Union, it could expect liberal terms on other points. The Southerners refused to come to Washington to negotiate.

**Assassination of Lincoln.** By the end of 1864, with Lincoln reelected and the victorious war winding down, both Hay and Nicolay let it be known that they desired different jobs. Soon after Lincoln's second inauguration in March 1865, the two secretaries were appointed to the US delegation in Paris: Nicolay as consul and Hay as secretary of legation. Hay wrote to his brother Charles that the appointment was "entirely unsolicited and unexpected", a statement that Kushner and Sherrill found unconvincing given that Hay had spent hundreds of hours during the war with Secretary of State William H. Seward, who had often discussed personal and political matters with him, and the close relationship between the two men was so well known that office-seekers cultivated Hay as a means of getting to Seward. The two men were also motivated to find new jobs by their deteriorating relationship with Mary Lincoln, who sought their ouster, and by Nicolay's desire to wed his intended – he could not bring a bride to his shared room at the White House. They remained at the White House pending the arrival and training of replacements.

Hay did not accompany the Lincolns to Fords Theatre on the night of April 14, 1865, but remained at the White House, drinking whiskey with Robert Lincoln. When the two were informed that the President had been shot, they hastened to the Petersen House, a boarding house where the stricken Lincoln had been taken. Hay remained by Lincoln's deathbed through the night and was present when he died. At the moment of Lincoln's death, Hay observed "a look of unspeakable peace came upon his worn features." He heard Secretary Edwin Staton's declaration, "Now he belongs to the ages."

According to Kushner and Sherrill, "Lincolns death was for Hay a personal loss, like the loss of a father ... Lincoln's assassination erased any remaining doubts Hay had about Lincoln's greatness." In 1866, in a personal letter, Hay deemed Lincoln, "the greatest character since Christ." Taliaferro noted that "Hay would spend the rest of his life mourning Lincoln ... wherever Hay went and whatever he did, Lincoln would always be watching."

**Early diplomatic career.** Hay sailed for Paris at the end of June 1865. There he served under U.S. Minister of France, John Bigelow. The workload was not heavy, and Hay found time to enjoy the pleasures of Paris. When Bigelow resigned in Mid-1866, Hay, as was customary, submitted his resignation, though he was asked to remain until Bigelow's successor was in place, and stayed until January 1867. He consulted with Secretary of State Seward, asking him for "anything worth having." Seward suggested the post of Minister to Sweden, but reckoned without the new president, Andrew Johnson, who had his own candidate. Seward offered Hay a job as his private secretary, but Hay declined, and returned home to Warsaw, Illinois.

Initially happy to be home, Hay quickly grew restive, and he was glad to hear, in early June 1867, that he had been appointed secretary of legation to act as *charge d'affaires* at Vienna. He sailed for Europe the same month, and while in England visited the House of Commons, where he was greatly impressed by the chancellor of the Exchequer, Benjamin Disraeli. The Vienna post was only temporary until Johnson could appoint a *charge d'affaires* and have him confirmed by the Senate, and the workload was light, allowing Hay, who was fluent in German, to spend much of his time traveling. It was not until July 1868 that Henry Watts became Hay's replacement. Hay resigned, spent the remainder of the summer in Europe, then went home to Warsaw.

Unemployed again, in December 1868 Hay journeyed to the capital, writing to Nicolay that he "came to Washington in the peaceful pursuit of a fat office. But there is nothing just now available." Seward promised to wrestle with Andy "for anything that turns up," but nothing did prior to the departure of both Seward and Johnson from office on March 4, 1869. In May, Hay went back to Washington from Warsaw to press his case with the new Grant administration. The next month, due to the influence of his friends, he obtained the post of secretary of legation in Spain.

Although the salary was low, Hay was interested in serving in Madrid both because of the political situation there – Queen Isabella II had recently been deposed – and because the U.S. Minister was the swashbuckling former congressman, General Daniel Sickles. Hay hoped to assist Sickles in gaining U.S. control over Cuba, then a Spanish colony. Sickles was unsuccessful and Hay resigned in May 1870, citing the low salary, but remaining in his post until September. The two legacies of Hay's time in Madrid were magazine articles he wrote that became the basis of his first book, *Castilian Days*, and his lifelong friendship with Sickles's personal secretary, Alvey A. Adee, who would be a close aide to Hay at the State Department.

**Wilderness years (1870-1897). Tribune and marriage.** While still in Spain, Hay had been offered the position of assistant editor at the New York Tribune – both the editor, Horace Greeley, and his managing editor, Whitelaw Reid, were anxious to hire Hay. He joined the staff in October 1870. The Tribune was the leading reform newspaper in New York, and through mail subscriptions, the largest circulating newspaper in the nation. Hay wrote editorials for the Tribune, and Greeley soon proclaimed him the most brilliant writer of "breviers" (as such editorials were called) that he had ever had.

With his success as an editorial writer, Hay's duties expanded. In October 1871, he journeyed to Chicago after the great fire there, interviewing Mrs. O'Leary, whose cow was said to have started the blaze, describing her as "a woman with a lamp [who went] to the barn behind the house, to milk the cow with the crumpled temper, that kicked the lamp, that spilled the kerosene, that fired the straw that burned Chicago." His work at the Tribune came as his fame as a poet was reaching its peak, and one colleague described it as "a liberal education in the delights of intellectual life to sit in intimate companionship with John Hay and watch the play of that well-storied and brilliant mind." In addition to writing, Hay was signed by the prestigious Boston Lyceum Bureau, whose clients included Mark Twain and Susan B. Anthony, to give lectures on the prospects for democracy in Europe, and on his years in the Lincoln White House.

By the time President Grant ran for reelection in 1872, Grant's administration had been rocked by scandal, and some disaffected members of his party formed the Liberal Republicans, naming

Greeley as their candidate for president, a nomination soon joined in by the democrats. Hay who was unenthusiastic about the editor-turned-candidate, and in his editorials mostly took aim at Grant, who, despite the scandals, remained untarred, and who won a landslide victory in the election. Greeley died only weeks later, a broken man. Hay's stance endangered his hitherto sterling credentials in the Republican Party.

By 1873, Hay was wooing Clara Stone, daughter of Cleveland multimillionaire railroad and banking mogul Amasa Stone. Their marriage in 1874 made the salary attached to office a small consideration for the rest of his life. Amasa Stone needed someone to watch over his investments and wanted Hay to move to Cleveland to fill the post. Although the Hays initially lived in John's New York apartment and later in a townhouse there, they moved in June 1875 to Stone's ornate home on Cleveland's Euclid Avenue, "Millionaire's Row" and a mansion was quickly under construction for the Hays next-door.

On December 29, 1876, a bridge over Ohio's Ashtabula River collapsed. The bridge had been built from metal cast at one of Stone's mills and was carrying a train owned and operated by Stone's Lake Shore and Michigan Railway. Ninety-two people died; it was the worst rail disaster in American history up to that point. Blame fell heavily on Stone, who departed for Europe to recuperate and left Hay in charge of his businesses. The summer of 1877 was marked by labor disputes; a strike over wage cuts on the Baltimore and Ohio Railroad soon spread to the Lake Shore, much to Hay's outrage. He blamed foreign agitators for the dispute and vented his anger over the strike in his only novel, *The Bread-Winners* (1883).

**Return to politics.** Hay remained disaffected from the Republican Party in the mid-1870s. Seeking a candidate of either party he could support as a reformer, he watched as his favored Democrat, Samuel Tilden, gained his party's nomination, but his favored Republican, James G. Blain, did not, falling to Ohio Governor Rutherford B. Hayes, whom Hay did not support during the campaign. Hayes' victory in the election left Hay an outsider as he sought a return to politics, and he was initially offered no place in the new administration. Nevertheless, Hay attempted to ingratiate himself with the new president by sending him a gold ring with a strand of George Washington's hair, a gesture that Hayes deeply appreciated. Hay spent time working with Nicolay on the Lincoln biography and traveling in Europe. When Reid, who had succeeded Greely as editor of the Tribune, was offered the post of Minister to Germany in December 1878, he turned it down and recommended Hay. Secretary of State William M. Everts indicated Hay "had not been active enough in political efforts," to Hay's regret, who told Reid that he "would like a second-class commission uncommonly well."

From May to October 1879, Hay set out to reconfirm his credentials as a loyal Republican, giving speeches in support of candidates and attacking the Democrats. In October, President and Mrs. Hayes came to a reception at Hay's Cleveland home. When Assistant Secretary of State Frederick W. Seward resigned later that month, Hay was offered his place and accepted, after some hesitancy because he was considering running for Congress.

In Washington Hay oversaw a staff of eighty employees, renewing his acquaintance with his friend Henry Adams, and substituting for Everts at Cabinet meetings when the Secretary was out of town. In 1880 he campaigned for the Republican nominee for president, his fellow Ohioan, Congressman James A. Garfield. Hay felt that Garfield did not have enough backbone and hoped that Reid and others would "inoculate him with the gall which I fear he lacks." Garfield consulted Hay before and after his election as president on appointments and other matters but offered Hay only the post of private secretary (though he promised to increase its pay and power), and Hay declined. Hay resigned as assistant secretary effective March 31, 1881, and spent the next seven months as acting editor of the Tribune during Reid's extended absence in Europe. Garfield's death in September and Reid's return the following month left Hay again on the outside of political power looking in. He would spend the next fifteen years in that position.

**Wealthy Traveler (1881-1897) Author and dilettante.** After 1881 Hay did not again hold public office until 1897. Amasa Stone committed suicide in 1883; his death left the Hays very wealthy. They spent several months in most years traveling in Europe. The Lincoln biography absorbed some of Hay's time, the hardest work being done with Nicolay in 1884 and 1885; beginning in 1886 portions began appearing serially and the ten-volume biography was published in 1890.

In 1884, Hay and Adams commissioned architect Henry Hobson Richardson to construct houses for them on Washington's Lafayette Square; these were completed in 1886. Hay's house, facing the White House and fronting on sixteenth Street, was described even before completion as the finest house in Washington. The price for the combined tract, purchased from William Wilson Cocoran, was $73,800, of which Adams paid a third for his lot. Hay budgeted the construction cost at $50,000; the ornate 12,000 square feet mansion eventually cost over twice that. Despite their possession of two lavish houses, the Hays spent less than half the year in Washington and only a few weeks a year in Cleveland. They also spent time at The Fells, their summer residence in Newbury, New Hampshire. According to Gale, “for a full decade before his appointment in 1897 as ambassador to England, Hay was lazy and uncertain.”

Hay continued to devote much of his energy to Republican politics. In 1884, he supported Blain for president, donating considerable sums to the senator’s unsuccessful campaign against New York governor Grover Cleveland. Many of Hay’s friends were unenthusiastic about Blain’s candidacy, to Hay’s anger, and he wrote to editor Richard Watson Gilder, “I have never been able to appreciate the logic that induces some excellent people every four years because they cannot nominate the candidate they prefer to vote for the party they don’t prefer.” In 1888 Hay had to follow his own advice as his favored candidate, Ohio senator John Sherman, was unsuccessful at the Republican convention. After some reluctance, Hay supported the nominee, former Indiana senator Benjamin Harrison, who was elected. Though Harrison’s appointment whom Hay supported, included Blaine, Reid and Robert Lincoln, Hay was not asked to serve in the Harrison administration. In 1890 Hay spoke for Republican congressional candidates addressing a rally of 10,000 people in New York City, but the party was defeated, losing control of Congress. Hay contributed funds to Harison’s unsuccessful re-election effort, in part because Reid had been made Harrison’s 1892 running mate.

**McKinley backer.** Hay was an early supporter of Ohio’s William McKinley and worked closely with McKiney’s political manager, Cleveland industrialist Mark Hanna. In 1889 Hay supported McKinley in his unsuccessful effort to become speaker of the House. Four years later, McKinley – by then Governor of Ohio – faced a crisis when a friend whose notes he had imprudently co-signed went bankrupt during the Panic of 1893. The debts were beyond the governor's means to pay, and the possibility of insolvency threatened McKinley's promising political career. Hay was among those Hanna called upon to contribute, buying up $3,000 of the debt of over $100,000. Although others paid more, "Hay's checks were two of the first, and his touch was more personal, a kindness McKinley never forgot." The governor wrote, "How can I ever repay you and other dear friends?"

The same panic that nearly ruined McKinley convinced Hay that men like himself must take office to save the country from disaster. By the end of 1894 he was deeply involved in efforts to lay the groundwork for the governors 1896 presidential bid. It was Hay's job to persuade potential supporters that McKiney was worth baking. Nevertheless, Hay found time for a lengthy stay in New Hampshire – one visitor at The Fells in mid-1895 was Rudyard Kipling – and later in the year wrote, "the summer wanes and I have done nothing for McKinley." He atoned with a $500 check to Hanna, the first of many. During the winter of 1895-96 Hay passed along what he heard from other republicans influential in Washington, such as Massachusetts senator Henry Cabot Lodge.

Hay spent part of the spring and early summer of 1896 in the United Kingdom and elsewhere in Europe. There was a border dispute between Venezuela and British Guiana, and Cleveland's Secretary of State, Richard Olney, supported the Venezuelan position, announcing the Olney interpretation of the Monroe Doctrine. Hay told British Politicians that McKinley, if elected, would be unlikely to change course. McKinley was nominated in June 1896; still many

Britains were minded to support whoever became the Democratic candidate. This changed when the 1896 Democratic National Convention nominate former Nebraska congressman William Jennings Bryan on a "free silver" platform; he had electrified the delegates with his Cross of Gold speech. Hay reported to McKinley when he returned to Britain after a brief stay on the Continent during which Bryan was nominated in Chicago: "they were all scared out of their wits for fear Bryan would be elected, and very polite in their references to you."

Once Hay returned to the United States in early August, he went to The Fells and watched from afar as Bryan barnstormed the nation in his campaign while McKinley gave speeches from his front porch. Despite an invitation from the candidate, Hay was reluctant to visit McKinley at his home in Canton. "He has asked me to come, but I thought I would not struggle with the millions on his trampled lawn." In October, after basing himself at his Cleveland home and giving a speech for McKinley, Hay went to Canton at last, writing to Adams,

*I had been dreading it for a month thinking it would be like talking in a boiler factory. But he met me at the railroad station, gave me meat and took me upstairs and talked for two hours as calmly and serenely as if we were summer boarders in Bethlehem, at a loss for means to kill time. I was more struck than ever with his mask. It is a genuine Italian ecclesiastical face of the XVth Century.*

Hay was disgusted by Bryan's speeches, writing in Language that Taliaferro compares to The Bread-Winners that the Democrat "simply reiterates the unquestioned truths that every man with a clean shirt is a thief and ought to be hanged: that there is no goodness and wisdom except among the illiterate and criminal classes." Despite Bryan's strenuous efforts, McKinley won the election easily, with a campaign run by himself and Hanna, and well financed by supporters like Hay. Henry Adams later wondered, "I would give sixpence to know how much Hay paid for McKiney. His politics must have cost."

**Ambassador. Appointment.** In the post-election speculation as to who would be given office under McKinley, Hay's name figured prominently, as did that of Whitelaw Reid; both men sought high office in the State department, either as secretary or one of the major ambassadorial posts. Reid, in addition to his vice-presidential run, had been Minister to France under Harrison. An asthmatic, he handicapped himself by departing for Arizona Territory for the winter, leading to speculation about his health.

Hay was faster than Reid to realize that the race for these posts would be affected by Hanna's desire to be senator from Ohio, as with one of the state's places about to be occupied by the newly elected Joseph B. Foraker, the only possible seat for him was that held by Senator Sherman. As the Septuagenarian senator had served as Treasury Secretary under Hayes, only the secretaryship of state was likely to attract him and cause a vacancy that Hanna could fill. Hay knew that with only eight cabinet positions, only one could go to an Ohioan, and so he had no chance for a cabinet post. Accordingly, Hay encouraged Reid to seek the State position, while firmly ruling himself out as a possible candidate for that post and quietly seeking the inside track to the ambassador to London. Zeitz states that Hay "aggressively lobbied" for the position.

According to Taliaferro, "only after the deed was accomplished and Hay was installed as the ambassador to the Court of St. James's would it be possible to detect just how subtly and completely, he had finessed his ally and friend, Whitelaw Reid." A telegraph from Hay to

McKinley in the latter's papers, dated December 26 (most likely 1896) reveals the formers suggestion that McKinley tell Reid that the editor's friends had insisted that Reid not endanger his health through office, especially in London's smoggy climes. The following month, in a letter, Hay set forth his own case for the ambassadorship and urged McKinley to act quickly, as suitable accommodation in London would be difficult to secure. Hay gained his object (as did Hanna) and shifted his focus to appeasing Reid. Taliaferro states that Reid never blamed Hay, but Kushner and Sherrill recorded, "Reid was certain that he had been wronged" by Hay, and the announcement of Hay's appointment nearly ended their 26-year friendship.

Reaction in Britain to Hays appointment was generally positive, with George Smalley of The Times writing to him, "we want a man who is a true American yet not anti-English." Hay secured a Georgian house on Carlton House Terrace overlooking the Horse Guards parade with 11 servants. He brought with him Clara, their own silver, two carriages and five horses. Hay's salary of $17,000 "did not even begin to cover the cost of their extravagant lifestyle."

**Service.** During his service as ambassador, Hay attempted to advance the relationship between the U.S. and Britain. The United Kingdom had long been seen negatively by many Americans, a legacy of its role during the American revolution that was refreshed by its neutrality in the American Civil War when it allowed merchant raiders such as the *Alabama* to be constructed in British ports, which then preyed on the US-flagged ships. In spite of these acts, differences according to Taliaferro, "rapprochement made more sense than at any time in their respective histories." In his Thanksgiving Day address to the American Society in London in 1897, Hay echoed these points, "The great body of people in the United

States and England are friends … sharing that intense respect and reverence for order, liberty, and law which is so profound a sentiment in both countries." Although Hay was not successful in resolving specific controversies in his year and a third as ambassador, both he and British policymakers regarded his tenure as a success, because of the advancement of good feelings and cooperation between the two nations.

An ongoing dispute between the U.S. and Britain was over the practice of pelagic sealing, that is the capture of seals offshore of Alaska. The U.S. considered them American resources; the Canadians (Britain was still responsible for that dominion's foreign policy) contended that the mammals were being taken on the high seas, free to all. Soon after Hay's arrival, McKinley sent former Secretary of State John W. Foster to London to negotiate the issue. Foster quickly issued an accusatory note to the British that was printed in the newspapers. Although Hay was successful in getting Lord Salisbury, then both prime Minister and Foreign Secretary, to agree to a conference to decide the matter, the British withdrew when the U.S. also invited Russia and Japan, rendering the conference ineffective. Another issue on which no agreement was reached was that of bimetallism: McKinley had promised silver-leaning Republicans to seek an international agreement varying the price ratio between silver and gold to allow for free coinage of silver, and Hay was instructed to seek British participation. The British would only join if the Indian colonial government (on a silver standard until 1893) was willing; this did not occur and coupled with an improving economic situation that increased support for bimetallism in the United States, no agreement was reached.

Hay had little involvement in the crisis over Cuba that culminated in the Spanish-American War. He met with Lord Salisbury in October 1897 and gained assurances Britain would not intervene if the U.S. found it necessary to go to war against Spain. Hay's role was "to make friends and to pass along the English point of view to Washington." Hay spent much of early 1898 on an extended trip to the Middle East and did not return to London until the last week of March, by which time the USS *Maine* had exploded in Havana harbor. During the war he worked to ensure U.S-British amity, and British acceptance of the U.S. occupation of the Philippines – Salisbury and his government preferred that the U.S. have the islands than have them fall into the hands of the Germans. Hay succeeded in making sure that the British were "kept in the loop" with regards to the U. S. invasion of Cuba, and in both reassuring the British that none of their interests in Cuba would be harmed by the invasion, while simultaneously communicating those interests to the McKinley administration (McKinley was himself keen on maintaining a good relationship with the British.)

In its early days, Hays described the war "as necessary as it is righteous." In July, writing to former Assistant Secretary of the Navy Theodore Roosevelt, who had gained wartime glory by leading the Rough Riders volunteer regiment. Hay made a description of the war for which, according to Zeitz, he "is best remembered by man students of American history."

*It has been a splendid little war, begun with the highest motives, carried on with magnificent intelligence and spirit, favored by that Fortune that loves the brave. It is now to be concluded, I hope, with that fine good nature which is, after all, the distinguishing trait of the American character.*

Secretary Sherman had resigned on the eve of war, and was replaced by his first assistant, William R. Day. One of McKinley's Canton cronies, with little experience of statecraft, Day was never intended a more than a temporary wartime replacement. With America about to splash her flag across the Pacific, McKinley needed a secretary with stronger credentials. On August 14, 1898, Hay received a telegram from McKinley that Day would head the American delegation to the peace talks with Spain, and that Hay would be the new Secretary of State. After some indecision, Hay, who did not think he could decline and still remain as ambassador, accepted. British response to Hay's promotion was generally positive, and Queen Victoria, after he took formal leave of her at Osborne House, invited him again the following day, and subsequently pronounced him, 'the most interesting of all the Ambassadors I have known."

**Secretary of State. McKinley years.** John Hay was sworn in as Secretary of State on September 30, 1898. He needed little introduction to Cabinet meetings and sat at the president's right hand. Meetings were held in the Cabinet Room of the White House, where he found his old office and bedroom each occupied by several clerks. Now responsible for 1,300 federal employees, he leaned heavily for administrative help on his old friend Alvey Adee, the second assistant.

Hay believed that Americas most valuable foreign relationship by far was its relationship with Great Britain. As Secretary of State, he did everything he could to cultivate a positive relationship with London. Eventually this proved successful, one example of this success being the Hay-Pauncefote Treaty. Hay formed a habit of confiding in the British and sharing sensitive intelligence with them, while at the same time shutting out the governments of Spain, France, Germany and Russia. Senator Mark Hanna remarked that "Hay and McKinley are outrageously pro-British." The French ambassador remarked that "Hay is friendly to the British and unfriendly to us, we should regard him with much suspicion."

By the time Hay took office, the war was effectively over, and it had been decided to strip Spain of her overseas empire and transfer at least part of it to the United States. At the time of Hay's swearing-in, McKinley was still undecided whether to take the Philippines, but by October finally decided to do so, and Hay sent instructions to Day and the other peace commissioners to insist on it. Spain yielded, and the result was the Treaty of Paris, narrowly ratified by the Senate in February 1899 over the objections of anti-imperialists.

Hay signs the Treaty of Paris 1899

**Open Door Policy.** By the 1890s China had become a major trading partner for Western nations and newly westernized Japan. China had its army severely weakened by several disastrous wars and several foreign nations took the opportunity to negotiate treaties with China that allowed them to control several coastal cities known as treaty-ports for use as military bases or trading centers. Within those jurisdictions, the nation in possession often gave preference to its own citizens in trade or in developing infrastructure such as railroads. Although the United States did not claim any parts of China, a third of the China trade was carried in American ships, and having an outpost near there was a major factor in deciding to retain the former Spanish colony of the Philippines in the Treaty of Paris.

Hay had been concerned about the Far East since the 1870s. As Ambassador, he had attempted to forge a common policy with the British, but the United Kingdom was willing to acquire territorial concessions in China (such as Hong Kong) to guard its interests there whereas McKinley was not. In March 1898 Hay warned that Russia, Germany and France were seeking to exclude Britain and America from the China trade, but he was disregarded by Sherman, who accepted assurances to the contrary from Russia and Germany.

McKinley was of the view that equality of opportunity for American trade in China was key to success there, rather than colonial acquisitions; that Hay shared these views was one reason for his appointment as Secretary of State. Many influential Americans, seeing coastal China being divided into spheres of influence, urged McKinley to join in; still, in his annual message to Congress in December 1898, he stated that as long as Americans were not discriminated against, he saw no need for the United States to become "an actor in the scene."

As Secretary of State, it was Hay's responsibility to put together a workable China policy. He was advised by William Rockhill, an old China hand. Also influential was Charles Beresford, a British Member of Parliament who gave a number of speeches to American businessmen, met with McKinley and Hay, and in a letter to the secretary stated that "it is imperative for American interests as well as our own that the policy of the 'open door' should be maintained." Assuring that all would play on an even playing field in China would give the foreign powers little incentive to dismember the Chinese Empire through territorial acquisition.

In mid-1899 the British inspector of Chinese maritime customs, Alfred Hippisley, visited the United States. In a letter to Rockhill, a friend, he urged that the United States and other powers agree to uniform Chinese tariffs, including in the enclaves. Rockhill passed the letter on to Hay, and subsequently summarized the thinking of Hippisey and others, that there should be "an open market through China for our trade on terms of equality with all foreigners." Hay was in agreement, but feared Senate and popular opposition, and wanted to avoid Senate ratification of a treaty. Rockhill drafted the first Open Door note, calling for equality of commercial opportunity for foreigners in China.

Hay formally issued his Open Door note on September 6, 1899. This was not a treaty and did not require the approval of the Senate. Most of the power had at least some caveats, and negotiations continued through the remainder of the year. In March, 1900, Hay announced that all powers had agreed, and he was not contradicted. Former secretary Day wrote to Hay congratulating him, "moving at the right time and in the right manner, you have secured a diplomatic triumph in the 'open door' in China of the first importance to your country."

**Boxer Rebellion.** Little thought was given to the Chinese reaction to the Open-Door note. The Chinese minister in Washington, Wu Ting-fang, did not learn of it until he read of it in the newspapers. Among those in China who opposed Western influence there was a movement in Shantung Province in the north, that became known as the Fists of Righteous Harmony, or Boxers, after the martial arts they practiced. The Boxers joined by imperial troops had cut the railroad between Peking and the coast, killed many missionaries and converts, and besieged the foreign legations. Hay faced a precarious situation; how to rescue the Americans trapped in Peking, and how to avoid giving the other powers an excuse to partition China, in an election year when there was already Democratic opposition to what they deemed American imperialism.

As American troops were sent to China to relieve the nation's legation, Hay sent a letter to foreign powers (often called the Second Open Door note). Stating while the United States wanted to see lives preserved and the guilty punished, it intended that China not be dismembered. Hay issued this on July 3, 1900, suspecting that the powers were quietly making private arrangements to divide up China. Communication between the foreign legations and the outside world had been cut off, and their personnel there were falsely presumed slaughtered, but Hay realized that Minister Wu could get a message in, and Hay was able to establish communication. Hay suggested to the Chinese government that it now cooperate for its own good. When the foreign relief force, principally Japanese but including 2,000 Americans, relieved the legations and sacked Peking, China was made to pay a huge indemnity but there was no cessation of land.

**Death of McKinley.** McKinley's vice president, Garret Hobart, had died in November 1899. Under the laws then in force, he made Hay next in line to the presidency should anything happen to McKinley. There was a presidential election in 1900, and McKinley was unanimously renominated at the Republican National Convention that year. He allowed the convention to make its own choice of running mate, and it selected Roosevelt, by then governor of New York. Senator Hanna bitterly opposed that choice, but nevertheless raised millions for the McKinley/Roosevelt ticket, which was elected.

Hay accompanied McKinley on his nationwide train tour in mid-1900, during which both men visited California and saw the Pacific Ocean for the only times in their lives. The summer of 1901 was tragic for Hay; his older son, Adelbert, who had been consul in Pretoria during the Boer War and was about to become McKinley's personal secretary, died in a fall from a hotel window.

Secretary Hay was at The Fells when McKinley was shot by Leon Czolgosz, an anarchist, on September 6 in Buffalo. With Vice President Roosevelt and much of the cabinet hastening to the bedside of McKinley, who had been operated on (it was thought successfully) soon after the shooting Hay planned to go to Washington to manage the communication with foreign governments, but presidential secretary George Cortelyou urged him to come to Buffalo. He traveled to Buffalo on September 10; hearing on his arrival an account of the Presidents recovery, Hay responded that McKinley would die. He was more cheerful after visiting McKinley, giving a statement to the press, and went to Washington, as Roosevelt and other officials also dispersed. Hay was about to return to New Hampshire on the 13th when word came that McKinley was dying. Hay remained at his office and the next morning, on the way to Buffalo, the former Rough Rider received from Hay his first communication as head of state, officially informing President Roosevelt of McKinley's death.

**Theodore Roosevelt Administration. Staying on.** Hay, again next in line to the presidency, remained in Washington as McKinley's body was transported to the capital by funeral train, and stayed there as the late president was taken to Canton for interment. He had admired McKinley, describing him as "awfully like Lincoln in many respects" and wrote to a friend, "what a strange and tragic fate it has been of mine – to stand by the bier of three of my dearest friends, Lincoln, Garfield, and McKinley, three of the gentlest of men, all risen to be head of the State, and all done to death by assassins."

By letter, Hay offered his resignation to Roosevelt while the new president was still in Buffalo, amid newspaper speculation that Hay would be replaced. When Hay met the funeral train in Washington, Roosevelt greeted him at the station and immediately told him that he must stay on as secretary. According to Zeitz, "Roosevelt's accidental ascendance to the presidency made John Hay an essential anachronism --- the wise elder statesman and senior member of the cabinet, he was indispensable to TR, who even today remains the youngest president ever."

The deaths of his son and of McKinley were not the only griefs Hay suffered in 1901 – on September 26, John Nicolay died after a long illness, as did Hay's close friend, Clarence King on Christmas Eve.

**Panama.** Hay's involvement in the efforts to have a canal joining the oceans in central America went back to his time as Assistant Secretary of State under Hayes, when he served as translator for

Ferdinand de Lesseps in his efforts to interest the American government in investing in his canal company. President Hayes was only interested in the idea of a canal under American control, which de Lesseps project would not be. By the time Hay became Secretary of State, de Lesseps's project in Panama (then a Colombian province) had collapsed, as had an American-run project in Nicaragua. The 1850 Clayton-Bulwer Treaty (between the United States and Britain) forbade the United States from building a Central American canal that it exclusively controlled, and Hay from early in his tenure, sought the removal of this restriction. But the Canadians for whose foreign policy Britain was still available, saw the canal matter as their greatest leverage to get other disputes resolved in their favor, persuaded Salisbury not to resolve it independently. Shortly before Hay took office, Britain and the U.S. agreed to establish a Joint High Commission to adjudicate the unsettled matters, which met in late 1898 but made slow progress, especially on the Canada-Alaska boundary.

The Alaska issue became less contentious in August 1899 when the Canadians accepted a provisional boundary pending final settlement. With Congress anxious to begin work on a canal bill, and increasingly likely to ignore the Clayton-Bulwer restriction, Hay and British Ambassador Julian Paunceforte began work on a new treaty in January 1900. The first Hay-Paunceforte Treaty was sent to the Senate the following month, where it met a cold reception, as the terms forbade the United States from blockading or fortifying the canal, that was to be open to all nations in wartime as in peace. The Senate Foreign Relations Committee added an amendment allowing the U.S. to fortify the canal, then in March postponed further consideration until after the 1900 election. Hay submitted his resignation, which McKinley refused. The treaty, as amended, was ratified by the senate in December, but the British would not agree to the changes.

Despite the lack of agreement, Congress was enthusiastic about a canal, and was inclined to move forward with or without a treaty. Authorizing legislation was slowed by a discussion on whether to take the Nicaraguan or Panamanian route. Much of the negotiation was a revised treaty allowing the U.S. to fortify the canal, took place between Hay's replacement in London, Joseph H. Choate, and the British Foreign Secretary, Lord Lansdowne, and the second Hay-Paunceforte Treaty was ratified by the senate by a large margin on December 6, 1901.

Seeing that the Americans were likely to build a Nicaragua Canal, the owners of the defunct French company, including Philippe Bunau-Varilla, who still had exclusive rights to the Panama route, lowered their price. Beginning in early 1902 President Roosevelt became a backer of the latter route, and Congress passed legislation for it, if it could be secured within a reasonable time. In June, Roosevelt told Hay to take personal charge of the negotiations with Colombia. Later that year, Hay began talks with Colombia's acting minister in Washington, Tomas Heran. The Hay-Herran Treaty, granting $10 million to Colombia for the right to build a canal plus $250,000 annually, was signed on January 22, 1903, and ratified by the United States Senate two months later. In August, however, the treaty was rejected by the Colombian Senate.

Roosevelt was minded to build the canal anyway, using an earlier treaty with Colombia that gave the U.S. transit rights in regard to the Panama Railroad. Hay predicted "an insurrection on the Isthmus of Panama against the regime of folly and graft ... at Bogota." Bunau-Varilla gained meetings with both men and assured them that a resolution and a Panamanian government more friendly to a canal was coming. In October, Roosevelt ordered Navy ships to be stationed near Panama. The Panamanians duly revolted in early November 1903, with Colombian interference deterred by the presence of U.S. forces. By prearrangement, Bunau-Varilla was appointed representative of the nascent nation in Washington, and quickly negotiated the Hay-Bunau-Varilla Treaty, signed November 18, giving the United States the right to build the canal in a zone 10 miles (16 km) wide, over which the U.S. would exercise full jurisdiction. This was less than satisfactory to the Panamanian diplomats who arrived in Washington shortly after the signing, but they did not dare renounce it. The treaty was approved by the two nations and the work on the Panama Canal began in 1904. Hay wrote to Secretary of War Elihu Root praising "the perfectly regular course which the President did follow as much preferable to armed occupation of the isthmus."

**Relationship with Roosevelt, other events.** Hay had met the President's father, Theodore Roosevelt, Sr. during the Civil War and during his time at the Tribune came to know the adolescent "Teddy", twenty years younger than himself. Although before becoming president, Roosevelt often wrote fulsome letters of praise to Secretary Hay, his letters to others then and after were less complimentary. Hay felt Roosevelt too impulsive and privately opposed his inclusion on the ticket in 1900, though he quickly wrote a congratulatory note after the convention.

As President and Secretary of State, the two men took pains to cultivate a cordial relationship. Roosevelt read all ten volumes of the Lincoln biography and in mid-1903 wrote to Hay that by then "I have had a chance to know far more fully what a really great Secretary of

State you are." Hay for his part publicly praised Roosevelt as "young, gallant, able and brilliant," words that Roosevelt wrote that he hoped would be engraved on his tombstone.

Privately and in correspondence with others, they were less generous: Hay grumbled that while McKinley would give him his full attention, Roosevelt was always busy with others, and it would be "an hour's wait for a minute's talk." Roosevelt, after Hay's death in 1905, wrote to Senator Lodge that Hay had not been "a great Secretary of State ... under me he accomplished little ... his usefulness to me was almost exclusively the usefulness of a fine figurehead." Nevertheless, when Roosevelt successfully sought election in his own right in 1904, he persuaded the aging and infirm Hay to campaign for him, and Hay gave a speech linking the administration's policies with those of Lincoln: "there is not a principle avowed by the Republican party today which is out of harmony with his [Lincoln's] teaching or inconsistent with his character." Kushner and Sherrill suggested that the differences between Hay and Roosevelt were more style than ideological substance.

In December 1902, the German government asked Roosevelt to arbitrate its dispute with Venezuela over unpaid debts. Hay did not think this appropriate as Venezuela also owed the U.S. money, and quickly arranged for the International Court of Arbitration in The Hague to step in. Hay supposedly said, as final details were being worked out, "I have it all arranged. If Teddy will keep his mouth shut until tomorrow noon!" Hay and Roosevelt also differed over the composition of the Joint High Commission that was to settle the Alaska boundary dispute. The commission was to be composed of "impartial jurists' and the British and Canadians duly appointed notable judges. Roosevelt appointed politicians, including Secretary

Root and Senator Lodge. Although Hay was supportive of the Presidents choices in public, in private he protested loudly to Roosevelt, complained by letter to his friends, and offered his resignation. Roosevelt declined it, but the incident confirmed his belief that Hay was too much of an Anglophile to be trusted where Britain was concerned. The American position on the boundary dispute was imposed on Canada by a 4-2 vote, with one English judge joining the three Americans.

One incident involving Hay that benefitted Roosevelt politically was the kidnapping of Greek-American playboy Ion Perdicaris in Moracco by chieftain Mulai Ahmed er Raisuli, an opponent of Sultan Abdelaziz. Raisuli demanded a ransom, but also wanted political prisoners to be released and control of Tangier in place of the military governor. Raisuli supposed Perdicaris to be a wealthy American and hoped United States pressure would secure his demands. In fact, Perdicaris, though born in New Jersey, had renounced his citizenship during the Civil War to avoid Confederate confiscation of his property in South Carolina, and had accepted Greek naturalization, a fact not generally known until years later, but that decreased Roosevelt's appetite for military action. The sultan was ineffective in dealing with the incident, and Roosevelt considered seizing the Tangier waterfront, source of much of Abdelaziz's income, as a means of motivating him. With Raisuli's demands escalating, Hay, with Roosevelt's approval, finally cabled the consul-general in Tangiers, Samuel Gummere: "We want Perdicaris alive or Raisuli dead. We desire least possible complications with Morocco or other Powers. You will not arrange for landing marines or seizing customs house without specific direction from the State department."

The 1904 Presidential National Convention was in session, and the Speaker of the House, Joseph Cannon, its chair, read the first sentence of the cable – and only the first sentence – to the convention, electrifying what had been a humdrum coronation of Roosevelt. "The results were perfect. This was the fighting Teddy that America loved, and his frenzied supporters – and American chauvinists elsewhere – roared in delight." In fact, by then the sultan had already agreed to the demands, and Perdicaris was released. What was seen as tough talk boosted Roosevelt's election chances.

**Final months and death.** Hay never fully recovered from the death of his son, Adelbert, writing in 1904 to his close friend Lizzie Cameron that the death of our boy made my wife and me old, at once and for the rest of our lives. Although Hay gave speeches in support of Roosevelt, he spent much of the Fall of 1904 at his New Hampshire house or with his younger brother Charles, who was ill in Boston. After the election Roosevelt asked Hay to remain another four years. Hay asked for time to consider, but the President did not allow it, announcing to the press two days later that Hay would stay at his post. Early 1905 saw futility for Hay as a number of treaties he had negotiated were defeated or amended by the senate – one involving the British dominion of Newfoundland due to Senator Lodge's fears it would harm his fisherman constituents. Others promoting arbitration were voted down or amended because the Senate did not want to be bypassed in the settlement of international disputes.

By Roosevelt's inauguration on March 4, 1905, Hay's health was so bad that both his wife and his friend Henry Adams insisted on his going to Europe, where he could rest and get medical treatment. Presidential doctor Presley issued a statement that Hay was suffering from overwork, but in letters the secretary hinted his conviction that he did not have long to live. An eminent physician in Italy prescribed medicinal bathes for Hay's heart condition, and he duly journeyed to Bad Nauheim, near Frankfurt Germany. Kaiser Wilhelm II was among the monarchs who wrote to Hay asking him to visit, though he declined; Belgian King Leopold II succeeded in seeing him by showing up at his hotel unannounced. Adams suggested that Hay retire while there was still enough life left in him to do so, and that Roosevelt would be delighted to act as his own Secretary of State. Hay jokingly wrote to sculptor Augustus Saint-Gaudens that "there is nothing the matter with me except old age, the Senate, and one or two other mortal maladies."

After the course of treatment, Hay went to Paris and began to take on his workload again by meeting with the French foreign minister, Theophile Delcassse. In London, King Edward VII broke protocol by meeting with Hay in a small drawing room, and Hay lunched with Whitelaw Reid, ambassador in London at last. There was not time to see all who wished to see Hay on what he knew was his final visit.

On his return to the United States, despite his family's desire to take him to New Hampshire, the secretary went to Washington to deal with departmental business and "say *Ave Caesar!* to the President," as Hay put it. He was pleased to learn that Roosevelt was well on his way to settling the Russo-Japanese War, an action for which the President would win the Nobel Peace Prize. Hay left Washington for the last time on June 23, 1905, arriving in New Hampshire the following day. He died there on July 1 of his heart ailment and complications. Hay was interred in Lake View Cemetery in Cleveland, near the grave of Garfield, in the presence of Roosevelt and many dignitaries, including Robert Lincoln.

American Heritage Magazine

Volume 63, Issue 1 - Spring, 2018

# Lincoln's Boys

## Joshua Zeitz

***John Nicolay and John Hay were Lincoln's two closest aids in the White House and helped to craft the image of the President we have today.***

Less than three weeks before his death, John Milton Hay awoke in his cabin room on the RMS Baltic as the great ocean liner, still the jewel of the White Star Line, steamed a course from Liverpool to New York. He reached for his diary and composed one of its final entries.

It was June 1905. Electric lights and street cars lined hundreds of American towns. Phonographs and telephones were quickly becoming common fixtures in middle-class living rooms, and for a nickel city folk could gaze into large wood and steel boxes and marvel at moving picture images of prizefighters, ballplayers, and ballerinas. John D. Rockefeller and Andrew Carnegie represented the extremes of American wealth and power. It had already been two years since the Wright brothers conducted the first manned test flight of an airplane. In Germany, the theoretical physicist Albert Einstein had recently published a paper on the "photoelectric effect" and was fast at work developing his theory of relativity. In Vienna, Sigmund Freud published his path-breaking volume, Three Essays on the Theory of Sexuality.

In his youth, John Hay could scarcely have imagined this world. A child of the western prairie, he was raised in the age of iron and grew to manhood in the age of steel. A noted poet and historian, former newspaper editor and railroad executive, Hay had served as U.S. ambassador to Britain and since 1898, Secretary of State – first under President William McKinley and then, after 1901, under President Theodore Roosevelt. He was one of the most powerful men in the world. But his bright spirit was fast burning out a frail body. In his final weeks his mind wandered back to the simpler world of his youth.

"I dreamed last night that I was in Washington," Hay confided to his diary, "and that I went to the White House to report to the President, who turned out to be Mr. Lincoln. He was very kind and considerate, and sympathetic about my illness. He gave me two unimportant letters to answer. I was pleased that this slight order was within my power to obey. I was not in the least surprised at Lincolns presence in the White House. But the whole impression of the dream was one of overpowering melancholy."

John Hay and John Nicolay were prairie boys who met in 1851 and forged a close friendship that endured over a half century. Fortune placed them in the right place (Springfield, Illinois) at the right time (1860) and offered them a front-row seat to one of the most tumultuous political and military upheavals in American History, then or since.

As Abraham Lincoln's private secretaries, they became, both literally and figuratively, closer to the president than anyone outside his immediate family. Still young men in their twenties, they lived and worked on the second floor of the White House performing the roles and functions of a modern-day chief of staff, press secretary, political director, and presidential body man. Above all, they guarded the "last door which opens into the awful presence" of the commander in chief, in the words of Noah Brooks, a journalist and one of many Washington insiders who coveted their jobs, resenting their influence, and thought them a little too big for their britches ("a fault for which it seems to me either nature or our tailors are to blame,"

Hay once quipped.) "These secretaries are young men," Brooks grumbled, "and the least said of them the better, perhaps."

In demeanor and temperament, they could not have been more different. Short-tempered and dyspeptic, Nicolay cut a brooding figure to those seeking the president's time or favor. William Stoddard, an assistant secretary under their supervision, later remarked that Nicolay was "decidedly German in his manner of telling men what he thought of them... People who do not like him – because they cannot use him perhaps – say he is sour and crusty, and it is a grand good thing, then, that he is."

Hay cultivated a softer image. He was, in the words of his contemporaries, a "comely young man with peach-blossom face – very witty – boyish in his manner, yet deep enough – bubbling over with some brilliant speech." An instant fixture in Washington social circles, fast friend of Robert Todd Lincoln's, and favorite among Republican congressmen who haunted the White House halls, he projected a youthful dash that balanced out Nicolay's more grim bearing.

Hay and Nicolay were party to the president's greatest official acts and most private moments. They were in the room when he signed the Emancipation Proclamation, and they were by his side at Gettysburg when he first spoke to the nation of "a new birth of freedom." When he could not sleep, which as the war progressed was often, Lincoln walked down the corridor to their private quarters and passed the time reciting Shakespeare or mulling over the day's political and military development. When his son Willie passed away in 1862, the first person to whom Lincoln turned was John Nicolay. When the president drew his last breath in April 1865, John Hay was by his bedside.

For the rest of their lives, even as they built their own families and career, Hay and Nicolay inspired a certain measure of wonder and awe. The greater Lincoln grew in death, the greater they grew for having known him so well and so intimately in life. Everyone wanted to know them, if only to ask what it had been like – what he had been like. It was a tough question to answer. Abraham Lincoln worked hard at being inscrutable. "The tones, the gesture, the kindling eye, and the mirth-provoking look defy the reporter's skill," wrote Brooks. William Herndon, Lincoln's law partner could fairly claim to have known him as well as any man during the Springfield days. But to Herndon, the future president "was the most-shut-mouthed man who ever lived. He always told only enough of his plans and purpose to induce the belief that he had communicated all," observed another friend, "yet he had reserved enough to have communicated nothing."

If anyone knew the mind of the inner president, it was the two secretaries. Witty and prolific letter writers, observant and incisive diarists, Hay and Nicolay left a remarkable record of Lincoln's evolution as chief executive. By their later account, they "came from Illinois to Washington with him, and remained at his side and in his service – separately or together – until the day of his death. "We were the daily and nightly witnesses of the incidents, the anxieties, the fears, and the hopes which pervaded the Executive Mansion and the National Capital during the war." Better than anyone else, they knew where the president was, what he was doing, and what he was thinking at almost every turn. It is little wonder that historians of the era consult their writings freely and frequently. But their life's work after the Civil War is a forgotten story.

"The boys" as the president affectionately called them, became Lincoln's official biographers. Enjoying exclusive access to his papers, which the Lincoln family closed to the public until 1947, they undertook a twenty-five-year mission to create a definitive and enduring historical image of their slain leader. It became the great undertaking of their lives. The culmination of these efforts – their exhaustive ten-volume biography which was widely serialized between 1885 and 1890 – constituted one of the most successful exercises in historical revisionism in American History. Writing against the rising currents of Southern apologia and a popular vogue for reunion and reconciliation, Hay and Nicolay pioneered the "Northern" interpretation of the Civil War – an interpretation whose influence waxed and waned but that created a standard against which every other historian and polemicist had to stake out his or her position. Hay and Nicolay helped invent the Lincoln we know today: the Great Emancipator, the sage father figure, the military genius, the greatest American orator, the brilliant political tactician, the master of a fractious cabinet who forged a "team of rivals" out of erstwhile challengers for the throne of the Lincoln Memorial Lincoln.

Abraham Lincoln was all of these, in some measure, there can be no doubt. But it is easy to forget how widely underrated Lincoln the president, and Lincoln the man, were on the eve of his death and how successful Hay and Nicolay were in elevating his place in the nation's collective historical memory. While Lincoln prided himself on his deep connection to "the people" – that nebulous body politic in whose collective wisdom he developed an almost mystic faith – he never succeeded in translating his immense popularity with the Northern public into similar regard among the nation's political and intellectual elites. The profound emotional bond that he shared with Union soldiers and their families, and his stunning electoral success in two successive presidential elections, never fully inspired an equivalent level of esteem by the influential men who governed the country and guarded its official history. To many of these men he remained in death what he was in life: the rail-splitter and country lawyer – good, decent and ill-fitted to the immense responsibilities that befell him in times of war.

Leading into the 1864 election cycle, many prominent members of Lincoln's own party agreed with the Iowa senator James Grimes that the administration "has been a disgrace from the very beginning to everyone who had anything to do with bringing it into power."

Charles Sumner the radical antislavery leader, fumed that the nation needed "a president with brains; one who can make a plan and carry it out." From across the political spectrum, influential writers and politicians blamed Lincoln for four years of military stalemate and setbacks and for a series of political blunders that cost his party dearly in the 1862 midterm elections. John Andrew, the governor of

Massachusetts, spoke for many Republicans when he explained his support of Lincoln's reelection. "The president," he said, "was essentially lacking in the quality of leadership, but now that he has been renominated, correction is possible ... Massachusetts will vote for the Union Cause at all events and will support Mr. Lincoln so long as he remains the candidate."

Years later, Hay remarked that had Lincoln "died in the days of doubt and gloom which preceded his reelection," rather than in the final weeks of the war, as the Union moved to secure its great victory, he would almost certainly have been remembered differently, despite his great acts and deeds.

But that is not how it happened. Assassinated on Good Friday, Lincoln became a Christ figure to many Americans who sought to make sense of the carnival of death and destruction that touched virtually every community over the preceding four years. But apotheosis was not Hays or Nicolay's objective. They sought to canonize their boss as a great leader among men, not a saint or a martyr. They remembered him as an innate leader of men, with a powerful grasp of political and military strategy. He was steadfast where other men wavered; he saw the long game, where others staggered from crisis to crisis; he alone enjoyed the trust of the Northern people. Americans today understand Abraham Lincoln much as Nicolay and Hay hoped they would. Theirs was a deliberate project of historical creation. They were "Lincoln men," Hay asserted, and they meant to tell their story so that the rest of the word would know the man whom they had known so intimately in their youth.

It was not an easy task to complete. Hay and Nicolay had to slug it out with lesser figures who had their own ideas about Lincoln's place in history. They were especially troubled by the historical amnesia that was quickly taking hold over the reunited states. In popular literature and journalism, the war was being recast as a brother's squabble over abstract political principles like federalism and states' rights, rather than as a moral struggle between slavery and freedom. Magazines and newspapers commonly took to celebrating the miliary valor of both Confederate and Union soldiers, as though bravery, rather than morality, were the chief quality to be commemorated. They also reimagined Lincoln as a conciliatory figure who was above politics and sectionalism, conveniently forgetting the social revolution unleashed by emancipation and ignoring his admonition – just weeks before his death – that "if God wills that [the war] continue until all the wealth piled by the bondsman's two hundred and fifty years of unrequited toil shall be sunk, and until every drop of blood drawn with the lash shall be paid by another drawn with the sword, as was said three thousand year ago, so still it must be said "'the judgments of the Lord are true and righteous altogether.'"

Nicolay and Hay viewed this revisionist tendency with alarm. While their editor and publisher hoped that the Nicolay-Hay volumes would "help unite the North and South as never before, around the story and experiences of the great President" the authors pointedly rejected the vogue for sectional reconciliation and emphasized the salient moral and political issues that divided the two sections before, and in many respects after the war. The war had been caused by "an uprising of the national conscience against a secular wrong" that could never be blotted out by romance of reunion. Though the influence of their interpretation of events would wax and wane over time it established the terms of a historiographical debate that persists to this day. As the only authorized biographers of Abrahan

Lincoln, they played a central role in determining how future generations would understand and imagine the sixteenth president.

More than just a story of history and memory, this book also addresses the ideological journey traveled by many men who came of age during the Civil War. Jolted to consciousness by the national debate over slavery, they were America's first "hope and change" generation. They forged new and expansive ideas about national citizenship on the fields of Shiloh and Gettysburg and in the halls of Congress. Yet in the decades that followed the war, many young men who began public life as antislavery crusaders seemed to be evolving into relatively conservative adults.

In some respects, there was great consistency in this evolution. The Republican Party, an organization that would remain central to the political identities of men like Hay and Nicolay, was founded on the laissez-faire proposition that free labor is always superior to slave labor. Regardless of color, people should be afforded the right to rise or fall on their talents and industry. Most Republicans continued to embrace this free market understanding of the world, but by the 1870s that vision was divorced from its radical antislavery roots and became a natural point of opposition to labor unions and advocates of urban and working-class Americans. During the war, Republicans had forged a strong alliance with capital and industry to subdue the South. After the war they saw no reason to divorce the party from its interests. Many men like Hay and Nicolay, who cut their teeth on antislavery politics, were comfortable with the inequalities that modern capitalism wrought. In their youth they were reformers; as they grew old, they became conservatives. It was not their thinking that changed as much as their context.

Little has been written about Nicolay's postwar career, as so much of it was devoted to preserving the memory of Lincoln. More has been written about Hay's literary career, his friendship with Henry Adams, and his service as Secretary of State under McKinley and Roosevelt. In many ways, he was one of the most extraordinary men of his generation.

www.ingramcontent.com/pod-product-compliance
Lightning Source LLC
LaVergne TN
LVHW090556110826
845146LV00001B/149

* 9 7 9 8 9 9 0 6 9 1 1 0 0 *